EVOLUTION AND SOCIETY

EVOLUTION AND SOCIETY

A STUDY IN VICTORIAN SOCIAL THEORY

BY

J. W. BURROW

Lecturer in History in the University of Sussex

CAMBRIDGE
AT THE UNIVERSITY PRESS
1970

Published by the Syndics of the Cambridge University Press
Bentley House, 200 Euston Road, London, N.W.1
American Branch: 32 East 57th Street, New York, N.Y. 10022

© Cambridge University Press 1966

Standard Book Numbers:
521 04393 X clothbound
521 09600 6 paperback

Library of Congress Catalogue Card Number: 66–21075

First Published 1966
Reprinted 1968, 1970

First printed in Great Britain
at the University Printing House, Cambridge

Reprinted by Offset in Great Britain by
Alden & Mowbray Ltd
at the Alden Press, Oxford

TO MY FATHER AND MOTHER

CONTENTS

PREFACE

This book attempts to investigate a phase of Victorian social thought which has an intrinsic interest as part of the history of ideas in nineteenth-century England. It would be gratifying if it should also be regarded by social scientists as a contribution to the history of their disciplines, but it is almost certainly not the kind of contribution a social scientist himself would be likely to make. The chief object has been to understand how and why theories of social evolution in Victorian England emerged and took shape as they did; it has not been to arrange the Victorian social theorists in an order of merit according to the extent to which they seem to have anticipated the methods and concepts of modern sociology and anthropology.

Nevertheless, the subsequent revolution in the methods and assumptions of the social sciences which underlies the vast differences between the preoccupations of the modern social scientist and those of his Victorian predecessors has led inevitably to a reinterpretation of the earlier revolution with which this book is primarily concerned. Its repudiation by modern British sociologists and anthropologists is a fact about evolutionary social theory of which any attempt to understand it and put it in historical perspective must take account. Questions—even historical questions—can now be asked about Victorian social theory which the Victorians themselves could not, or would not, have asked, because the concepts in terms of which they have to be put had not been made explicit, or did not seem important.

The most obvious of these questions is, why did so many Victorians conceive the major task of social science to be the study of social evolution? It is an obvious question because it is in this respect that the approach of modern social scientists is most at variance with that of the Victorians, and an attempt is made in this book to answer it, and to explain the hold that the idea of social evolution had upon the minds of Victorian intellectuals.

In making use, up to a point, of the more familiar concepts of the modern social sciences to ask historical questions about Victorian social theory, two difficulties in particular have to be faced.

First, there is the obvious danger of displaying *naïveté* in a field of study other than the author's own. Social scientists may find irritating the airy use here of terms such as 'functionalism', 'social system' and the like which they have either abandoned or are engaged in reconsidering and refining. An attempt has been made to keep the use of such terms to a minimum, using them where they seemed essential for brevity or precision, but not attempting to break them down by introducing distinctions not strictly necessary at this level of analysis. If the result seems to some crude and irritating this is perhaps in the nature of the case, quite apart from whatever avoidable errors and gaucheries there may be.

The second difficulty is more serious; as an historian, it has not been my intention to pass judgement on Victorian theories of society from the standpoint of the modern social scientist, nor am I qualified to do so. On the other hand, to employ some of the concepts and distinctions suggested by the subsequent development of the social sciences in analysing Victorian social theories often involves appearing to make an evaluation. To ask why someone did *not* think in a particular way may be taken to carry the implication that he ought to have done so.

To this again, there appeared no acceptable alternative

and no attempt has been made to write in an absolutely neutral manner. This probably does not matter, provided it is remembered that such evaluations as there may be do not form part of the chief object in writing the book, which has been to understand and explain. The questions asked and the analyses undertaken have this as their ultimate object, and are not introduced primarily to convict the Victorians of sociological unsophistication. This is not an attempt to avoid responsibility for the evaluations made—obviously responsibility for them must be accepted, whatever the purpose in making them. But a mere attack on the Victorian social theorists would be undesirable for many reasons: it would be unnecessary; it would not be very interesting; the present writer is not particularly qualified to undertake it; and it would be historically irrelevant.

It remains true, however, that the legacy of the evolutionary anthropologists and sociologists of the nineteenth century has been largely repudiated by their twentieth-century successors, particularly in Britain. Contemporary social anthropologists do not regard it as their task to collect information about primitive peoples with a view to reconstructing the prehistory of civilization, nor do sociologists try to elicit laws of social evolution; indeed, one of the accusations made against certain influential contemporary sociological theories is that they cannot account for social change.

The repudiation of the evolutionary tradition by modern sociology and anthropology has made a reappraisal of the historical significance of that tradition inevitable. This reappraisal does not, of course, necessarily involve a rejection of the evolutionists' claim to have replaced theories of society deduced from psychological assumptions by the study—however heavily charged with preconceptions—of actual social phenomena in a systematic way. Modern anthropology goes back to Malinowski and Radcliffe-Brown, Durkheim and Weber, but it also, in a sense and more remotely, goes back to the evolutionists and polygenists, the travellers and cranks, who founded the Anthropological Society of London in 1863, 'with the object of promoting the study of Anthropology in a strictly scientific manner'. To some extent, the link is purely verbal, but there is also a genuine though loose connection, in their insistence on anthropology as an empirical and systematic subject, taking the world for its province and regarding nothing as too strange, remote, irrational or disgusting to be of potential importance. There was a notable change in the methods and intentions of social theory in the third quarter of the nineteenth century.

The rejection of evolutionism, however, has inevitably led to a reassessment of its historical importance. This reassessment, most elaborately expounded by Talcott Parsons, in *The Structure of Social Action*, depreciates the importance of the revolution of the mid-nineteenth century by pointing to a persisting framework of ideas—positivism —within which it took place, positivism being defined by Parsons as the belief that 'positive science constitutes man's sole possible significant cognitive relation to external reality'.

It may be asked, why bother with evolutionary positivism? Who now, as Talcott Parsons pointedly asks at the beginning of *The Structure of Social Action*, reads Spencer? And if the answer is no one, is that not as it should be? There are a number of answers to this. The history of ideas is not necessarily, like the old school history books, a record of victories. Moreover, there *was* a revolution in the mid-nineteenth century which requires explanation and which has not, apart from the hopeful use of 'Darwin' as a magic password, really received it.

But there is also an answer more directly related to the reappraisal mentioned above which bears upon the question of what Lord Annan has called 'the curious strength of positivism in English thought'. The study of evolutionary positivism may not show why it did not disintegrate ten, twenty or even thirty years earlier, but it should help to explain how evolutionism became so strongly entrenched as the prevailing orthodoxy, and hence so hard to uproot. Even today, among educated laymen, a vague kind of evolutionary positivism often seems to play a considerable part in their unstated assumptions about the social sciences, while Weber and Durkheim are little more than names. To show how it became so strongly established would be to find out something not only about the intellectual needs and preoccupations of the Victorians but about the history of social theory.

It will be argued in this book that the seeds of modern sociological theory were to a considerable extent implicit in the doctrines which were becoming current in the eighteen-sixties, but they were stifled by the overriding needs of an evolutionism which provided more satisfactorily what the Victorians sought in theories of society.

The Introduction (chapter 1) and chapter 2 deal in a fairly summary way with the prehistory of social evolutionism. This seemed necessary because there is no single work to which the reader can confidently be referred for such a prehistory. Chapter 2, in particular, deals with the question of the relations between English utilitarianism and embryonic social evolutionism. Parts of this story are familiar enough; others perhaps less so.

Evolutionary social theory proper is considered primarily with reference to three outstanding figures: Sir Henry Maine, Herbert Spencer and E. B. Tylor. There are good reasons for the choice of these three in particular. Maine was the first, and in many ways the most thorough, student of institutions by the new methods. Spencer, as well as making contributions to social theory which still arouse the interest of contemporary sociologists, was the philosopher of the whole movement, ambitiously relating his social theories to a total theory of existence. His name, more than any other, symbolized evolutionary social theory for the ordinary reader. Tylor was the chief channel through which social anthropology passed from being the concern of a few eccentrics in the early eighteen-sixties to acceptance as a profession and an academic discipline. There are other candidates for consideration—most notably J. F. McLennan and Sir John Lubbock, who are discussed in less detail. Any selection must be to some extent arbitrary, but the selection of these three—Maine, Spencer and Tylor— seems more defensible than any other.

A word must be said about the treatment of continental theorists. Evolutionary social theory was not an isolated, purely English phenomenon. It was, for a while, the orthodox social theory of most of the countries of Europe, and also of the United States. Where continental theories appear to have been relevant to the development of evolutionary social theory as a method, as in the case of Comte and Savigny, these have been discussed at some length. Where they seem to have contributed concepts and methods merely within an already established tradition of inquiry—the tradition of evolutionary social theory—they have been ignored, partly from lack of competence to deal with them, partly because their contribution is of interest only at a level of technical complexity which this book does not aspire to reach. The reader will therefore find no estimate of the contribution of such continental anthropologists as Wundt, Klemm and Waitz.

To the establishment of evolutionary social theory, however, continental influences were profoundly important. Evolutionary social theory in England is seen, in the following pages, very largely as the outcome of a tension between English positivistic attitudes to science on the one hand and, on the other, a more profound reading of history, coming to a large extent from German romanticism, which made the older form of positivist social theory, philosophic radicalism, seem inadequate. The tension between the romantic-historical and the positivist approaches to society could only be reconciled, for the Victorians, by some theory of social evolution. This book is an attempt to understand why, and so to explain the hold which theories of social evolution had over so many Victorian intellectuals.

I wish to thank the Master and Fellows of Christ's College, Cambridge, for electing me into the Research Fellowship during the tenure of which most of the research for this book was done. I am also grateful to the Twenty-Seven Foundation for a grant to cover the costs of preparing the manuscript.

I wish to thank the Editor of *Victorian Studies* for permission to publish part of Chapter 4 which first appeared as 'Evolution and Anthropology in the 1860s: The Anthropological Society of London, 1863–71' in *Victorian Studies*, VII, December 1963.

In writing this book I have become indebted to too many colleagues to mention them all by name; I hope that they will accept this expression of my gratitude. A few of these debts, however, call for specific mention. Dr G. Kitson Clark, who supervised the book's progress from its inception, allowed me to benefit from many helpful suggestions and from his intimate knowledge of nineteenth-century England. Without his help at crucial stages the book would never have been completed. The criticisms and encouragement of Professor Meyer Fortes have done much to make me feel rather less gauche and uneasy in my trespasses into anthropology. To Professor Graham Hough and Mr Quentin Skinner I am indebted not only for reading the manuscript and making helpful criticisms and suggestions but for many stimulating conversations. When I attempt to estimate how different my career would have been without the generosity of Professor J. H. Plumb, which only the many others who have experienced it will be able to appreciate, I am defeated by the extent of my indebtedness; of one thing I am certain: it would not have included writing this book. To these and many others this book owes much; I alone am responsible for its errors and inadequacies. I must also thank Mrs Hazel Treleaven, who typed the manuscript, and my wife for her criticisms and her forbearance.

J.W.B.

PREFACE TO PAPERBACK IMPRESSION

I should first of all like to thank those critics and correspondents who have kindly sent me factual corrections. Unfortunately I cannot acknowledge each of these here separately, but I do want to take this opportunity of considering some more fundamental objections to the overall strategy of *Evolution and Society*. For an author to offer second thoughts after only three years may perhaps raise suspicions of light-mindedness. However, the gestation of a book is a lengthy process and it is only exceptionally that one can think equally intensively about all its parts at once; much in the pre-history of *Evolution and Society* prior to its publication in 1966 is, I find it salutary to recall, now a decade old. In particular I have been helped in reappraising it by the work and criticisms of Professor George Stocking.[1]

Essentially I think that the criticisms I would now accept are those which show that I have not always been sufficiently rigorous in applying the methodology I professed; the latter I continue to think sound, at least in essentials. I should like, therefore, both to consider and briefly acknowledge some of these deficiencies in execution and confusions in strategy and also to reaffirm and slightly amplify the theoretical allegiance of the book.

There is first of all, however, an objection which, though in a sense one of detail, does deserve to be mentioned here since it bears directly on one of the chief claims of the book to offer an historical explanation. In a number of places,

---

[1] G. W. Stocking Jnr., *Race, Culture and Evolution* (Free Press, New York, 1968).

developing historically a point originally made by Professor Talcott Parsons, I attempted a general historical explanation of social evolutionism by pointing to the fact that a wider sociological knowledge raised the spectre of relativism. I still think that this is an important point and a vital clue. I now think, however, that in some particular cases the point is overstressed or at least oversimplified. There seems to be virtually no direct evidence, for example, that Tylor was bothered by relativism. What he was bothered by, as Professor Stocking has pointed out to me, was polygenism. This, in a sense, is relativism in another form, but I think I insufficiently stressed the different forms it could take. In the case of Maine, I recognised the problem, but in an unsatisfactory way. On p. 155 I said 'This is not meant to imply that, psychologically speaking Maine felt in any danger of falling into relativism but merely that this was the logical function of his method'. Indeed it was, but I am not now very happy about the status of this kind of 'functionalism' in intellectual history.

My view of the overall strategy adopted in *Evolution and Society* is, as I have said, still essentially that put forward in the original preface. What is at issue, and where I am inclined to give ground, is the adequacy with which this strategy is carried out, which is related to the degree of clarity with which I conceived it. The fundamental point was that it was not a history of British 'social anthropology' in the Victorian period. This was partly due to a necessary modesty. To write such a history would be to provide a good deal more in various directions than *Evolution and Society* even pretends to offer. It was also, however, intended as a warning that a good deal in the way of historical explanation is likely to be missed if we approach the subject with preconceptions conditioned by a phrase like 'social anthropology'. In particular it seemed profitable to regard the Victorians who are usually picked out, for good reasons, as pioneers of social anthropology, as being concerned to a considerable extent with the same problems as, for example, the utilitarians of the early nineteenth century, who are not often considered in this context. To this extent *Evolution and Society* was conceived quite deliberately as a repudiation of the Whiggish way of looking at the history of the social sciences, which seemed to distort the understanding of the past by insisting on distinctions, for example between political theory and sociology, which have less application to the nineteenth century than they have had since (see p. 17).

So far so good. But in the preface I made another point which I also continue to adhere to, namely that the subsequent development of the social sciences has thrown into relief certain conceptual and methodological issues which can be, as it were, reflected back upon the past and used to ask genuinely historical questions. These two assertions seem *prima facie* incompatible. I believe, and shall try later to show, that they are not. What is undoubtedly true, however, is that to attempt to maintain both raises grave dangers of inconsistency in the actual execution of a work, and these I think I did not always avoid.

Most seriously, a critic might well ask why I selected the figures I did for special treatment and virtually ignored others. My dismissal of the Social Darwinists. (e.g. p. 115) —which I now feel sure was unjustifiably brusque, especially in the case of Bagehot—seems fishy, and a critic might object, though so far as I am aware no one has, that it runs the danger of making my denial that Darwin was a major influencing on evolutionist sociology seem only trivially true, by arbitrarily excluding from it those writers who were evidently influenced by him. I do not think matters are quite so bad as this, but it does seem in retrospect that my reasons for neglecting Social Darwinism look suspiciously Whiggish. Other matters seem unduly neglected for the same reason, and their exclusion suggests a certain cloudiness of aims. For in disclaiming both the scope and the possibly anachronistic limitations of a 'history of Victorian anthropology', I necessarily raise the question: if that is not the subject of the book, what is? The obvious short answer would be 'Victorian social evolutionism'. The exclusion of Bagehot and Leslie Stephen, or, somewhat earlier, of authors like Bray, Hennell and R. W. Mackay, then becomes indefensible. Again, if one is going to discuss evolutionist debates of the eighteen sixties, as distinct from picking out figures the twentieth century happens to find interesting, then debates between monogenists and polygenists, and between the evolutionist and degenerationist accounts of savagery should certainly bulk larger than they do in *Evolution and Society*.[1]

For the latter omissions, however, I think a slightly more respectable explanation can be offered than for the exclusion of the Social Darwinists. I concentrated not merely on social evolutionism but also—with the regrettable omissions of Stephen and Bagehot—specifically on attempts to construct a social *science*. This still seems to me legitimate as an attempt at a scholarly division of labour, though the lines of demarcation are admittedly very hard to draw and are not in fact drawn at all clearly. Nevertheless, the attempt, even if its difficulties were not at all fully understood, did make easier what does still seem to me a virtue of the book—the

[1] I do plead in some mitigation the slightly fuller treatment given to these matters in my article "The Uses of Philology in Victorian England" in R. Robson (ed) *Ideas and Institutions of Victorian Britain. Essays in honour of G. Kitson Clark* (London, 1967).

attempt to link social evolutionism with Philosophic Radicalism, considered as an earlier version of a 'science of social relations'. This in turn, however, does have its own kind of limitation of vision. In other words there seems to have been both a profit and loss account in my use of the Philosophic Radicals; it got me out of the limited context of 'histories of anthropology' only to suggest other limitations of its own.

It is time to return, however, to the main theoretical issue, and here I remain unrepentant. I still think, that is, that my original belief that the subsequent development of the social sciences suggests (legitimate) ways of looking at Victorian social evolutionism and providing valid historical explanations of it, is compatible in principle, however difficult to combine in practice, with the anti-Whiggish principles which I also asserted. It is true that there is a good deal that I now find tiresomely cumbersome and nagging about the constant contrasting of Spencer, Maine and Tylor with more recent sociology and social anthropology, but that is a complaint about execution, not an objection in principle. Nevertheless, the principle itself may not seem immediately acceptable. I recognized the difficulty when I pointed out (p. x) that 'To ask why someone did *not* think in a particular way may be taken to carry the implication that he ought to have done so'. What can one say about this? One can, of course, admit the reproach, but claim it as a necessary evil. We do expect people to think as we do, especially when their thinking is served up to us under labels—which may well be necessary to avoid intolerable circumlocutions—like 'social anthropology', 'sociology', 'science', etc. To make it clear that this was not the case, when it was not, is an indispensable classificatory activity, a necessary preliminary to an historical explanation. Anachronistic questions are preferable to anachronistic assumptions. It is a vital part of this defence, of course, that the ideas with which those of the past are to be contrasted are those most likely to be current among the historian's readers.

Again, so far so good. But why should we then use these particular differences in asking for an historical *explanation*? We may properly ask why we are not like our ancestors; there seems something odder about asking why our ancestors were not like us. Can we properly ask why their ideas were not ours? Why *ours*? To ask why something is as it is, is a legitimate though imprecise question. To ask whether something is or is not like something else is also a proper question. But to ask *why* it is not presupposes that there might be some reason for supposing that it might be. There seems no *prima facie* reason for supposing that everyone, or indeed anyone, in the past might have been like us. This defence therefore will not do.[1]

At this point one can fall back on another defence. This is to say that we may find that doing what *we* find it natural to expect was already, so to speak, 'on the cards'. This is what I tried to show on p. 83ff. If it is conceded that the study of the interrelation of institutions was, conceptually speaking, a 'real' option in mid-nineteenth century England, then the question why it was to such an extent sacrificed to the construction of evolutionary sequences becomes a proper and obvious historical question. This is one defence, but I am inclined to press the argument further. For I suspect that even without such evidence I should have been tempted to adopt the same strategy and I am not yet persuaded that I should have been wrong to do so.

---

[1] I am heavily indebted at this point to Quentin Skinner. "Meaning and Understanding in the History of Ideas". *History and Theory* VIII. No. I, 1969.

It still seems to me, for example, an important observation about Victorian social evolutionism that it was 'both relativist and not relativist' (p. 263). It is important both as a classification for us and as part of an explanation of what social evolutionism could do for Victorian intellectuals and hence of their possible motives in adopting it. Whether these were, or were relevant to, their actual motives then becomes a question to be determined by research. But, though Spencer, at least, recognized the point, it seems highly unlikely that the conceptual terms within which this research would be carried out would be arrived at simply by trying to see social evolutionism as its Victorian practitioners saw it. One needs also to be able to see it against a model of a social theory deliberately intended to be relativist: Malinowskian functionalism, for example. But the usefulness of the comparison is not affected one way or the other by whether social anthropologists now follow Malinowski, or even by whether a completely neutral social theory is possible. Any genuine conceptual distinction, once made, may be applicable to past debates, and hence may allow us to ask historical questions which we could not have asked otherwise, because it enriches our sense of the possibilities of a situation. The intellectual historian should not allow today's conceptual maps to obliterate or to distort those of the past, which it is his job to recover and explain, but he may quite properly allow the former to enrich his sense of the potentialities of the latter. The case with conceptual distinctions seems in this respect much like that of metaphors and explanatory models generally. They can be, and often are, inappropriately applied, but this is a matter of empirical tests; no limits at all can be set *a priori* (except tautologically) to their potential historical usefulness. They are neither automatically validated nor automatically disqualified if they happen to be currently fashionable among ourselves, nor are they automatically discredited if they are not.

J.W.B.

June 1969.

ABBREVIATIONS

The following abbreviations have been used:

The place of publication of all works cited is London unless otherwise stated. The customary abbreviations O.U.P. and C.U.P. have been used to denote the Oxford and Cambridge Presses. Where an edition other than the first has been used and the date of the first edition is of some importance it has been placed in brackets after the citation.

CHAPTER I

INTRODUCTION

1. THE PROBLEM OF THE IRRATIONAL

Whether the positivist tradition has been the dominant one in modern English intellectual life is perhaps a question too imprecise to be debated usefully. In a wider context than political theory, it is certainly possible—Professor Basil Willey, for example, has seemed at times to be engaged in doing it[1]—to present English intellectual history since the seventeenth century as a battle for survival by those who wished to give emotion and spontaneity their due, to defend intuition as a valid source of understanding, tradition as a valid justification, and the life of the imagination as something more than a holiday from reality, against an all-eroding positivism. This is to make Coleridge and Newman and Arnold—to go back no further than the nineteenth century —into a kind of opposition, voices crying in the wilderness. There is some truth in this, even if often it seems an unusually populous wilderness, noisy with major and minor prophets.

But of course the dominant positivist tradition—if dominant *is* correct—was never monolithic or invulnerable, not only because of what was formidable in its opponents' case, but because of the inconvenient surprises which its own programme, the attempt to apply scientific methods to as wide a variety of social phenomena as possible, inevitably laid in store for it. It is with some aspects of this vulnerability that this book is concerned. In particular it is con-

[1] Basil Willey, *The Seventeenth Century Background* (1934), *The Eighteenth Century Background* (1940), and *Nineteenth Century Studies* (1949).

cerned with the attempts of an initially rationalist, utilitarian approach to the study of social relations and institutions to comprehend non-rational modes of thought and conduct and the existence and viability of institutions which seem, though cherished, to serve no purpose that is readily describable in utilitarian terms.

'Non-rational' conduct may be regarded, for our present purpose, as conduct which is reverential, ceremonial, status-ordered, as distinct from practical, calculating, 'useful'. Another way of putting it might be to consider it in terms of its opposite, rational conduct, which in turn might be negatively described as conduct which does not *per se* invite sociological explanation, for example, selling at the highest price and buying at the lowest. Hence the connection, which will be stressed throughout this book, between awareness of the problem of non-rational behaviour and rejection, in favour of sociological investigation, of a model of society as a set of rational, calculated relationships entered into for the sake of the advantages they confer.

Such difficulties present themselves with peculiar acuteness in the case of alien and, above all, of primitive societies, on whose behalf familiarity and acceptance are not available to turn aside awkward questions. One light in which this book can be regarded is as an attempted contribution to the history of social anthropology, but it has also a wider relevance than this. One of the ways in which men are led to make most vividly manifest the values and habits of thought which underlie their own social attitudes is by contact with ways of life and thought which are alien to them. Recognition of this has contributed to one of the stock devices of satire. The situation is potentially a tragic one, particularly where there are great disparities of power between the two societies; and any attempt by intellect, imagination, and whatever hints may be provided by established intellectual disciplines to produce some ordered appraisal of it is worthy of attention.[1]

At this point a word of warning is appropriate. We shall not be directly concerned, though free to refer to it whenever it may seem convenient, with the problem as it presented itself to colonists or to the rulers of Empire, but as it presented itself to intellectuals trying to answer historical and moral, as well as political, questions. Nor, however, need much notice be taken of the occasional use of what would now be called anthropological data to reinforce a purely philosophical argument: for example, its use in the debate about the existence of innate ideas, and particularly the idea of God. Of course, such preoccupations could lead to a serious interest in primitive societies, but we are concerned with them only *in so far as* they did, not with their merely random and occasional use in controversy.

The 'savage' had always represented a potential problem for the theodicies, moral ideas, and philosophies of history of civilized men. His existence can readily offend against too tidy an idea of the Divine plan, too narrow a view of human history, or against moral and political creeds and susceptibilities based on too ready an assumption that the people one has to deal with are, in point of beliefs and way of life, roughly similar to oneself. This egalitarian assumption was given a dogmatic foundation in the seventeenth and eighteenth centuries by the widely held belief in the universal and more or less equal diffusion of reason among men; hence the savage, if one allowed oneself to think about him at all seriously, badly needed accounting for.

---

[1] For an account of European attitudes towards the tribes with whom the traffic in slaves was carried out, see K. George, 'The Civilized West looks at Primitive Africa, 1400–1800', *Isis*, XLIX (1958).

It is certainly an oversimplification, but perhaps a venial one, to represent attitudes to the savage in the seventeenth and eighteenth centuries as oscillating between two extremes, either of which, taken seriously, withdraws the savage from scrutiny as a problem. One view, by a denial of his humanity, entails that whatever problems his existence may pose they are not problems concerning the nature of man; the other, by regarding him as the exemplar of essential human nature, converts him from a problem into a measure of other problems—those of civilization.

The former view, the assertion of the non-humanity, or at least the essentially different humanity, of, let us say, the negro, functions more obviously as an apology for vested interests in exploitation than as an intellectually considerable thesis,[1] though, as we shall see, it was sometimes to put on the academic dress of scientific ethnology.[2]

The second view is essentially that embodied in the concept of the Noble Savage, and is worth more prolonged attention because of its relation to some of the most enduring myths of harassed mankind, the myths of innocence: the Blessed Isles, the Earthly Paradise, the Golden Age and the Garden of Eden. It has affinities with both the classical pastoral and the Tolstoian peasant.[3] It is closely related to the distinction between nature and convention which is central to European political thought till the end of the eighteenth century. The amiable savages discovered by Columbus, 'guileless, and liberal of all they have',[4] had a

---

[1] Cf. for Spanish attitudes to the Indians of the New World, Lewis Hanke, *Aristotle and the Indians* (1959).

[2] It also found a place in the 'Chain of Being' theory. In the eighteenth century some writers saw the Hottentots as a link between anthropoids and man. A. O. Lovejoy, *The Great Chain of Being* (Harvard, 1936), p. 234.

[3] H. N. Fairchild, *The Noble Savage* (New York, 1928), esp. pp. 2–3.

[4] *Select Letters of Christopher Columbus*, trans. R. H. Major (2nd ed. 1870), p. 7.

mythological and philosophical world already waiting for them to step into.

Nevertheless, it is difficult to see the concept of the Noble Savage—in the sense of an equation of the 'natural man' of theory with actual contemporary primitives—as a serious contribution to social thought, even in the eighteenth century. Judged by these standards, the Noble Savage has very much the air of a rococo toy, part of the furniture of a *fête champêtre*, rather than of a tool of social understanding. It was an essentially literary rather than theoretical concept, an ornament of rhetoric or a peg for satire. It has the characteristic of a literary symbol, which is not shared by theoretical postulates, of being readily discardable without any question of culpable inconsistency arising. Voltaire, usually regarded as sharing Dr Johnson's objections to cant about savages,[1] introduces a noble Huron as the hero of his story *L'Ingénu*. This tale belongs to the genre of philosophic fables, the typical protagonists of which are ingenuous or ignorant strangers, innocently, devastatingly inquiring. This cult of the innocent eye, a kind of fictional, semi-playful version of the Cartesian method, had a use for the Noble Savage. He has a niche in its gallery of ingenuous youths and suave orientals. No beliefs about actual primitives are entailed, however, any more than about actual Persians, though in both cases, perhaps, a favourable predisposition is implied, a generous inclination towards unprejudiced cosmopolitanism. Men of the eighteenth century, one might say, were prepared to believe in the wisdom and virtue of savages, if the savages would only co-operate.

The Noble Savage idea, in fact, was anchored only very

---

[1] Certainly he did not share Rousseau's views, but see the section 'Sauvages' in Voltaire, *Essai sur les Mœurs. Œuvres* (Paris, 1878), vol. ii, Introduction.

lightly, if at all, in knowledge of actual primitive peoples. Rousseau's reference to the Caribs of Venezuela[1] has an agreeably specific air, but the connection with fact is obviously tenuous, and, as Rousseau himself admits,[2] his descriptions of the pre-social state are not dependent on factual evidence. In any case, his references to pre-social man are notoriously ambivalent.

Diderot's *Supplément au Voyage de Bougainville*[3] is more specific still; the place is Tahiti, the time the present. But this is a mere backdrop to the discussion between the French monk and the untutored but dialectically adroit islander, which is, of course, wholly to the advantage of the latter. The *Encyclopédie*, however, tells a different story. There the Noble Savage is by no means adopted unquestioningly. This is not, of course, to say that the distinction between nature and convention which the notion of the Noble Savage was used to illustrate was not taken seriously by Diderot—on the contrary it was cardinal to his thinking, as to that of the other *philosophes*. All that is in question is the seriousness with which actual primitives were conceived as representing 'nature' in this—primarily normative—sense.[4]

---

[1] *Discours sur l'origine et les fondements de l'inégalité parmi les hommes* (C.U.P. 1941), p. 29 (1755).

[2] See below, p. 25.

[3] Not published till 1796. Reprinted in Diderot, *Selected Philosophical Writings* (ed. J. Lough, C.U.P. 1953).

[4] 'L'existence sans lois, sans police, sans propriété, sans religion surtout, sera exaltée comme l'état le plus heureux de l'homme. Il ne reste pas moins vrai que ce n'est là qu'argument polémique, et que, lorsqu'ils se bornent à assembler des faits, pour en tirer une vue et un jugement, d'ensemble, les Encyclopédistes n'ont vanté ni l'état, ni l'innocence de l'homme sauvage' (René Hubert, *Les Sciences sociales dans l'Encyclopédie* (Paris, 1923), p. 88).

2. THE 'SOCIOLOGY OF ERROR'

In fact, neither of the extreme attitudes to the savage—the denial of his humanity or the assertion of his goodness and even rationality—had, it seems, anything to offer any serious attempt to come to grips with the facts of primitive social life. This does not mean, however, that we have exhausted the attitudes to the savage current in the eighteenth century. Primitive religion, in particular, was a constant source of interest and speculation, and was variously interpreted as allegory, personification of dead heroes or historical events, placation of the terrible gods suggested by a harsh and incalculable environment, or as a political device, justified —like the 'noble lie' in Plato's Republic—or unjustified, of the ruling caste for maintaining its authority. These interpretations have been made the subject of an extremely comprehensive study by Professor Manuel[1] to which reference should be made.

The two schools of thought most relevant to the development of an essentially evolutionary approach to the problems raised by primitive societies, the approach with which this book is directly concerned, are represented by the *histoires raisonnées* or philosophic histories produced by the Enlightenment in France and Scotland respectively. The nineteenth-century descendant of the first is Comte and of the second James Mill. It would be a specialist task in itself to trace the relations between the two traditions, though Montesquieu is clearly a key figure in both. All that can be offered here is a brief outline of each.

In France, the philosophies of history of the Enlightenment characteristically derive their theories of progress from

[1] F. E. Manuel, *The Eighteenth Century Confronts the Gods* (Harvard, 1959).

the central concept of rationality.[1] The Cartesian doctrine of the infallibility of clear and distinct ideas, and of their accessibility to all men, seemed, quite apart from the philosophical difficulties it raised, incompatible with the known facts of human life, particularly of life in primitive societies, and of the past history of civilized peoples. Error and irrationality became, given the acceptance of this doctrine, not a normal part of the fabric of life, but pathological, something requiring explanation. Much the same implications ensued from belief in the 'natural goodness' of man. Somewhere, somehow, something has happened which should not have happened, something not predictable from the model of human nature which has been set up. That something is the register of crimes and follies which made up, for Gibbon, the history of mankind.

This discrepancy between the ideal model and the actual record underlies, in the form of the nature–convention dichotomy, much of the social and political thought of the Enlightenment; indeed, it is this distinction, and the contribution it could make, if any, to the study of primitive peoples, which we have been considering in connection with the idea of the Noble Savage. But in the course of the eighteenth century the discrepancy gave rise not merely to ironical denunciation and conceptual distinctions, but also to attempts at explanation, to what Professor Frankel calls a 'sociology of error'.[2] This is achieved by a kind of rewriting, *en philosophe*, of the Providential versions of history produced by Christians attempting the essentially similar task of justifying the ways of God to men—a reminder that the problem of evil was not invented by

[1] There have been a number of studies of the idea of Progress in the eighteenth century. The one on which the account given above relies most heavily is Charles Frankel, *The Faith of Reason* (New York, 1948).

[2] Frankel, *op. cit.* pp. 136–40.

Cartesian rationalism. Given the initial assumption, the goodness of God or the rationality of man, the problem becomes less to explain why progress has occurred than why so slow and painful a process has been necessary at all. And the *philosophes'* answer, broadly speaking, was that reason, though always present, has often had to operate in circumstances which prevent it reaching its goal, or at least cloud and distort the truths to which it attains. There are distinct stages through which reason must pass on its pilgrimage to the illumination to which its nature destines it. A version of the Comtist law of three stages (theological, metaphysical and positivist, i.e. scientific) is first to be found in Turgot.[1] The process is necessary and inevitable: 'All the ages are linked by a series of causes and effects which bind the present situation of the world to all those which have preceded.'[2] The triumph of Enlightenment is assured, because reason is self-corrective. Even error itself —*O felix culpa*—is a necessary aspect of this self-correcting progress.

Condorcet is in this respect more peevish than Turgot.[3] Vested interests play a part which is merely pernicious; knowledge becomes the possession of a class, which uses it as the instrument of political domination, turning science into mystification. But ultimately no such monopoly can be maintained, and progress resumes its march. Moreover, reason brings not merely truth but goodness, for moral knowledge is no less sure than any other kind. Morality, no less than understanding and control, is a matter of knowing the truth; indeed, it is a branch of understanding. Obviously much of Comtism is incipient here.

[1] *Ibid.* p. 123.   [2] *Ibid.* p. 121.   [3] *Ibid.* pp. 133–40.

3. CONJECTURAL HISTORY AND THE
COMPARATIVE METHOD

The philosophic historians of the Scottish Enlightenment, most notably Adam Ferguson, Adam Smith and John Millar,[1] are less easy to summarize, and have more affinities with Marx than with Comte.[2] The 'stages' of human history they discuss are not based on the intellectual categories singled out by Turgot, or upon others like them, but are the economic ones: hunting, pastoral, agricultural and commercial.[3] The division of labour, rather than intellectual inquiry, tends to be regarded as the primary cause of social progress. The Scots tended in general to be more appreciative of the unplanned though beneficial character of human institutions. 'Nations stumble upon establishments, which are indeed the result of human action, but not the execution of any human design',[4] as Ferguson put it.

The Scottish Enlightenment, and the social theories it threw out, require a book to themselves.[5] They force themselves, however, upon the attention of anyone concerned

[1] For studies of the philosophy of history of the Scottish Enlightenment, see G. Bryson, *Man and Society. The Scottish Enquiry of the Eighteenth Century* (Princeton, 1945); W. C. Lehmann, *Adam Ferguson and the Beginnings of Modern Sociology* (New York, 1930); and *John Millar of Glasgow, 1735–1801* (C.U.P. 1960).

[2] See R. L. Meek, 'The Scottish Contribution to Marxist Sociology' in J. Saville (ed.), *Democracy and the Labour Movement* (1954). The major works of the school are Adam Ferguson, *An Essay on the History of Civil Society* (1767); John Millar, *Observations concerning the Distinction of Ranks in Society* (1771) (the revised edition, 1779, was renamed *The Origin of the Distinction of Ranks*); William Robertson, *A History of America* (1777); and of course the works of David Hume and Adam Smith.

[3] See Duncan Forbes, 'Scientific Whiggism—Adam Smith and John Millar', *Cambridge Journal*, VII (1954), 648 ff.

[4] Quoted Meek, *op. cit.* p. 88. Cf. Adam Smith, *Lectures on Justice, Police, Revenue and Arms* (ed. E. Cannan, O.U.P. 1896), p. 168.

[5] On this subject I am heavily in debt to the writings of Mr Duncan Forbes.

with evolutionary theories of society in nineteenth-century England, partly because of their perception, as in the sentence quoted above, of the inadequacy of the notion of society as an artifact, partly because of the anticipation of what came in the nineteenth century to be called the Comparative Method.

The fundamental assumption of the Comparative Method is so simple that it is not surprising that its history can, if one is so inclined, be traced back almost indefinitely. It consists in the recognition of similarities between the practices and beliefs of contemporary primitive or barbaric peoples and those recorded in the past history of civilization. Such resemblances were freely played upon in the early eighteenth century,[1] and Professor Manuel sees this largely as an aspect of the denigration of the Greeks and Romans in the battle between 'Ancients' and 'Moderns'[2] —the reappraisal which stood at the very beginning of the modern doctrine of progress, which was to make such extensive use of the Comparative Method.

There is, however, a difference between pointing out similarities merely in order to illuminate the less by the more familiar, or even in order to throw new light on the latter, and using them as a basis for systematic classification, with the object of constructing a hypothetical sequence illustrating the development of civilization. It was this that the Scots attempted. As Sir James Mackintosh (1765–1832) put it:

We can [now] examine almost every variety of character, manners, opinions and feelings and prejudices of mankind into which they can be thrown either by rudeness of barbarism or by the

---

[1] Manuel, *The Eighteenth Century Confronts the Gods*, pp. 16–19. See also F. Meinecke, *Die Entstehung des Historismus. Werke*. Band III (Munich, 1959), pp. 70–2.   [2] Manuel, *op. cit.* p. 19.

capricious corruptions of refinement...History...is now a museum, in which specimens of every variety of human nature may be studied. From these great accessions to knowledge... moralists and political philosophers may reap the most important instruction.[1]

History and the variety of contemporary social life could be used to illuminate one another. For the most part, however, it was the illumination of the past by the exotic present which was chiefly stressed. It was a kind of history which, if it was forced to rely heavily, as Dugald Stewart noted,[2] upon conjecture to take the place of evidence about the earliest stages of history, relied also on the assumption illustrated by Ferguson when he wrote: 'It is in their [the Indians'] present condition that we are to behold, as in a mirror, the features of our own progenitors.'[3] To compare this assertion, and the practice of much of the so-called 'conjectural history' produced by the Scottish Enlightenment, with an exposition of the Comparative Method put forward by an anthropologist of the later nineteenth century is to be struck at once by the similarities.

Let us take as an example of the latter the remarks of J. F. McLennan. He begins by observing that 'the preface to general history may be compiled from the materials of barbarism',[4] and then continues:

...the first thing to be done is to inform ourselves of the facts relating to the least developed races...Their condition, as it may today be observed, is truly the most ancient condition of man. It is the lowest and simplest...and...in the science of history

---

[1] Sir James Mackintosh, *The Law of Nature and of Nations* (1798) quoted Lehmann, *John Millar of Glasgow*, p. 120.

[2] Adam Smith, *Essays on Philosophical Subjects—to which is prefixed a Life and Writings of the Author by Dugald Stewart* (1795), p. xli.

[3] Adam Ferguson, *The History of Civil Society* (1767) (new ed. Basil, 1789), p. 123.

[4] *Studies in Ancient History* (2nd series, 1896), p. 10.

old means not old in chronology but in structure. That is the most ancient which lies nearest the beginning of human progress considered as a development.[1]

This is one statement of the Comparative Method, but many others could have been chosen which would serve as well. There are several implications to be noted. McLennan holds:

(*a*) That contemporary primitive peoples represent the earliest stages of human development.

(*b*) That in the 'science of history', there is a distinction, or may be a distinction, between simple chronological sequence and 'human progress considered as a development'.[2]

(*c*) That it is possible to classify societies by their structure, as higher or lower (in the manner of comparative anatomy), in the scale of development.

But how is it possible to make a transition from a static classification by structure, a sort of *Scala Naturae* of social life, to a classification into stages of development, more or less 'advanced'? What is the guarantee that the higher forms have passed through the lower stages—the assumption which alone can make the series a temporal one? The answer given in the eighteen-sixties was partly that the way in which degrees of primitiveness shade off into each other suggests different stages of advancement along the same

[1] *Ibid.* p. 16.
[2] Dugald Stewart had drawn the distinction that is implied in McLennan's words about 'old' in structure and 'old' in chronology: '... the real progress is not always the most natural. It may have been determined by particular accidents, which are not likely again to occur, and which cannot be considered as forming any part of that general provision which nature has made for the improvement of the race' (Stewart, introduction to Adam Smith, *Essays on Philosophical Subjects*, p. xlvi). In the form Stewart puts it in, the distinction between 'actual' and 'natural' is based explicitly on a teleology. In McLennan—'human progress considered as a development'—this is not perhaps quite so clear.

road, partly that not all sections of the community 'move' at the same speed. Thus, there are traces in each community of its own past, i.e. elements which have not kept pace with the others.[1] This is the concept of 'survivals', elaborated by E. B. Tylor. Just as retarded communities reveal the earliest ages of mankind, so retarded elements within a community reveal its own past and, by their similarity to the practices of contemporary communities at a lower 'stage', guarantee the truth of the original assumption that these 'lower stages' may be taken, roughly, as representing the past condition of the higher ones. The conclusion is that 'the history of human society is that of a development following very closely *one general law*, and that the variety of forms of life—of domestic and civil institutions—is ascribable mainly to the *unequal development* of the different sections of mankind'.[2]

Even in the nineteenth century, as we shall see later, there were different ways of handling the Comparative Method. To examine in detail the extent to which McLennan's formulation fits eighteenth-century practice would entail far closer attention to the Scots than can be given here. Nevertheless, it is apparent that in the Scottish Enlightenment we find the outlines of an attitude and a method which, if still arrogantly European in that it forced knowledge of alien and primitive societies into a preconceived model of the progress of civilization,[3] did offer a framework within which such knowledge could be ordered, and neither romanticized or dismissed.

It is possible, therefore, to argue with some justification that the Scottish intellectual tradition, by the beginning of

[1] McLennan, *Studies in Ancient History*, pp. 14–15.

[2] *Ibid.* p. 9. Italics mine.

[3] See Duncan Forbes, 'James Mill and India', *Cambridge Journal*, v (1951–2), 31.

the nineteenth century, encouraged a more controlled attention to non-rational conduct and primitive institutions than
anything English intellectual life could offer, in spite of
Burke and in spite of the romantic cult of the primitive.
The paradox is that in a period when Scottish intellectual
influence on England seemed greater than ever before,[1] so
much that was distinctive in the Scottish approach to the
study of society should have been lost.

James Mill, who had attended Stewart's lectures at Edinburgh[2] and was familiar with the works of Ferguson and
Millar[3] as well as Adam Smith, ended his life as Bentham's
chief disciple; when his son felt the need of a wider understanding of social life than Bentham plus Malthus could
provide, it was not primarily to Ferguson and Millar
that he turned but to the heir of Condorcet, Auguste
Comte.[4]

Dugald Stewart had written at the end of his survey of
the distinctive historical methods of the Scottish Enlightenment that 'in proportion as the experience and reasonings
of different individuals are brought to bear upon the same
objects, and are combined in such a manner as to illustrate
and to limit each other, the science of politics assumes more
and more that systematical form which encourages and aids

[1] In no earlier period would young English aristocrats like the future
Lords Lansdowne and Melbourne have been sent to Scottish universities.
The most obvious example of Scottish cultural influence is the *Edinburgh
Review*, but Political Economy was, at least till Ricardo, a distinctly Scottish
export and was disseminated by Scots like James Mill and McCulloch.
Brougham's biographer says of the new University of London that 'the
Scottish influence was predominant both in outline and detail' (Chester W.
New, *The Life of Henry Brougham to 1830* (O.U.P. 1961), p. 375).

[2] Alexander Bain, *James Mill* (1882), p. 16.

[3] *Ibid.* pp. 18–19, 56, 426. Cf. Forbes, 'James Mill and India', *passim*.

[4] But Mill did point out to Comte the affinity between Scottish eighteenth-
century and French thought: J. S. Mill, *Earlier Letters, 1812–48* (ed. F. E.
Mineka), *Collected Works*, XIII (1963), 638. Mill compares Millar's historical
ideas to those of Guizot (*ibid.* p. 683). Cf. Forbes, 'Scientific Whiggism', p. 669.

the labours of future enquirers'.[1] Stewart clearly believes
that broad lines of inquiry have already been laid down,
and that in consequence 'the science of politics' can now
be cultivated co-operatively, with all the advantages that
this implies. In fact, Stewart stood not near the beginning
of an intellectual tradition but virtually at the end of one.

As the distinctive Scottish educational tradition declined,[2]
conjectural history declined also; in fact it declined even
faster, for Professor Davie, in his study of the Scottish
educational system, dates the crucial changes from the
eighteen-thirties onwards,[3] while it is difficult to find much
that can be regarded as continuing the tradition of Ferguson
and Millar in the early nineteenth century at all.[4]

4. CONJECTURAL HISTORY AND 'SOCIAL DARWINISM'

In the development of social anthropology—to speak
anachronistically—the first half of the nineteenth century
was a fallow period, though important for ethnography and
physical anthropology.[5] It is not, therefore, sufficient to say
of the development of social anthropology that 'we have
already in the speculations of these eighteenth-century
writers all the ingredients of anthropological theory in the
following century'.[6] We need to know whether these anticipations imply an actual influence, and if so—or even if not

[1] Stewart, introduction to Adam Smith, *Essays on Philosophical Subjects*,
pp. lxiii–lxiv.
[2] For this whole subject see G. E. Davie, *The Democratic Intellect* (Edinburgh U.P. 1961).
[3] *Ibid*. pp. xvi, 287.
[4] An interesting example which deserves to be better known is Hugh
Murray, *Enquiries Historical and Moral respecting the Character of Nations
and the Progress of Society* (Edinburgh, 1808).
[5] See below, chapter 4.
[6] E. E. Evans-Pritchard, *Social Anthropology* (1954), p. 25.

—why there is this puzzling gap in the first half of the nineteenth century.

It is here that modern specialization, the acceptance of lines of division between anthropology and history and philosophy, however necessary today, does a disservice to the study of a past to which such rigidity has no application.

The lines of demarcation would often have seemed arbitrary or meaningless to the men whose ideas are being discussed. To some extent this conflict is inevitable: not all the past is equally interesting, and our evaluations are often different from those current in the past. In some types of history this perhaps does not matter, but in the history of ideas we are avowedly concerned with what was thought, and hence with what was thought important. Of course there are still limits to human patience and interest, and doubtless many an audience which would listen patiently to an account of Comte's contribution to sociology would disintegrate if given an exposition of the Comtist Religion of Humanity. Nevertheless, we should at least be aware of the price we pay for not being bored.

The history of the development of evolutionary social theory has tended to be told in two separate compartments; in the histories of anthropology on the one hand and in the histories of political thought on the other. Thus, from the one side one hears about Lyell and Boucher de Perthes but little or nothing of J. S. Mill and Buckle, while the other tends to be equally sketchy in its treatment of the scientific background and of men who, like J. F. McLennan and E. B. Tylor, wrote nothing overtly political or philosophical but played a considerable part in the creation of a new climate of opinion.

A direct consequence of this is the mystery of the missing

half-century in the history of social anthropology to which we have just referred. It is widely recognized that the central idea of evolutionary anthropology—that contemporary primitive societies can be used as evidence for reconstructing the past of our own—was current in the eighteenth century, and that it provided a focal point for the theories of the Scottish school. By contrast, the neglect of the early nineteenth century is very noticeable. In the older general histories of anthropology—Haddon's or Lowie's for example[1]—the vacuum is filled by accounts of the development of ethnology and prehistoric archaeology. Evans-Pritchard's historical introduction—a brief one admittedly —ignores this period altogether.[2] This is understandable given the limited intentions of these histories. If no important advances were being made in anthropology during a particular period, that period has no interest for them. It would be unreasonable to expect them to try to explain *why* nothing of interest was happening—an inquiry which would lead them straight into the jungle of general social and intellectual history.

This has been recognized by at least one writer on the history of the social sciences. Professor Donald MacRae has remarked that 'the reasons for its [i.e. the Scottish school's] ultimate failure in Scotland would provide material for a pretty essay in the sociology of knowledge—it would, alas, be irrelevant'.[3] 'Alas' is disarming, and presumably implies reluctant submission to the exigencies of space and editors, but the remark itself indicates a state of affairs which is depressing. It suggests that the history of the social sciences

[1] A. C. Haddon, *A History of Anthropology* (1934); R. H. Lowie, *The History of Ethnological Theory* (1938).

[2] Evans-Pritchard, *Social Anthropology*.

[3] D. G. MacRae, in J. S. Roucek (ed.), *Contemporary Sociology* (1959), p. 700.

is still left largely a prey to the Whig interpretation of history. All that is relevant in it for the modern social scientist can be depicted as a series of 'discoveries', sometimes, it is true, misunderstood and misapplied, but somehow leading inexorably up to modern sociology and anthropology. This is the kind of picture presented in most histories of anthropology and sociology.[1] The impression conveyed is that the history of the social sciences is to be written by isolating 'anticipations' of modern concepts and methods from the irrelevant, because outmoded, theories of which they formed part. 'In Maine's work we can excise the genetic argument and still profit from the discussion which remains.'[2] Of course, such a search for friends in the past, who may or may not be ancestors as well as precursors, is both legitimate and interesting, and must form part of any adequate history of the subject, but it does not by itself constitute such a history, and is not converted into one by arranging the portraits of putative ancestors in chronological order. To do this may be to chart the development of social anthropology; it does not explain it.

Another striking result of the inadequacy of this method *as history* has been the over-use of Darwin in accounting for the rapid development of anthropology in the third quarter of the last century. The hopeful employment of 'Darwinism' as a blanket explanation is obviously related to the neglect, already referred to, of the first half of the nineteenth century, and both are the natural consequence of the separation of the history of anthropology from that

---

[1] There are, of course, noteworthy exceptions, such as E. R. Leach's essay on the background of Malinowski's ideas ('The Epistemological Background to Malinowski's Empiricism') in R. Firth (ed.), *Man and Culture* (1957), and T. S. and M. B. Simey, *Charles Booth—Social Scientist* (Oxford, 1960).

[2] A remark which is admitted to be 'patronizing', D. F. Pocock, *Social Anthropology* (1961), p. 24.

of social and political thought. Despite objections,[1] dogmatic assertions of the impact of Darwinism have provided
a convenient substitute for actual inquiry both to anthropologists not primarily concerned with history and to
historians largely ignorant of the development of social
anthropology.[2]

Of course there were attempts to apply Darwin's theories
to society, and for these 'Social Darwinism' is an appropriate enough label.[3] There were writers in the latter part
of the last century who took Darwin's specific contribution
to evolutionary theory—the concept of Natural Selection—
as the central theme of evolutionary sociology, and who,
naturally believing that their own work represented the
main stream of sociological thinking, helped to create the
myth that Darwin's theory represented a turning-point in
social thought. Bagehot's *Physics and Politics* (1869) was an
early example. Benjamin Kidd, contributing the article on
sociology to the eleventh edition of the *Encyclopaedia
Britannica* in 1911, devoted half his space to Darwin. For
Leslie Stephen also, Darwin's theory set the dividing line
between the old and the new in sociological theory.[4]

There is no doubt that the *Origin of Species* was a turning-
point in Stephen's own life; his unbelief sprang from it

[1] See, for example, Kenneth E. Bock, 'Darwin and Social Theory',
Philosophy of Science, XXII (1955) and the essay by Professor D. G. MacRae
in S. A. Barnett (ed.), *A Century of Darwin* (1958).

[2] E.g. E. H. Carr, *What is History?* (1961), 'Then Darwin made another
scientific revolution; and social scientists, taking their cue from biology,
began to think of society as an organism' (pp. 50–1).

[3] Such as, for example, the material examined by Professor Hofstadter in
his *Social Darwinism in American Thought, 1860–1915* (Harvard, 1944),
though in many cases 'Spencerianism' would be equally appropriate. By
the eighteen-seventies, and below a certain level of sophistication, there is
really no point in making the distinction.

[4] See his essay on Buckle, 'An Attempted Philosophy of History', *Fortnightly Review*, n.s., XXVII (1880).

rather than from the German biblical criticism, or the utilitarian objections to the Athanasian Creed, which unsettled many of his contemporaries.[1] But even in his own case he was overstating, for Sidgwick later forced him to admit that his sociological thinking owed more to Comte than he had acknowledged.[2] In generalizing from his own case to that of his contemporaries, moreover, he was ignoring the fact, if it was known to him, which in most instances it probably was not, that Maine, McLennan, Spencer, Pitt-Rivers and possibly even Tylor—the founders of the new evolutionary sociology—had all, before 1859, written on or become interested in the subjects which were later to make them famous. Nor was this because they had advance knowledge of Darwin's theory. The only one who had was Lubbock[3] and he came to anthropology primarily as an extension of his archaeological interests.

The issues involved are sufficiently complicated to make a simple denial of Darwinian influence on the development of theories of social evolution inappropriate. Nevertheless, it is sufficiently obvious that they were not simply a by-product of *The Origin of Species*. It is only the relative dearth, in the first half of the nineteenth century, of social theories of an evolutionary kind that makes such a view plausible at all. To explain this hiatus we have to look at English intellectual life, or at least certain aspects of it, in the early nineteenth century.

This was the period in which the aspiration to create a science of morals and legislation, the central ambition of social thinking of a positivist complexion since the seventeenth century, was incarnated in utilitarianism. And in turning to the utilitarians one is made immediately aware

[1] See N. G. Annan, *Leslie Stephen* (1951).
[2] *Ibid*. pp. 212, 321.   [3] See below, chapter 7.

of a tradition of eighteenth-century theorizing—that of Hartley and Priestley in England and Condillac and Helvétius in France—quite distinct from the Enlightenment philosophies of history we have been considering up to now. It originated in the empiricist epistemology derived from Locke, according to which all complex ideas were derived initially from sensations, bound together in the mind by memory and association, and could be resolved into those sensations by reversing the steps of the associations. All sensations were either pleasant or unpleasant, either directly or by association, and it was a universal propensity of human nature to seek the former and avoid the latter.

The springs of human motivation being thus, it seemed, revealed, there appeared to be no reason why education—conditioning rather—and wise legislation should not, by appropriate rewards and sanctions, produce an unprecedented degree of social harmony and well-being. If the human mind was a blank sheet upon which experience wrote, and if the laws of its calligraphy were understood, it seemed up to the schoolmaster and legislator to supersede the haphazard scribbling of chance and custom by judicious and benevolent controls. As David Hartley, the father of association psychology, put it:

It is of the utmost importance to morality and religion that the affections and passions should be analysed into their simple compounding parts, by reversing the steps of the associations which concur to form them. For then we can learn to cherish and improve good ones, and check and root out such as are mischievous and immoral.[1]

References to 'static' eighteenth-century thinking are not, unelaborated, very illuminating. Hartley's law of the association of ideas is a law of mental dynamics; it is as

[1] D. Hartley, *Observations on Man* (1749), p. 81.

much an intended explanation of development as is the theory of Natural Selection, and is equally retrospective; that is, it is based on the reconstruction of a past and, in a literal sense, for each individual, irrecoverable process. Nevertheless, there is an obvious gulf between Hartley's remark, quoted above, and the guiding assumptions of Scottish conjectural history. What becomes of 'the establishments which are, indeed, the result of any human action, but not the execution of any human design'?[1] Hartley's theory calls for a Lycurgus—the role for which Bentham cast himself. Millar, representing the Scottish tradition, characteristically thought that Lycurgus and all such creative legislators were essentially the products, rather than the creators, of social circumstances.[2] It is to the rival English view that we must now turn.

[1] See above, p. 10.
[2] John Millar, *The Origin of the Distinction of Ranks* (3rd ed. 1779), reprinted in Lehmann, *John Millar of Glasgow*, part III, pp. 177–8.

CHAPTER 2

A KNOWLEDGE OF HUMAN NATURE

1. UTILITARIANISM AND THE ANALYSIS OF SOCIETY

Bentham, in rejecting natural rights as an adequate basis for political thinking, did not alter the characteristic structure of political theory, but merely some of its postulates. A political theory could still be presented, as in James Mill's *Essay on Government*,[1] in the form of a set of deductions from certain essential attributes of mankind, the difference being that for the utilitarian the initial premiss consisted of the attribution to all men, not of certain inalienable natural rights, but of a certain fundamental and ineradicable inclination, namely to pursue pleasure and avoid pain.[2] This substitution was the basis of the utilitarian claim to have given morals and politics an empirical foundation, to have grounded them not in fictional rights but in actual wants.

Traditionally, the axioms of deductive political philosophy—propositions attributing a certain property to mankind *qua* mankind—had been arrived at by introspection, though introspection of a peculiar kind, designed to overcome the difficulty of performing controlled experiments in the study of society. It involved an abstraction of the essential from the inessential in order to arrive at the universal elements in human nature. 'He that is to govern a whole nation, must read in himself *not this or that particular*

[1] James Mill, *Essay on Government* (C.U.P. 1937) (1820).
[2] E.g. J. Bentham, *Introduction to the Principles of Morals and Legislation* (Blackwell, Oxford, 1948) (1789), ch. 1.

man, but mankind.'[1] It was this method of abstraction which justified the hypothetical reconstructions of the State of Nature. 'Commençons donc par écarter tous les faits, car ils ne touchent point à la question.'[2] And again: 'O homme! de quelque contrée que tu sois, quelles que soient tes opinions, écoute: voici ton histoire.'[3] Rhetoric apart, the similarity to the quotation from Hobbes above is striking. Rousseau explicitly makes the distinction between actual history and an explanatory model, and draws the analogy with physics: 'Il ne faut pas prendre les recherches dans lesquelles on peut entrer sur ce sujet pour des vérités historiques, mais seulement pour des raisonnements hypothétiques et conditionnels, plus propres à éclaircir la nature des choses qu'à en montrer la véritable origine et semblables à ceux qui font tous les jours les physiciens sur la formation du monde.'[4]

It was a matter of 'thinking away' society and all the inessentials of the human mind, of stating what *would* be the case if certain disturbing causes did not produce variations. That there is an analogy with Newton's first law of motion is obvious. Malthus's population principle is essentially of the same character: 'Population, *when unchecked*, increases in a geometrical progression.'[5]

The atomic unit of these systems of explanation is the isolated free individual, intelligently and self-interestedly adapting means to ends. Civil society is analysable in terms of such behaviour because it is an intelligent creation of the

[1] Hobbes, *Leviathan* (Blackwell, Oxford, 1946), p. 6. Italics mine.
[2] Rousseau, *Discours sur l'inégalité*, p. 23.
[3] *Ibid.* p. 34.   [4] *Ibid.* p. 23. Cf. Hobbes, *Leviathan*, p. 83.
[5] T. R. Malthus, *A Summary View of the Principle of Population*, reprinted in D. V. Glass (ed.), *Introduction to Malthus* (1953), p. 138; italics mine. For a discussion of the analogy between Malthus's law and those of classical physics, see A. G. N. Flew, 'The Structure of Malthus' Population Theory', *Australasian Journal of Philosophy*, xxxv (1957).

human will to some human purpose. As Hobbes put it: 'Geometry, therefore is demonstrable, for the lines and figures from which we reason are drawn as described by ourselves; and civil philosophy is demonstrable because we make the commonwealth ourselves.'[1] Since political society is a human artifact, the best analogy for it is a mechanical model and the method of understanding it is to take it to pieces and examine the components:

Everything is best understood by its constituent causes. For as in a watch, or some such small engine, the matter, figure and motion of the wheels cannot well be known, except it be taken insunder and viewed in parts; so to make a more curious search into the rights of states and duties of subjects, it is necessary, I say not to take them insunder, but yet that they may be so considered as if they were dissolved.[2]

There is, of course, an ambiguity in this. It is akin to the ambiguity in the Contract theory itself. Is Hobbes here describing the method of discovering the causes of political society, or offering criteria for judging it? The watch analogy suggests the former, the reference to rights and duties the latter. It may be argued that in the work of the later utilitarians, who had discarded the Contract and the conjectural state of nature,[3] the ambiguity has disappeared —that James Mill is not offering an explanation at all. It still remains arguable, however, that the utilitarians, generally speaking, found a model whose components are

[1] Quoted R. Peters, *Hobbes* (1956), p. 71. For my present purpose it does not much matter whether the view of Hobbes implied in what is said here is the correct one or not. It merely provides a useful paradigm of the arguments I wish to discuss. For a summary of the reasons why it has seemed to some scholars that Hobbes's political theory is not deduced from his psychological premisses, see C. B. Macpherson, *The Political Theory of Possessive Individualism* (O.U.P. 1962), pp. 10–13.

[2] Peters, *op. cit.* p. 74.

[3] E.g. J. Bentham, *Fragment on Government* (Blackwell, Oxford, 1948) (1776), p. 36.

unchanging principles of human nature a satisfactory one both for understanding society and as a basis for making political recommendations. To the utilitarian, no less than for Hobbes, society was an artifact.[1] The difficulties recognized by James Mill in the *Essay on Government* are those raised by the unchanging factor of human egotism, not by historically conditioned manners, habits, morals and modes of thought.

James Mill's *Essay* attempts a proof of the necessity of democracy by deducing it from the propensity of each man to pursue his own interest as he understands it. The end of government is prescribed by the utilitarian maxim that we should aim at the greatest happiness of the greatest number; in other words, the task of government is to provide the conditions in which each man can obtain the maximum of what he wants.[2] Essentially James Mill's argument runs: if you want x—and you do want x, for it is your nature to want it—this is the way, your nature and that of your fellows being what it is, to achieve it.[3] 'The question with respect to government is a question about the adaptation of means to an end.'[4] The problem has been shifted from the realm of ends to that of means. It is an attempt to solve problems of social conflict in an impartial and purely quantitative manner, as with a problem in mechanics.

[1] In *The History of British India* James Mill gives an entirely Hobbesian account of the origin of the state: 'The misery and disorder which overspread human life, wherever self-defence rests wholly upon the individual, are the cause to which government owes its origin. To escape from these evils, men agree to transfer to the magistrate powers sufficient for the defence of all: and to expect from him alone that protection from evil, which they obtained so imperfectly, and with so many disadvantages, from their own exertions' (James Mill, *The History of British India* (3 vols. 1817), I, 150).

[2] James Mill, *Essay on Government*, p. 3.

[3] It is not proposed to discuss here the notorious difficulties involved in the utilitarians' alleged combination of a hedonist psychology and an altruistic ethic.   [4] *Essay on Government*, p. 1.

The second and third quarters of the nineteenth century witnessed a number of attacks on this type of social and political theory, and a progressive weakening of the pristine confidence felt in it. One such attack came from the Idealist theory of ethics, which, by refusing to accept human wants as ultimate data and classifying them instead in terms of autonomous will and mere appetite, reintroduced qualitative distinctions into ethical and political theory. It is not, however, with this kind of attack that we are concerned. Both Spencer and Maine announced themselves prepared to accept the utilitarian formula—the greatest happiness of the greatest number—as the end of social life and political action. Their objection was not to the ethics of utilitarianism, but to its allegedly deductive, psychologically based social and political analysis.

It is at this point that doubts and qualifications begin to intrude. Are we really justified in placing so much emphasis on one essay, and was James Mill's *Essay* really, as Leslie Stephen called it, 'the essence of utilitarian politics'?[1] Can we speak of an essence of utilitarianism at all,[2] and were the utilitarians really so neglectful of what Bentham called 'the influence of Time and Place in Matters of Legislation'?[3] How can we say that philosophic history in the Scottish manner was moribund, for is not James Mill's *History of British India* a notable example of it? Mr Forbes has claimed that 'the widespread diffusion in the later nineteenth century of the belief in "progress" has perhaps

[1] Leslie Stephen, *The English Utilitarians* (3 vols. 1900, repr. 1950), II, 84.

[2] Perhaps we shall save ourselves fruitless searches by recalling the difficulties encountered in searching for the essential Marx. We are perhaps less self-conscious in talking about the utilitarians, and references to the essence of utilitarianism might pass without comment in circles where a similar reference to Marxism would immediately set nominalist antennae waving.

[3] *Of the Influence of Time and Place in Matters of Legislation*. Bentham, *Works* (ed. J. Bowring, 11 vols, 1843), vol. I.

obscured the fact that for the utilitarians belief in progress was not Utopian but rested on a clear-cut and "scientifically" established philosophy of history.'[1] In other words there was another, historically oriented, strain besides associationist psychology, underlying the utilitarian's belief in progress. It is true that Forbes concludes that because of the limitations of this philosophy of history 'Mill's method in the *History of India* was really deductive, as in the *Essay on Government*'.[2] Nevertheless, the sharp lines of our original picture of a utilitarian political theory depending solely upon propositions deduced directly from psychology have been blurred, and need to be redrawn.

The historiography of English utilitarianism does not, at the present time, readily yield the non-specialist a quick summary. Nevertheless, our overall purpose exacts at least some account of the state of play.

The classical picture of the development of utilitarian ideas was provided by Leslie Stephen[3] and Elié Halévy.[4] Stephen saw utilitarianism through the eyes of a man for whom all things, including social theory, had been made new by the Darwinian revelation. Utilitarianism, though on the right track in ethics, was inadequate because it was not sociological and evolutionary—Stephen tends to make the two criticisms mean pretty much the same thing.[5] In this respect he was typical of the social theorists of the second half of the last century, and his book, while still useful as history and even analysis, is also an historical document. For him, utilitarianism was essentially a psychological

---

[1] Forbes, 'James Mill and India', p. 32.

[2] *Ibid.* p. 29.

[3] Leslie Stephen, *The English Utilitarians.*

[4] E. Halévy, *The Growth of Philosophic Radicalism*, English trans. by M. Morris (1952 ed.).

[5] Stephen, *op. cit.* III, 375.

theory, and hence insufficient, because, as he had written of Hartley's association theory, it 'needs to be supplemented by a study of the reciprocal action upon each other of different members of the race'[1]—by a theory of social relations, in fact. Bentham, according to Stephen, 'starts from the "ready-made man" and deduces all institutions or legal arrangements from his properties'.[2] Stephen's view of utilitarian political theory is sufficiently indicated by his remark, quoted above, that James Mill's *Essay on Government* gives the essence of it.

He recognizes that the philosophy of history of the Enlightenment has a place, though a subordinate one, in utilitarianism. His criticisms of it, from what he thought of as a 'Darwinian' position, will be considered later. For him the limitations of the utilitarians' notion of what constituted a 'science of man' led to an irreconcilable tension between their empirical aspirations and their simplifying generalizations, or, to put it another way, between utilitarian psychological and historical thinking. They desire, says Stephen, 'on the one hand to be scientific, and on the other hand to be thoroughly empirical. The result is to divide the two spheres: to enlarge as much as possible on the variability of human society in order to be "empirical"; and to regard the constituent atoms as unchangeable.'[3]

Halévy too postulates an unresolved dilemma at the heart of utilitarianism, between its psychology and its philosophy of history, though the terms in which he presents it are somewhat different. The former he derives from Helvétius, the latter from Adam Smith, and to him they represent the unsolved conflict within utilitarianism between the 'arti-

[1] Leslie Stephen, *History of English Thought in the Eighteenth Century* (2 vols. 1876) (3rd ed. 1902), II, 70.
[2] *The English Utilitarians*, I, 301.   [3] *Ibid.* III, 332.

ficial identification' and the 'natural identity' of interests. Utilitarian association psychology, the doctrine of Hartley, Helvétius and Bentham, implies the former—the need for pedagogue and legislator to adjust the sources of pleasure and pain for each individual so as to supply him with adequate motives for good behaviour and so contribute to the maximization of social well-being. The utilitarian philosophy of history, however, according to Halévy implies that this can be achieved simply by the unhampered operation of economic laws, without legislative interference.

This interpretation forms the core of Halévy's book, which ends with the triumph of the *laissez-faire* strain over the Benthamite 'artificial identification of interests'; philosophic radicalism dies in giving birth to *Manchestertum*.[1] Halévy is not so interested as Stephen in the utilitarian philosophy of history *per se*, since for him what is most significant in it—the theory of the natural identity of interests —is most clearly seen in classical economics.[2] But, like Stephen, he sees the tension between it and the deductive, psychologically based arguments of utilitarianism as one which the utilitarians were never able to resolve.

The attempts which have been made of recent years to rescue Bentham and the classical economists—James Mill appears as yet to have found no partisan—from the interpretations of Stephen and Halévy have been, on the whole, less coherent, and even run at times the risk of being suspected of concentrating on marginalia. Thus, when Lord Robbins instances in partial rebuttal of the claim that the utilitarians were unhistorical Bentham's remark, in a

---

[1] Halévy, *The Growth of Philosophic Radicalism*, p. 514.

[2] If Halévy's notion of what, for the utilitarians, constituted the philosophy of history seems odd, it must be remembered that he paradoxically regards the work of Ricardo and Malthus not as less 'historical' than Smith's, but more so (*ibid.* p. 274).

footnote, that in some countries the state needs to interfere
more than in others,[1] one feels inclined to observe that, after
all, it *is* a footnote. Leslie Stephen noticed that

when accused...of laying down absolute principles in such
cases, they reply that they are only speaking of 'tendencies',
and recognise the existence of checks. They treat of what would
be, if certain forces acted without limit, as a necessary step
towards discovering what is when the limits exist. They appear
to their opponents to forget the limits in the practical conclusions.[2]

Clearly some distinction is needed between a man's
theories and his views. He may recognize limitations to the
scope of his theory, may insert qualifications which he is
yet unable to integrate into the theory itself. Thus he may,
as an individual, if he is cautious enough—and how cautious
he is is not perhaps of very much interest—escape charges
of superficiality and oversimplification which nevertheless
continue to lie against his theory. It is no defence, for
example, of a sociological theory which lies under the im-
putation of being unable to account for social change, to say
that its author is aware of the problem.

This is one potential source of confusion. Another is more
fundamental still, since it questions whether one can talk of
utilitarian theory at all. All one has is various works by
different authors on political theory, psychology, jurisprudence and history. Pressed to its limits, this approach would
leave us with nothing to do but quote or paraphrase. It is,
however, a useful reminder that one does not rebut objections to, for example, James Mill's *Essay on Government*
by pointing to the *History of British India*. Again we are
reminded of the difference between men and theories.

[1] Lionel Robbins, *The Theory of Economic Policy in English Classical
Political Economy* (1952), pp. 39–40.
[2] *The English Utilitarians*, II, 90.

A third source of confusion is the fact that criticisms and rebuttals—if we must talk in these terms, which is itself unfortunate—may miss each other by being couched in terms of different standards. Thus Mrs Mack's illustration of Bentham's alleged sense of history—his use of apparently random historical examples[1]—might well seem to others with more exacting standards to illustrate precisely the opposite: that he lacked one. And when she claims that Bentham was a sociologist[2] one suspects that she is using the term in a much more generous sense than most sociologists would be prepared to allow.

Again, when Professor Baumgardt claims, on the evidence of the essay *Of the Influence of Time and Place*, that 'Bentham proves to be one of the most clear-sighted forerunners of the nineteenth century's ethnological school in ethics',[3] one can only assume that he is pitching the requirements for being considered a forerunner, and a clear-sighted one at that, pretty low.

This point is vital to the argument of this book, for, if Professor Baumgardt and Mrs Mack were correct, the evolutionists of the latter half of the last century who thought they were in revolt against 'Benthamism' would have been deceiving themselves. It will be contended in this book that they were to a considerable extent deceived, but about themselves, not about Bentham. It is essential, therefore, that these confusions should be, at least partially, cleared up.

Frequently, in the nineteenth century, the debate between 'inductive' and 'deductive' political theories was conducted

---

[1] Mary P. Mack, *Jeremy Bentham. An Odyssey of Ideas, 1748–1792* (1962), p. 280.

[2] *Ibid*. p. 10.

[3] D. Baumgardt, *Bentham and the Ethics of Today* (Princeton U.P. 1952), p. 364.

around the proposition 'Human nature is everywhere the same'. Both sides could be satisfied with the justice of their case, because the assertion is true or false according to the sense in which it is understood. There must be some basic similarities to render the concept 'man' applicable at all; in this sense the statement is tautological. Even taking it in a non-tautological sense, there is a distinction to be made between modes of feeling—loving, hating, fearing, etc., to say nothing of the still higher-level concept 'desiring'—and their forms of expression.

The modern debate has clung uncomfortably closely to the terms in which the nineteenth-century argument about utilitarian political theory was conducted; terms which presupposed a suspicion of 'hypotheses'[1] and an oversimplified notion of what constituted 'inductivism'. James Mill had impatiently to protest that there was nothing inherently vicious in 'theory';[2] and it is worth recalling that even Darwin was to suffer from the exaggerated 'Baconianism' of his contemporaries.[3] Their Whig opponents attacked the utilitarians for violating the principles of sound 'Baconian' inductivism;[4] the latter, convinced that their methods were empirical, were at a loss to know what the fuss was about.[5]

[1] See below, p. 35 n. 1,

[2] Bain, *James Mill*, p. 465. Cf. J. S. Mill, *Autobiography* (O.U.P. 1955) (1873), p. 27.

[3] Darwin was emphatic that he had begun his work on the origin of species on sound 'Baconian' principles. See his *Autobiography* in F. Darwin (ed.), *Life and Letters of Charles Darwin* (3 vols. 1887), I, 83. Nevertheless, it was one of the points of Wilberforce's attack on the *Origin* that it offended against the stern 'Baconian' law of observation, and Darwin's defenders had to defend the use of 'probable hypotheses' as a legitimate procedure (Gertrude Himmelfarb, *Darwin and the Darwinian Revolution* (1958), pp. 225, 244).

[4] Cf. Mackintosh's attack on Hobbes, and Mill's reply: James Mill, *A Fragment on Mackintosh* (1835), esp. pp. 22–6.

[5] The Benthamite *London and Westminster Review* carried on its title-page the motto from Bacon 'Legitimae inquisitionis vera norma est, et nihil veniat in practicam, cuius non fit etiam doctrina aliqua et theoria'.

Bentham regarded Bacon as one of his masters,[1] while James Mill claimed that the argument of his *Essay on Government* was 'a case of the strictest adherence to the precepts of Bacon'.[2]

This disagreement and mutual incomprehension can be seen as a continuation of the eighteenth-century debate between adherents of sensation psychology, particularly Hartley and Priestley, and the Scottish philosophers of 'Common Sense'.[3] In fact, no sense can be made of the debate in these terms. There is no point in trying to decide whether association psychologists or defenders of Common Sense are the more genuinely 'inductive'. The former claim to provide a model of the way the mind works which is more precise and has greater explanatory power than the ordinary, everyday account of concepts and motives. The Common Sense school denies this and, broadly speaking, stands by the interpretations embodied in ordinary language.[4] In the absence of crucial experiments and an agreed language in which their results could be expressed, the argument remains a philosophical one.

A question which does arise out of this, which is highly germane to the matter in hand, is whether there is an inherently unhistorical or anti-historical bias in associationism and, conversely, whether there was anything, other than perhaps patriotism and personalities, in the Scottish Common Sense doctrine, the philosophical orthodoxy of

---

[1] See Mack, *Jeremy Bentham*, esp. pp. 129 ff.

[2] James Mill, *A Fragment on Mackintosh*, pp. 296–7. Cf. the belief of John Austin, byword among the historical jurists of the latter part of the century as an 'unhistorical' legal analyst, that his was the truly historical method in jurisprudence (Stephen, *The English Utilitarians*, III, 320).

[3] S. A. Grave, *The Scottish Philosophy of Common Sense* (O.U.P. 1960), esp. ch. III, section 2; for Reid on Bacon see pp. 7, 132, 135, 141, 147–8.

[4] *Ibid.* esp. pp. 77, 131, 133–4. For the debate about the validity of 'hypotheses' see ch. IV, section 2, esp. pp. 134–9.

eighteenth-century Scotland, which would naturally or logically ally it with historical studies in general and Scottish philosophic history in particular, so that the fortunes of both might be expected to wax and wane together. Associationism was obviously a tempting thesis for philanthropists in a hurry, for it seemed to offer, as in the passage from Hartley quoted above, a short cut to a manipulated millennium. There is much of this, undeniably, in Bentham.

Where then in Bentham's work is one to look for Professor Baumgardt's proto-ethnologist and Mrs Mack's sociologist 'immensely aware of the power of habit and tradition'[1] who came 'to recognise the endless varieties of human motives'?[2] Again we have to ask what exactly is being claimed. To be 'aware of' the power of tradition and habit is a very much smaller matter than to understand its functions, and may in fact be a very small matter indeed if one interprets that power simply in terms of vested interests and human laziness.[3] To 'recognise' the variety of motives is not in itself a very striking feat. Bentham certainly recognized that race, for example, could affect in unaccountable ways the 'bias of sensibility', that is, a man's disposition to find pleasure in one thing rather than another.[4] But this recognition appears as an isolated *aperçu*, not as part of the theoretical texture of the work in which it occurs. Indeed Bentham obviously experienced a sense of defeat, rare in him, in contemplating the diversity of men's inclinations.[5]

But, fundamentally, such recognition of diversity on Bentham's part is of limited importance, though it may be used to rebut the more loosely phrased charges against him, because he is primarily concerned not to explain but simply

---

[1] Mack, *Jeremy Bentham*, p. 9.
[2] *Ibid.* p. 211.   [3] *Ibid.* pp. 166, 294.
[4] Bentham, *Morals and Legislation*, pp. 164, 182.
[5] *Ibid.* p. 166 n. 1.

to indicate and categorize.[1] Bentham's 'logic of the will', as Mrs Mack explains, is not a psychology but a system of definitions, whose organizing principle is the notion of utility and whose purpose is to make possible the appraisal of motives and actions, divested of the associations of praise and blame with which their common descriptions invest them, simply in terms of their tendency to produce pleasure and pain. It derives its point and its interest simply through its relevance to a particular moral doctrine—utilitarianism.

2. BENTHAM ON TIME AND PLACE

Much may yet be held to depend, however, on Bentham's more peripheral writings, and in particular the essay *Of the Influence of Time and Place in Matters of Legislation*. It is here, if anywhere, that one might expect the influence of the eighteenth-century philosophic historians to show itself. Certainly Bentham was not entirely ignorant of their works. His admiration for Montesquieu was strictly limited,[2] but he cites Ferguson,[3] and Kames's *History of Man*,[4] with approval. He even uses the Comparative Method, though only in an attempt to write a conjectural history of language.[5] According to Mrs Mack:

Bentham wrote the history of civilization in several ways, and one of his tests of progress was the relative force of a given sanction at a given time. In the most primitive societies men were wholly absorbed in caring for their physical needs. Gradually, supernatural forces were invoked to terrify them into

[1] Cf. Halévy, *The Growth of Philosophic Radicalism*, part III, ch. iii, section 2.
[2] Mack, *Jeremy Bentham*, p. 113. Cf. Bentham, *Time and Place*, p. 173. Also *Fragment on Government*, p. 54 n. 1, and *Morals and Legislation*, p. 428 n. 1.
[3] Baumgardt, *Bentham and the Ethics of Today*, p. 20.
[4] Bentham, *Chrestomathia*, *Works*, VIII, 115. Cf. *Fragment*, p. 39 n. 15.
[5] 'In New South Wales may be seen the immediate progeny of Adam and Eve' (quoted Mack, *Jeremy Bentham*, p. 157).

social order. In the third stage of civilization secular law began to replace religious sanctions. Finally, men developed enough moral imagination and self-control to live peaceably together without threats and punishments.[1]

This sketch of social evolution has much in common with, for example, Herbert Spencer,[2] and suggests a gradualist approach to problems of legislation and social change. When we turn for confirmation, however, to the *Influence of Time and Place*, its most striking feature is precisely the absence of any social evolutionary framework, any attempt to use Time and Place to illuminate each other through the notion of 'stages' of development, in the manner of the Comparative Method. Despite the exaggerated claims which have been advanced for it, it amounts to little more than a man-of-the-world injunction to be cautious when making laws for prejudiced people. He allows that prejudices usually have some function, but there is no attempt to elaborate on this, and Bentham is, of course, far from the optimistic determinism which holds that the laws a people have evolved are necessarily the best for them: 'Laws need not be of the wild and spontaneous growth of the country to which they are given: prejudice and the blindest custom must be humoured; but need not be the sole arbiters and guides.'[3]

Apart from noting the absence of an evolutionary framework of the kind offered by the Comparative Method, one can by selective quotation make pretty much what one likes of the *Influence of Time and Place*. Bentham is asserting that local prejudices need to be taken into account, but that they need not be slavishly followed. To anyone but a doctrinaire believer in the sanctity of an indigenous and historically evolved legal system, there is nothing very

---

[1] *Ibid.* p. 292. Unfortunately Mrs Mack gives no citation at this point.
[2] See below, chapter 6.   [3] *Influence of Time and Place*, p. 180.

outrageous in this, or anything very impressive either. Whether it is to be counted merely as a grudging admission that foreigners can be odd, and need to be handled with care, or as a considerable step towards historical and cultural relativism depends largely upon the *tone*, which can only be properly appreciated by reading the essay in full. It is difficult, in fact, to believe that most readers of the essay have not agreed with Leslie Stephen that 'the real assumption is that all such circumstances [i.e. of time and place] are superficial, and can be controlled and altered indefinitely by the legislator',[1] though perhaps entering a small caveat about the word 'indefinitely'.

Bentham begins the essay by recognizing, as in his *Introduction to the Principles of Morals and Legislation*, to which he refers the reader, that what evokes pleasure in one man or one country may not do so in another,[2] and that the legislator must take account of 'the imperious and oftentimes unchangeable circumstances of the people to be governed'.[3] But one wonders what to make of a passage like the following:

Legislators who, having freed themselves from the shackles of authority, have learnt to soar above the mists of prejudice, know as well how to make laws for one country as for another: all they need is to be possessed fully of the facts; to be informed of the local situation, the climate, the bodily constitution, the manners, the legal customs, the religion, of those with whom they have to deal; possessed of these data, all places are alike.[4]

It is extraordinary, at least to a modern eye, because of the disparity between the comprehensiveness of the programme outlined, which, apart perhaps from a slight quibble at the

---

[1] Stephen, *The English Utilitarians*, I, 300.
[2] *Influence of Time and Place*, p. 172. Cf. *Morals and Legislation*, ch. VI.
[3] *Influence of Time and Place*, p. 177.
[4] *Ibid.* pp. 180–1.

insensitive phrase 'the facts'—as though referring to some
readily comprehended heap of objects—is acceptable
enough, and the breezy confidence with which it is put
forward. 'Possessed of these data, all places are alike';
apart from all their distinguishing characteristics, all objects
whatever are alike.

The impression produced by this passage is confirmed
when one turns to Bentham's *Codification Proposal*: 'In
comparison of the universally-applying, the extent of the
exclusively-applying circumstances will be found very
inconsiderable.'[1]

Even if this interpretation of the essay on Time and Place
is rejected, it is impossible to regard Bentham's call for
'tables or short accounts of the moral, religious, sympathetic
and antipathetic biases of the people'[2] as a demand for a
comparative sociology. All he does is to recommend the
collection of information and suggest a few headings under
which it may be arranged.

To judge Bentham's essay by these standards may perhaps seem unduly ponderous but it has been made necessary
by the claims Professor Baumgardt has made for it.[3] There
are, however, more interesting things to be said about the
essay. Most notable is the relative neglect of Time compared
with Place. One explanation readily suggests itself: Bentham's concerns were always practical, and the past is
inaccessible to the most determined philanthropy; no utilitarian legislator could alleviate its ills. The notion, moreover,
that the past, considered as an unfolding evolutionary development, might be useful as a guide to the present and
future, is precisely what is missing from Bentham's essay.
The past is used only in the crudest fashion, as a store of

---

[1] Bentham, *Works*, IV, 561. Cf. *Fragment*, Preface, section 56, p. 25.
[2] *Influence of Time and Place*, p. 173.   [3] See above, p. 33.

randomly chosen examples, as when Bentham uses the precedent of Mahomet to dispose of the argument that new laws cannot be successfully foisted upon a backward people.[1]

But, of course, not merely was the past irrelevant for Bentham because untouchable by the reforming hand, it was also suspect as part of the conservatives' stock-in-trade. The doctrine of the wisdom of our ancestors, and the more subtle argument that past and present form a living, connected tissue which must not be rudely broken, were his particular abhorrences.[2]

The same sort of objections as he applied to the wisdom of our ancestors underlay his suspicion of claims to superior wisdom by the men on the spot—the fear of vested interests.

To Anglo-Indian officials like Sir Henry Maine and Sir Alfred Lyall in the second half of the nineteenth century, with many years of sometimes mistaken but uncorrupt British government behind them, the most painful aspect of governing India, and the real impediment to governing it properly, was the difficulty of finding out what Indian life was really like, and of understanding it—the difficulty, in fact, of doing what Bentham so airily recommended in the *Influence of Time and Place*. To Bentham, however, the chief obstacles to good government in India, as in England, apart from unthinking bigotry, were vested interests and corruption. The superiority of the philosophic legislator in a distant land lay in his disinterestedness. When government is dirty it is easy to believe that to make it clean will virtually inaugurate the millennium. The social theorists of the second half of the century were often more sophisticated

---

[1] *Influence of Time and Place*, p. 191. Cf. the remarks on the usefulness of the history of jurisprudence, in *Morals and Legislation*, p. 428.

[2] For Bentham's conscious detestation of Savigny and the German historical school, see *Works*, x, 562; noted Halévy, *The Growth of Philosophic Radicalism*, p. 436.

in their approach to institutions because the more obvious abuses had already been dealt with. The utilitarians were too closely involved in the battle against prejudice and vested interests to be able to appraise them with detachment.

3. JAMES MILL AND THE SCOTTISH TRADITION

If Bentham's essay on the *Influence of Time and Place* is a peripheral work, the same cannot be said of James Mill's *History of British India*. It occupied him from 1806 to 1818, and upon it his contemporary reputation largely rested. Even after he had completed it he contemplated another work in the same genre.

> The next work which I meditate is a History of English law, in which I mean to trace, as far as possible, the expedients of the several ages to the state of the human mind, and the circumstances of society in those ages, and to show their concord or discord with their standard of perfection.[1]

His failure to write this projected work, both Benthamite and yet thoroughly in the tradition of Scottish philosophic history, takes us to the heart of the puzzle of his intellectual career. Of course, the project may have always been merely one of those hypothetical books which so many scholars cherish but know that they have no real intention of writing. The *History of British India*, after all, had cost Mill much toil and many years; indeed, he openly said that if he had known the cost in advance he would never have begun.[2] Something must be allowed to weariness of the flesh—even for James Mill. But much must also be laid to the account of the increasing pressure of radical politics upon Mill's time and intellectual energy. What needs explaining, perhaps, is not so much his failure to follow the *History* by

[1] Bain, *James Mill*, p. 174.   [2] *Ibid.* p. 62.

another work of the same kind, but his failure to adopt in his more directly polemical, political writings more of the characteristic stance of a Scottish philosophic historian. For after all, the *History* is not a work of detached scholarship. Mill's prose is often harsh with the grinding of axes. Not merely does it not aspire to that sympathetic understanding which was beginning to be postulated as the goal of historical writing, it does not aim even at the ironical superiority of a Gibbon.

In fact Mill's *History* both represented and reinforced a current of contemporary opinion within which the urbane tolerance and even qualified admiration of the eighteenth century for alien and barbaric cultures was giving way to censoriousness and denigration. More than ever, contemporary Europe was being taken as the measure of all excellence.

Mill's standpoint in the *History* is that strictly qualified relativism which is the hallmark of 'philosophic' history, as distinct from *Historismus*, on the one hand, and naïve utopianism on the other. There *is* an absolute standard of judgement—in Mill's case, utility—but the 'improvement' of backward societies must be a slow and cautious business, and must be related to the 'stage' of civilization they have reached. Books II and III of Mill's *History* are an attempt to determine the stage of civilization reached by the native population of India.[1]

No scheme of government can happily conduce to the ends of government, unless it is adapted to the state of the people for whose use it is intended. In those diversities in the state of civilization, which approach the extremes, this truth is universally acknowledged. Should anyone propose, for a band of roving Tartars, the regulations adapted to the happiness of a regular and polished society, he would meet with neglect or

[1] Forbes, 'James Mill and India', p. 27.

derision. The inconveniences are only more concealed and more or less diminished, when the error relates to states of society which more readily resemble one another.[1]

If we think the Hindus have a high civilization, the argument goes on, when in fact they have a low one, we shall misgovern them in consequence.[2]

Mill had no doubt that the civilization of the Hindus had been overrated and that the chief culprit was Sir William Jones, the distinguished orientalist and Sanskrit philologist. Jones, though a profound scholar, had much of the eighteenth-century notion of Asia as a source of wisdom. His recognition of the superiority of Europe in very many respects did not preclude the belief that from Asia 'many valuable hints may be derived for our own improvement and advantage'.[3] He was a defender of customary law[4]—the *bête noire* of the utilitarians. For British theorists, India provided the battle-ground for the dispute between advocates of codified and customary law which in Germany took the form of the conflict between Romanists and Germanists, and which provided much of the impetus to the development of the historical school of jurisprudence.[5] Jones's attitude, however, was really that of the urbane man of culture rather than that of a deliberate controversialist. He speaks approvingly of 'the gratification of a natural and

---

[1] James Mill, *History of British India*, I, 42.

[2] Cf. 'Doubtless the laws which are adapted to an impoverished state of society, would not be adapted to a state of society much behind. But it will not be difficult when we have a standard of excellence; to determine what is to be done, in all cases' (Mill to Ricardo, 27 December 1817, quoted in T. W. Hutchinson, 'James Mill and the Political Education of Ricardo', *Cambridge Journal*, VII (1954), p. 90).

[3] *Asiatic Researches*, Transactions of the Society instituted in Bengal for inquiry into the History and Antiquities and the Arts, Sciences and Literature of Asia, I (1798), 407.

[4] E.g. *Asiatic Researches*, III, 449.

[5] *Op. cit.* IV, p. 1.

laudable curiosity'[1] though he did hope that his work on Comparative Religion would help to confirm the essential truth of the book of Genesis.[2]

Much of the second book of Mill's *History of India* is devoted to an attempt to topple Hindu civilization from the pedestal on which he considered Jones had unjustifiably placed it. The result is frequently to a modern reader very odd indeed. Mill takes issue with many aspects of Hindu society as though he were attacking abuses in his own society. Hindu theology is examined to be rejected *as* theology. There is in fact almost certainly a sidelong glance at the Anglican Church in Mill's strictures on the Brahmins. Mill was enough of a *philosophe* to see the opportunities for oblique castigation. As the author of a recent study of British attitudes to India has said, 'Antipathy in Britain towards the social institutions of India was as much a general disapproval of the medieval and aristocratic society passing away as a failure to understand and appreciate institutions peculiar to India.'[3]

But if Mill tended, as he probably did in part, to see what he disliked in India as a reflection or even aggravation of what he disliked in England, this was probably the result of a rationalist, radical cast of mind applied to both societies rather than because he was using India primarily as a mask for an attack on English institutions. In early nineteenth-century England, though it was wise to publish attacks upon orthodox religion under a pseudonym,[4] no such elaborate

---

[1] Cf. 'Disquisitions concerning the manners and conduct of our species in early times, or indeed at any time, are always curious, at least, and amusing' (*op. cit.* I, 224).

[2] Jones, 'On the Gods of Greece, Italy and India' (*op. cit.* I, 225).

[3] G. D. Bearce, *British Attitudes towards India, 1784–1858* (O.U.P. 1961), p. 7. Cf. Forbes, 'James Mill and India', p. 26.

[4] E.g. Bentham's pamphlet, 'Not Paul but Jesus' (1823), which he published with the help of George Grote under the pseudonym 'Gamaliel Smith'.

deviousness was required as the shadow of the Bastille had taught eighteenth-century Frenchmen. In any case the subtler irony of the *philosophes* was alien to Mill's blunt censoriousness. His main purpose remained to fix Indian society in the scale of civilization.

Jones had gone wrong, he thought, because he had not, unlike Mill himself, had the advantage of a grounding in Scottish philosophic history.

Notwithstanding all that modern philosophy had performed for the elucidation of history, very little had been attempted in this great department, at the time when the notions of Sir William Jones were formed. The writings of Mr Miller (*sic*) of Glasgow, of which but a small part was then published, and into which it is probable that Sir William had never looked, contained the earliest elucidation of the subject. The suggestions offered in his successive productions, though highly important, were but detached considerations applied to particular facts, and not a comprehensive induction leading to general conclusions.[1]

Jones lacked, in consequence, an adequate sense of history. 'The term civilization was by him, as by most men, attached to no fixed and definite assemblage of ideas. With the exception of some of the lowest states of society in which human beings had been found it was applied to nations in all stages of social advancement.'[2] Mill's criterion of civilization is, unequivocally, utility, which seems to have more to do with Bentham than with Millar. 'Exactly in proportion as Utility is the object of every pursuit may we regard a nation as civilized.'[3] But Mill's chief explanation of progress—population increase[4]—is very Scottish.[5] The actual outline of

---

[1] Mill, *History of British India*, I, 431–2. [2] *Ibid*. p. 431.
[3] *Ibid*. p. 428. Cf. p. 263. [4] *Ibid*. pp. 104–6.
[5] For Mill's acknowledgements to the work of Scottish eighteenth-century historians of civilization other than Millar, see *History of British India*, I, 93, 117 (Robertson), 304, 375, 433 (Ferguson) and 398–9 (Adam Smith).

progress is etched in by the orthodox methods of conjectural history. Mill admits that

it is not easy to describe the characteristics of the different stages of social progress. It is not from one feature or from two, that a just conclusion can be drawn...It is from a joint view of all the great circumstances taken together, that their progress can be ascertained, and it is from an accurate comparison, grounded on these general views, that a scale of civilization can be formed, on which the relative position of nations may be accurately marked.[1]

And he goes on to cite Ferguson's *History of Civil Society*[2] to illustrate the complexity of the criteria of savagery and civilization.

Nevertheless, Mill is convinced that there is essentially one path which all nations follow. The following is worth quoting at length for its similarity to many statements of the eighteen-sixties:

As the manners, institutions and attainments of the Hindus have been stationary for many ages, in beholding the Hindus of the present day we are beholding the Hindus of many ages past, and are carried back, as it were, into the deepest recesses of antiquity. Nor is this all; of some of the nations, about which our curiosity is the most alive, and information the most defective, we acquire a practical, and what may be almost denominated a personal knowledge by our acquaintance with a living people, who have continued on the same soil from the very times of those ancient nations, partaken largely of the same manners, and are placed nearly at the same stage in the progress of society. By conversing with the Hindus of the present day, we, in some measure, converse with the Chaldeans and Babylonians of the time of Cyrus; with the Persians and Egyptians of the time of Alexander.[3]

---

[1] *Ibid.* p. 431.   [2] *Ibid.* p. 433 n.

[3] *History of British India*, I, 469. For Mill's use of travellers' accounts of contemporary savage and barbarous societies, see especially *ibid.* pp. 181–2, 194 n., 211 n.

Mill's book is not only the last, it is also the most elaborate
and detailed example of Scottish philosophic history.

At this point we seem to have reached a paradox. It was
suggested at the end of the previous chapter that conjectural
history, for all its defects, represented a basis for the serious
study of alien societies, and its decline a setback in the
development of what, with some anachronism, we may call
social anthropology. Yet in Mill's attack on Jones we see a
tolerant, even sympathetic approach to an alien culture,
assailed by a brash European censoriousness, and assailed,
moreover, from a basis of Scottish philosophic history,
ignorance of which is supposed largely responsible for
Jones's errors.

About this a number of observations may be made. It is
a characteristic of all theories to open some doors while
closing others. Some problems are brought into focus, others
fall into the background. A theory must set aside certain
possible lines of exploration as profitless if it is to be any
use at all. A guide is not a guide if he leads simultaneously
in all directions at once. In retrospect one may regret that
certain avenues were closed, certain attitudes proscribed,
yet still regard *some* theoretical framework as better than
none at all. Jones's theory, if we may call it that, was a theory
of cultural diffusion. He wanted to show that European,
Arabic and Indian culture sprang from a common source,
and thereby prove their cousinship. The cultural broad-
mindedness this belief encouraged may have been admirable,
and could lead to much useful work of a philological or
ethnographical kind, but from the point of view of developing
sociology and anthropology it was a blind alley. Conjectural
history, for all its ultimate parochialism, was not. Moreover,
a good deal depended on how it was written. Mill's tone is
notably more contemptuous of alien and barbaric societies

than is that of his eighteenth-century predecessors.[1] Mr Forbes, who stresses the weaknesses of the Scottish philosophy of history, also notes that Mill presents in some respects a cruder version of it and suggests what was surely a major cause of the decline of conjectural history in the early nineteenth century: 'The radical movement in England was responsible for a retrogression in historical thinking *within* the rationalist tradition.'[2] Mill's attack probably did grave damage to the prestige of oriental studies, but he did not succeed in rescuing conjectural history. In the event, both declined. Mill noticed the lacuna.

Unfortunately the subject, great as is its importance, has not been resumed. The writings of Mr Millar remain almost the only source from which the slightest information on the subject can be drawn. One of the ends which has at least been in view during the scrutiny conducted in these pages, has been to contribute something to the progress of so important an investigation.[3]

It is perhaps unfair, then, to blame Mill for the decline of an intellectual tradition to which he made a striking contribution.

4. THE DECLINE OF CONJECTURAL HISTORY

Nevertheless, the general tenor of Mill's political philosophy, and the contempt he tended to express for non-European peoples, can hardly have encouraged a scholarly interest in the comparative study of institutions. And if we look, for example, at some of Mill's Scottish-trained Whig contemporaries, we find parallels to Mill's contempt for oriental cultures actually accompanied by a rather brusque attitude to the leisurely, eighteenth-century Scottish com-

---

[1] Contrast the attitude of the Scottish historian Robertson. Bearce, *British Attitudes towards India*, pp. 20–1, 25.
[2] Forbes, 'Scientific Whiggism', p. 670.
[3] Mill, *History of British India*, I, 432.

bination of political philosophy and philosophic history. A new, a-theoretical impatience in politics was becoming apparent, and European parochialism tending to degenerate into European arrogance. The more complex, eighteenth-century theories of progress were coarsened in Macaulay's version of it. James Mill remained resolute in defence of theorizing—it was this that marked him off from the Whigs—but the impatience and the arrogance he had in full measure.

We may compare, for example, Mill's strictures on Voltaire's overestimation of Chinese civilization, and his remark that 'the state of belief in Europe has, gradually, through the scrutiny of facts, been of late approximating to sobriety on the attainments of the Chinese, and a short period longer will probably reduce it to reason and fact',[1] with Jeffrey's more laconic 'I had always a profound contempt for the Chineses'.[2] Philosophic Chinamen did not fit into the Edinburgh Reviewers' scheme of things.[3]

While trying to account for this growing lack of sympathy, we should, of course, recognize that some reappraisal was naturally to be expected as knowledge of the East became fuller. It was understandable that enthusiasm should diminish with closer acquaintance. Of course, counter-examples could easily be found of more subtle and sympathetic attitudes to the past, and to alien cultures. In England, this was, after all, the age of Scott—and of the Brighton Pavilion! In India, officials like Elphinstone and Munro[4] were very far from sharing the contempt for Indian culture and institutions of a Macaulay. We may profitably take Macaulay as the exponent of at least one powerful

---

[1] *History of British India*, I, 430. Cf. Mill's review of de Guignes, 'Voyage à Pékin', *ER*, XXVIII (1809). Attributed to Mill in Bain, *James Mill*, p. 100.
[2] Quoted in John Clive, *Scotch Reviewers. The Edinburgh Review, 1802–1815* (1957), p. 168.   [3] *Ibid.* pp. 167–71.
[4] Bearce, *British Attitudes towards India*, pp. 122–49.

trend of contemporary opinion, however; to anyone interested in the rise of social anthropology, Macaulay's attitudes are fascinating. To a friend who had been dabbling
in ethnology, he wrote from India begging him to translate
Herodotus instead:

Your talents are too great, and your leisure time too small, to be
wasted in inquiries so frivolous (I must call them), as those in
which you have of late been too much engaged; whether the
Cherokees are of the same race with the Chickasaws; whether
Van Diemen's Land was peopled from New Holland, or New
Holland from Van Diemen's Land; what is the precise mode of
appointing a headman in a village in Timbuctoo: I would not
give the worst page in Clarendon or Fra Paolo for all that ever
was, or ever will be, written about the migrations of the Leleges
and the laws of the Oscans.[1]

Macaulay's own leisure in India was spent in prodigious
reading of the classics, while his interest in the customs of
the peoples whose laws he was helping to codify can be
gauged from remarks like the following:

I have, as yet, seen little of the idolatry of India, and that little,
though excessively absurd, is not characterised by atrocity or
indecency...The Todas, the aboriginal population of these hills,
are a very curious race. They had a great funeral a little while
ago. I should have gone if it had not been a Council day; but
I found afterwards that I had lost nothing. The whole ceremony
consisted in sacrificing bullocks to the manes of the defunct...
I have not lived three and thirty years in this world without
learning that a bullock roars when he is knocked down, and that
a woman can cry whenever she chooses.[2]

It is a far cry to Maine, in the eighteen-seventies, insisting
on the respect due to, and the scientific interest of, Indian
institutions.

[1] Letter to T. F. Ellis, 1 July 1834, in G. O. Trevelyan, *Life and Letters
of Lord Macaulay* (1908 ed.), pp. 269–70. Compare Henry Sidgwick, 'We
don't want to know what particular black stones the aborigines worshipped
—at least I don't' [This was in 1866]. (*Henry Sidgwick, A Memoir*, by A.S.
and E.M.S. (1906), p. 140.) [2] Trevelyan, *op. cit.* pp. 271–2.

But, as with Bentham, it can be argued that Macaulay was too immersed in the contemporary struggle with obscurantism and lethargy to think otherwise. It was easy for Maine, in the eighteen-sixties, addressing the students of the University of Calcutta, to temper his criticisms of their Indian cultural heritage with an admission of its scholarly interest; yet it is arguable that, but for Macaulay's Minute on Education, there would have been no students for Maine to address.[1]

The Westernizers in India won a great victory with the admission of missionaries in 1813, and another with Macaulay's Minute on Education. His proposal to allow oriental literature to fall into neglect was largely accepted.[2] Meanwhile, in England, too, oriental studies had fallen into disrepute, partly perhaps as a result of Mill's attack in his *History*. The *Quarterly Review* noted that booksellers did not dare republish the oriental researches of the earlier period.[3] Jones's work on Sanskrit was not developed as it might have been, and it was left to the Germans to make it the basis of comparative philology.

The supersession of eighteenth-century tolerant cosmopolitanism by early nineteenth-century cultural chauvinism is many-faceted; it does not, moreover, fall neatly into periods in the way this sentence implies. If one must have a period, then that between 1770 and 1830 is the period of transition, during which the coexistence of the romantic sense of the past with a Whiggish and Evangelical passion for improvement, both equally alien to the cultural scene

---

[1] Even Maine sternly warned that the Indian must not be too enthusiastic about native culture: 'On the educated Native of India the Past presses with too awful and terrible a power for it to be safe for him to play or palter with it' ('Address to the University of Calcutta' (1866), in Sir Henry Maine, *Village Communities in the East and West* (3rd ed. 1876), p. 291 (1871).

[2] Bearce, *British Attitudes towards India*, p. 171.

[3] *Ibid.* p. 182.

of the early eighteenth century, defies easy classification. To explain it, and by implication the trends we have been considering, would be to write the history of European society during this period. It is nevertheless, perhaps, worthwhile to try to identify them, even though identification is not explanation. We may locate the issues with which we are concerned, the decline of conjectural history, the prospects, in the early nineteenth century, for the emergence of social anthropology in a pattern whose outlines, romanticism, evangelicalism, liberalism, industrialization,[1] rationalism and so on, however vacuous as explanations, are at least familiar as points of departure. And if there are no simple explanations, neither is there a simple profit and loss account. What we have been considering is a new censoriousness in attitudes to alien and primitive cultures.[2] It is easy to stigmatize this as blind arrogance and narrow intolerance, and to contrast it with easy-going, even up to a point open-minded, eighteenth-century urbanity. This is largely true. But the reverse side of nineteenth-century arrogance and censoriousness was a genuine humanitarianism and passion for improvement, just as the reverse side of eighteenth-century tolerance was often callousness and corruption.

There were, however, casualties, and one of them may

[1] The rhythms and festivities of an agricultural community were not yet altogether alien even to the most cultivated of eighteenth-century Englishmen. Of the mid-nineteenth century, however, Bearce can say, 'Many Britons, seeing such manifestations of a traditional peasant community as the squandering of a life's savings at a marriage or funeral ceremony, as well as the more obvious evils of caste and superstition, could only regard Indians as "enemies of God"' (*British Attitudes towards India*, p. 229). In the eighteenth century the poor were not yet expected to be 'good'.

[2] And to much else, of course; curiously, the characteristic counterpart of censoriousness appears to be not satire but jocularity. In Sydney Smith, in his capacity as an Edinburgh Reviewer, censoriousness and jocularity were united in the same person.

have been conjectural history. If so, it fell a victim not so much to censoriousness alone—Mill had shown that the two could be combined pretty effectively—but perhaps to impatience.

Dugald Stewart,[1] in his introduction to Adam Smith's *Essays on Philosophical Subjects*, was at pains to dissociate the method he was describing—the method of conjectural history—from political radicalism. It is true that the early seventeen-nineties was a bad moment to be radical, and that Stewart was doubtless trying to ensure that his hero should not suffer eclipse through conservative suspicion.[2] Stewart himself had in 1794 to apologize abjectly for having once referred to Condorcet with respect.[3]

Nevertheless, it is still possible to agree with his remarks about the political complexion of even the more radical members of the Scottish Enlightenment, Smith and Millar. Despite the anarchist strain on which Halévy placed so much emphasis, their approach is Whiggish rather than revolutionary, while the historical and determinist cast of their thinking, minus any drastic recipes for 'easing the birth pangs of the new society', implied a comforting gradualism. Indeed there are indications that the young Scottish-trained Whigs of the early nineteenth century found the characteristic method, if not the actual political views, of their early mentors altogether too leisurely and broadly based. Sydney Smith's complaint that the characteristic Scottish method was to begin every subject 'a few days before the flood, and come *gradually* down to the reign

---

[1] The discussion which follows professes to present only a bare outline of a possible solution of this problem. The whole question would repay further attention.

[2] Lehmann holds that suspicion of his radicalism was a major reason for the eclipse of Millar (Lehmann, *John Millar of Glasgow*, p. 148).

[3] Clive, *Scotch Reviewers*, p. 25.

of George the third"[1] was more than merely flippant. Brougham found Robertson's histories 'too general for practical use and application',[2] a significant phrase, and regretted his neglect of detail, while Jeffrey, the editor of the *Edinburgh Review*, actually protested against the proliferation of conjectural history, saying that it needed to be handled with great skill and care.[3]

In fact the characteristic Scottish method seems to have been altogether too 'philosophic' for the impatient pragmatism of the Edinburgh Reviewers—well enough to serve as the framework for a review of some 'instructive' book of travels,[4] but hardly relevant to the serious business of politics. The rough-and-ready common sense which Jeffrey turns against Bentham, and which also characterizes much of Macaulay—the impatient 'every schoolboy knows', a significant as well as characteristic stylistic trait—was really as much out of key with the constant reference to first principles of Scottish philosophic history as it was with utilitarianism.

The common impressions of morality, the vulgar distinctions of right and wrong, virtue and vice, are perfectly sufficient to direct and conduct the individual, and the judgment of the legislator, without any reference to the nature or origin of these distinctions. In many respects indeed, we conceive them to be fitter for these purposes than Mr Bentham's oracles of utility.[5]

But for the last four words, could one be sure that this was an attack upon utilitarianism rather than upon conjectural

---

[1] Quoted in New, *The Life of Henry Brougham to 1830*, p. 223. Italics original.

[2] *ER*, III (1803), 240; attributed to Brougham by Clive, *op. cit.* p. 176 n. 5.

[3] *ER*, III (1803), 206–7 noted Clive, *Scotch Reviewers*, p. 166.

[4] E.g. *ER*, XXX (1810), review of *Voyage aux Indes Orientales*, par le P. Paulin de S. Barthélemy.

[5] *ER*, VII (1804), attributed to Jeffrey by Clive, *op. cit.* 92.

history? Jeffrey was doubtless considered, and perhaps considered himself, to be continuing the war of the eighteenth-century Scottish Common Sense philosophers against sensation psychology, now represented by Bentham. But Jeffrey made it clear elsewhere that he understood the primacy of common sense as assigning to philosophy a much humbler role than the Scottish philosophers would have admitted. 'Everyone knows exactly what it is to perceive and to feel, to remember, imagine, and believe; and though he may not always apply the words that denote these operations with perfect propriety, it is not possible to suppose that anyone is ignorant of the things.'[1] Philosophical adherence to 'ordinary language' and common sense is constantly in danger of committing suicide, or turning itself into lexicography. This is an implication which Jeffrey accepts, which is tantamount to rejecting all the traditional claims of philosophy.

Leslie Stephen detected a natural affinity between Scottish Common Sense philosophy and a-theoretical Whiggism.[2] There is a great deal in this, and certainly it is no accident that Mackintosh the Whig was a defender of Common Sense, while James Mill the radical was a follower of Hartley, but it must be appreciated that Common Sense philosophy in Whiggish hands could become something very unphilosophical indeed, becoming literally common sense without capital letters—'What every schoolboy knows'. At this point, its connection with any philosophical school becomes negligible.

---

[1] *ER*, VI (1804), Review of Stewart's Life of Reid, p. 276; attributed to Jeffrey by Stephen, *The English Utilitarians*, I, 152.

[2] 'The Scottish philosophy was...in philosophy what Whiggism was in politics. Like political Whiggism it included a large element of enlightened and liberal rationalism; but like Whiggism it covered an aversion to thorough-going logic' (Stephen, *op. cit.* I, 167).

The decline of Common Sense philosophy was another aspect of the decline of the distinctive Scottish intellectual tradition in the early nineteenth century. With the work of Thomas Brown,[1] Scottish philosophy, as Stephen put it, virtually declared itself bankrupt,[2] though it was not until J. S. Mill's attack on Hamilton[3] that it received its *coup de grâce*.

The question has already been raised, but not discussed, whether there was some logical link, or at least some natural affinity, between Common Sense philosophy and conjectural history such that the decline of the former might entail or imply the decline of the latter. If so, we should know where to look for the answer to our problem—the long gap between the Scottish 'philosophic' histories and the emergence of evolutionary social theory in the eighteen-sixties. But is this in fact the answer?

The beginnings of the rival theories are not propitious for our thesis. The paternity of common-sense intuitionism has been fostered upon Shaftesbury[4] as that of sensationalist hedonism upon Mandeville.[5] But Mandeville wrote a conjectural history,[6] while Shaftesbury denied altogether the original primitive state of man.[7] The roles appear to be reversed. Perhaps, however, we need not take this too seriously. We can at least concede that between Common Sense philosophy and history there is no such disjunction as between associationism and history. Common Sense philosophy may not actually prescribe historical inquiry, but neither does it promise to render it unnecessary. If it

---

[1] For Brown, see Stephen, *The English Utilitarians*, II, ch. VII.
[2] *Ibid.* p. 285.
[3] J. S. Mill, *An Examination of Sir William Hamilton's Philosophy* (1865).
[4] Grave, *The Scottish Philosophy of Common Sense*, p. 7.
[5] Halévy, *The Growth of Philosophic Radicalism*, p. 16.
[6] Stephen, *History of English Thought in the Eighteenth Century*, II, 40.
[7] *Ibid.* p. 40.

offers a short cut to philosophical understanding, it does not do the same for social understanding. Does not the belief in universally valid intuitions, however, impose limits on historical relativism? If things are what they seem, then what they seem must remain pretty much the same if the implications are not to be very disturbing indeed. A sociologically based scepticism would have been as bad as Hume's logically based scepticism. In fact, however, conjectural history was not relativist. Mr Forbes has noticed that Millar, for one, uses the notion of the progress of society through different stages to account for the diversities which would otherwise have seemed irreconcilable with the idea of stability in the moral sentiments of mankind.[1]

Nevertheless, the connection between conjectural history and Common Sense philosophy appears to be a fairly loose one. It lies, if anywhere, in a suggested antipathy between Common Sense's epistemological rival, sensationalism, with its psychological development, associationism, on the one hand, and the serious study of history as a guide to the present, on the other.

But is this really the case? Certainly in the case of Bentham, as we have seen, the purity of his psychological approach to morals and politics is not adulterated in any significant way by attention to history. But what of James Mill? Did the author of the *History of British India* (certainly an example of 'committed' rather than academic historiography), the *Essay on Government*, the *Analysis of the Human Mind*, and the *Fragment on Mackintosh* succeed in marrying these diverse works into a coherent political philosophy, in which philosophic history and sensation psychology harmoniously cohabit? Or was the *History* merely his last tribute to his Scottish inheritance, while

[1] Forbes, 'Scientific Whiggism', p. 645.

the *Essay* was his first major contribution to English utilitarianism?

Mill was brought up on the philosophy of Reid and Stewart, the philosophical orthodoxy of the Scottish universities.[1] As late as 1806, the year in which he began the *History of British India*, he was still denouncing Hartley, Helvétius, and the associationist school of which he was later to become an ornament.[2] It was his connection with Bentham, according to Halévy, which changed all this: 'If James Mill had never known Bentham he would never have become the doctrinaire of the philosophy of the association of ideas and general utility.'[3] Mill continued, however, his work on the *History of British India*, and the projected work with which he intended to follow it[4] would indeed have been a kind of marriage of Benthamism with philosophic history. As it was, with the completion of the *History*, he seems to have abandoned serious work of this kind. Nevertheless, he could at least claim, with far more justice than Bentham, that he had made a contribution to explaining in what way the dictates of utility were to be adjusted to the stages reached by different societies.

How then are we to account for the notoriously deductivist and a-historical character of his later writings? The answer, if anywhere, lies not in the *Essay on Government*, whose brevity can be pleaded in extenuation, or in the *Analysis of the Human Mind*, which is avowedly a psychological work, but in the *Fragment on Mackintosh*, in which Mill, in defending Bentham against Mackintosh, is also, as he says, defending himself—referred to in the third person; the book was published anonymously—against

[1] Bain, *James Mill*, pp. 18–19.
[2] Halévy, *The Growth of Philosophic Radicalism*, p. 439.
[3] *Ibid.* p. 450.   [4] See above, p. 42.

Macaulay. Mackintosh had levelled the classic charge against the utilitarians: 'Mr Bentham, indeed, is much more remarkable for laying down desirable rules for the determination of rights and the punishment of wrongs, in general, than for weighing the various circumstances which require them to be modified in different countries and times.'[1]

To this, adverting with a certain understandable weariness—understandable, that is, in view of the half-baked 'Baconianism' of his opponents—to 'the beaten topic of theory and practice',[2] Mill has two answers. He claims, like Mrs Mack, that Bentham considered attention to such circumstances 'of primary importance'. Like Bentham himself, however, he greatly weakens the force of this claim and goes far to substantiate, inadvertently, Mackintosh's criticism, by his second defence. 'There are circumstances which all nations have in common. There are other circumstances, which each nation has peculiar to itself. The first set of circumstances, those which nations have in common; at least nations which are nearly on the same level in point of civilization; are beyond comparison the most important.'[3]

Mill has indeed inserted a qualification which Bentham does not make: 'on the same level in point of civilization'. What Mill means by this, in its application to contemporary Britain, becomes clear when he goes on to say that 'if any thing is really good for the people, it is rarely indeed a very difficult matter to make them see that it is so'.[4] If we assume that this sentence refers to contemporary England, but not to contemporary India, it becomes possible to reconcile the *Essay on Government* with the *History of British India*, and Mill's advocacy of democracy on theoretical grounds with

---

[1] Sir James Mackintosh, *A Dissertation on the Progress of Ethical Philosophy* (Edinburgh, 1836), p. 289.

[2] James Mill, *A Fragment on Mackintosh* (1835), p. 142.

[3] *Ibid.* p. 142.   [4] *Ibid.* p. 149.

his vehement denial that it was possible or appropriate for India: for a major step in the argument of the *Essay on Government* is that men can recognize their own interest. If this condition is not fulfilled, the conclusion of the argument does not follow. The implication is that it is fulfilled in contemporary England but not in India. One is reminded of his son's caveat, in his essay *On Liberty*, that his arguments apply only to men who have the capacity for being influenced by rational argument.

The result, in James Mill's case, is to preserve the congruity of his political philosophy with his philosophy of history, at the expense of making the latter irrelevant to contemporary politics, except where the government of a backward country like India is in question. As Mill retorted to Mackintosh, when accused of having, in the *Essay on Government*, tried to explain the complexity of political facts by a single simple principle, 'Mr Mill has not sought to explain the immense variety of political facts at all, all that Mr Mill attempted was, to show how a community could obtain the best security for good legislation.'[1]

We can now begin to understand the apparent paradox of Macaulay's and Mill's respective attitudes to India. In their approach to India, the Mill who wrote the *Essay on Government* and the Macaulay who attacked it appear to have changed places. They share a common contempt for Indian culture and institutions, but in an Indian context, as Dr Stokes points out, it is Macaulay who displays unbounded confidence and James Mill who is cautious and pessimistic.[2] The explanation is that Mill has a philosophy of history which teaches him to be a gradualist in India,

---

[1] *Ibid.* p. 293.
[2] See E. T. Stokes, *The English Utilitarians and India* (O.U.P. 1959), pp. 57–9.

just as he has a philosophy of mind which teaches him to be a democrat in England, while Macaulay has neither.

Nevertheless, if Mill's philosophy of history and his philosophy of politics were not inconsistent, the fact that the former applied directly only to the past or to backward peoples almost certainly conduced to its neglect in the excited political atmosphere of the eighteen-twenties and early eighteen-thirties, especially by a man so deeply politically committed as James Mill. This separation between modes of argument appropriate to the present and those appropriate only to the past, and to societies that represent the past, is one we shall find again in the second half of the century. But by then the atmosphere had changed, and what was required from a philosophy of history was not that it should be an engine of radical reform, but that it should provide something much more like cosmic reassurance. Only Marx could claim to have made the philosophy of revolution identical with the philosophy of history—and even here it is significant that Engels, late in the century, virtually abandoned the equation. James Mill's philosophy of history was congruous with his radical political philosophy; it was not identical with it, and this, in the circumstances of the time, was perhaps enough to account for its relative neglect.

It seemed important to the utilitarians rather to play down the lessons of history because they were associated with Burkean attitudes, just as, as we have seen in the case of Bentham, it seemed important to denigrate the acquired empirical wisdom of the professionals, because this was tainted, whether in English law or Indian government, with the notion of corruption and vested interest. What was needed was not the subtle understanding born of long experience, but above all impartiality, the impartiality of men schooled in first principles.[1] Vested interests were still the chief enemy, and pragmatic Whiggism seemed altogether too lenient to them. Mill follows his remark that men may readily be induced to see where their interest lies with the significant qualification, 'where much influence and artifice are not employed to delude them'.[2] Mackintosh's point about making laws adapted to circumstances is to Mill 'the slang of those who are the enemies of all reform. This serves for a while after the language of direct adherence to what is *contrary to reason* can no longer be held...it is an argument for everlasting postponement.'[3] To emphasize the importance of history seemed to the utilitarians dangerous. The only remedy would have been a philosophy of history as radical in its implications as Marx's was revolutionary. Halévy claims that in Political Economy the radicals had such a philosophy of history, but even if this view is accepted, this was not philosophic history as exemplified by James Mill's *History of British India*. Hence the latter tended to be left on the shelf when current political questions were debated.

Perhaps the most striking proof of James Mill's defection from the Scottish philosophy of history is, as Mr Forbes points out,[4] the neglect of it by his son. John Stuart Mill obviously knew the work of the Scottish eighteenth-century historians, but seems to have derived little inspiration from them as philosophers of history.[5] At all events, however strong the dose of them his education contained, it was insufficient to inoculate him against Comtism.

---

[1] James Mill, *History of British India*, Preface, pp. xiii–xix.
[2] *Fragment on Mackintosh*, p. 149.
[3] *Ibid.* p. 147. Italics mine.
[4] Forbes, 'Scientific Whiggism', p. 670.
[5] For Millar's possible influence on him see Lehmann, *John Millar of Glasgow*, pp. 152–3.

In many different ways, in the eighteen-twenties and eighteen-thirties, the current was running against the Scottish historical and philosophical tradition. Even in Political Economy, the gift from Scotland which England accepted, the greater theoretical refinement of the subject was detaching it from the broad historical and sociological context in which it had rested in the works of Adam Smith. From the eighteen-thirties onwards, the Scottish educational system itself, no longer the donor but the recipient of influences, began to decline.[1] The period of Whig domination saw the beginning of the deterioration of the distinctive Scottish educational tradition, just as it was the period of Whig victory, the early eighteen-thirties, that saw the influence of the Westernizers in India at its height.[2]

But the tide was about to turn, or rather, since the complexity of history sometimes obliges us to maltreat our metaphors, it was receding while it still rose.

[1] Davie, *The Democratic Intellect*, p. 3.
[2] Bearce, *British Attitudes towards India*, ch. VI.

CHAPTER 3

THE REASONED HISTORY OF MAN

I. THE CRITIQUE OF PHILOSOPHIC RADICALISM

The decline of the gospel of Hartley and Bentham was not
an autonomous development in English intellectual life.
'The influences of European, that is to say Continental
thought, and especially those of the reactions of the nineteenth century against the eighteenth were now streaming
in upon me.'[1] J. S. Mill went on to list them as Coleridge
and Carlyle as intermediaries, Goethe, and, above all, the
Saint-Simonians and Comte.[2]

J. S. Mill's *Autobiography* is an epitome of the transition,
both because of his birth in the utilitarian purple and because of his attempt to preserve a *via media*. The crucial
chapters of the book reveal two main sources of discontent
with his father's system. The first, which he derived chiefly
from the Continent, may be called 'historical relativism'.
The claim to be able, with only minor adjustments at the
most, to deduce the ends and necessities of any commonwealth, and to prescribe by reason its ideal constitution and
principles of legislation, was beginning to be rejected. Even
John Austin, the Benthamite jurist, according to Mill,
returned from a course of study in Germany and 'professed
great disrespect for what he called "the universal principles
of human nature of the political economists" and insisted
on the evidence which history and daily experience afford
of the "extraordinary pliability of human nature"'.[3] The

---

[1] J. S. Mill, *Autobiography*, pp. 136–7.   [2] *Ibid.* pp. 137–41.
[3] *Ibid.* p. 151. Austin was a curious case. He both knew and admired the
work of Savigny, but continued himself to write as a purely analytic jurist.
See Stephen, *The English Utilitarians*, III, 318–320.

constants in the utilitarian system were turning into
variables; and the natural result was a new interest in the
other factors in the social situation, history and society.

Existing standards of historiography were also beginning
to be regarded as inadequate. J. S. Mill, in an article on
Michelet for the *Edinburgh Review* in 1844, lamented that
'whatever may be the merits, in some subordinate respects,
of such histories as the last twenty years have provided
among us, they are distinguishable in no essential character
from the historical writings of the last century',[1] though he
exonerates Arnold and Carlyle. There was an impatience
with the triviality of an historiography concerned merely
with courts and dynasties, and a demand that it should
widen the area of its preoccupations. As G. H. Lewes put
it, 'Popes, kings and emperors—courts, camps and dun-
geons—these have filled the "swelling scene" to the exclusion of all that was important, vital—all that produced
them and much else.'[2]

This demand for a broader-based history was not confined to one generation, or to those who, like Lewes, believed that history could be made a science. Macaulay wrote
in his review of Mitford's *History of Greece*,

The happiness of the many commonly depends on causes independent of victories or defeats, of revolutions or restorations
—causes which can be regulated by no laws and which are
recorded in no archives. These causes are the things which it is
of main importance to us to know, not how the Lacedaemonian
phalanx was broken at Leuctra—not whether Alexander died of
poison or by disease.[3]

This is a declaration which forcibly recalls Voltaire's

[1] *ER*, CLIX (1844), p. 1.
[2] G. H. Lewes, 'The State of Historical Science in France', *British and
Foreign Review*, XXXI (1844), 74.
[3] Reprinted in *Miscellaneous Writings* (2 vols. 1860), I, 176–7.

biting insistence in the *Essai sur les Mœurs* that 'le but de ce travail n'est pas de savoir en quelle année un prince indigne d'être connu succéda à un prince barbare chez une nation grossière'[1] and looks forward to T. H. Huxley's demand that '*by and by*, we must have history treated not as a succession of battles and dynasties; not as evidence that Providence has always been on the side of either Whigs or Tories; but as the development of man in times past, and in other conditions than our own'.[2]

All these views represent a middle-class revolt against the treatment of history as a chronicle of the deeds of an aristocratic and military caste, and a demand instead for history which shall concern itself with the man in the street, his opinions, conditions of life and the factors which have made for his happiness and unhappiness.[3]

But this demand did not, in itself, represent a threat to deductive political theory, though it did involve an increasing interest in the texture of society. What brought the new historical attitude into conflict with the assumption of universal laws of human nature was the insistence on the unique character of different historical periods. In the article already cited, J. S. Mill praised Michelet, not merely for his concern to portray the lives of the masses, but because 'with him, each period has a physiognomy and a character of its own'.[4]

English historians, under the influence of German models, were beginning to stress the importance of this kind of approach. One of J. S. Mill's honourable exceptions, Arnold,

[1] Voltaire, *Essai sur les Mœurs*. Avant-propos.
[2] T. H. Huxley, 'A Liberal Education' (1868), reprinted in *Lay Sermons* (1871), p. 52. Italics mine.
[3] This is obviously paralleled by similar movements in literature, in the development of the novel and the 'Bürgerliches Trauerspiel'.
[4] J. S. Mill, *ER*, CLIX, 15.

had already written, 'It is important to look at an age and country in its own point of view',[1] and the other, Carlyle, pronounced that 'the inward condition of life...so far as men are not mere digesting machines, is the same in no two ages'.[2] Similar views were soon to be expressed by J. C. Hare, who condemned historians who, 'not having a right insight into the necessary distinctions of ages and nations...measure others by their own standard and so misunderstand and misjudge them',[3] while Stanley wrote, 'In historical matters, the power of seeing differences cannot be too highly prized. The tendency of ordinary men is to invest every age with the attributes of their own time.'[4]

An historiography based on recommendations like these obviously involved a very different approach to society from that of a political theory deduced from supposed laws of human nature, and this new historiography was very largely a continental import.

There was also, however, from the end of the eighteen-twenties, a purely indigenous type of opposition to some of the central tenets of philosophic radicalism. J. S. Mill's unhappiness and Macaulay's inspired common sense were native products which owed nothing to France or Germany.

Of the two types of criticism these two brought to bear, Macaulay's was the first and the more immediately telling, though J. S. Mill's recantation, long stifled out of consideration for his father, was to have more profound results in the long run. Their criticisms are the more striking in that both belonged, to a greater and lesser extent, to the tradition they attacked, for Macaulay, at Cambridge, had come under the

[1] D. Forbes, *The Liberal Anglican Idea of History* (C.U.P. 1952), p. 130.
[2] *Ibid.* p. 188.   [3] *Ibid.* p. 133.
[4] *Ibid.* pp. 191–2.

influence of Charles Austin, who, according to Mill, 'presented the Benthamic doctrines in the most startling form of which they were susceptible'.[1]

In three famous articles for the *Edinburgh Review* in 1829, Macaulay delivered a searching criticism of James Mill's *Essay of Government* and of the deductive method in general. The canons which he accused James Mill of having violated are not those of Comte, nor of German idealism, but of traditional British empiricism. Bacon is his sacred name, and he invokes him again and again.[2] When he offers a paradigm method for 'useful' history, it is by an example from *physics*, from Bacon's treatment of the problem of heat, in fact.[3] Macaulay's articles are doubly interesting: as a native reaction against deductivism, and as an indication of how limited and unsystematic a reaction it was.

Macaulay's most damaging criticism is one echoed by modern philosophers.[4] It consists in pointing to an ambiguity in the pleasure principle. Either the statement that all men desire pleasure and avoid pain is analytic, in which case it is true by definition but gives no information, or it is synthetic, in which case it is simply not true. Or, as Macaulay put it, more simply, either it is trivial or it is false.[5]

This criticism of the utilitarian generalization of ends as merely verbal leads Macaulay to a criticism of James Mill for being concerned simply with the form of institutions, instead of with the real distribution of power. Mill, in the *Essay*, was concerned with sovereignty and its forms; Macaulay is concerned with power. He insists that the

---

[1] J. S. Mill, *Autobiography*, p. 66.
[2] Macaulay, *Miscellaneous Writings*, I, 284–5, 346, 356.
[3] *Ibid.* pp. 363–4.
[4] E.g. A. J. Ayer, *Philosophical Essays* (1954), p. 266.
[5] Macaulay, *Miscellaneous Writings*, p. 318.

inductive method is the only appropriate one, and that 'our knowledge of human nature, instead of being prior in order to our knowledge of the science of government, will be posterior to it'.[1] But his account of this 'induction' is of the type which J. S. Mill (though not with reference to Macaulay) stigmatized as 'vulgar'.[2] Certainly Macaulay seems to ignore the problems of social morphology which his method raises, and to advocate an empiricism of the crudest type: 'We ought to examine the constitution of all those communities in which, under whatever form, the blessings of good government are enjoyed; and to discover, if possible, in what they resemble each other, and in what they differ from those societies in which the object of government is not attained.'[3]

Macaulay's attack is a good example of Graham Wallas's dictum that 'Bentham's utilitarianism was killed by the unanswerable refusal of the plain man to believe that ideas of pleasure and pain were the only sources of human motive'.[4] J. S. Mill was not a plain man, and he was not addicted to bald, 'unanswerable refusals', but he was deeply impressed, though not totally converted, by Macaulay's attack on his father's essay. His own objections were both more complicated and more personal, but they were directed at the same sensitive spot, the utilitarian generalization of ends. He became convinced that the utilitarian theory of ends was only satisfactory in the case of the 'purely physical and organic [desires]; of the entire insufficiency of which to make life desirable, no one had a stronger conviction that I had'.[5] Except in the case of these primary 'physical and

---

[1] *Miscellaneous Writings*, p. 345.
[2] J. S. Mill, *Auguste Comte and Positivism* (1865), p. 86.
[3] Macaulay, *ibid.* p. 364.
[4] Graham Wallas, *Human Nature and Politics* (1908), p. 13.
[5] J. S. Mill, *Autobiography*, p. 117.

organic' desires, the attachment of pleasure to objects was by association, and was entirely arbitrary.[1]

The result of analysing the relation would therefore be, as he believed to have happened in his own case, to destroy it, and leave one barren of desires. The tendency of analysis was to dispel prejudice, and if all secondary desires had no rational foundation, since the associations on which they were based were, unlike the perceptions of regularities in nature, accidental and arbitrary, it followed that they must be prejudices, and would be destroyed by analysis. 'Analytic habits may thus even strengthen the associations between causes and effects, means and ends, but tend altogether to weaken those which are, to speak familiarly, a *mere* matter of feeling.'[2]

J. S. Mill's objection to the orthodox theory of the formation of ends is, at least at first sight, less a true objection than a confession. He is complaining that he is in the position of the conjurer's assistant who is no longer amused by the tricks because he knows how they are done. His objection to the theory, or rather to his own knowledge of it, was that it seemed to have deprived him of any good reason for doing anything. The importance of this apparently purely private distress is that, like Macaulay's criticism, it involved looking behind the utilitarian generalization of ends and asking why men find pleasure in different things. And having done this, J. S. Mill found that immediately he was in the realm of the contingent and the arbitrary.

These criticisms of Macaulay and J. S. Mill struck at the root of utilitarian political theory. By going behind the utilitarian generalization of ends and asking: in what do

---

[1] 'The pains and pleasures thus forcibly associated with things are not connected by any natural tie' (*ibid.* p. 116).

[2] *Ibid.* p. 117. Italics original.

men find pleasure and pain, and why?, they exposed the utilitarian solution of the problem (of motives) as merely a verbal one.

It is significant that, in the predicament in which they placed themselves, both Macaulay and J. S. Mill, in their different ways, turned to history for help. J. S. Mill's criticism, indeed, is curious in that his dissatisfaction was a psychological and moral rather than a strictly intellectual one. The utilitarian account of motives had failed to provide him with a reason for living, and his search for one led him to the philosophy of history. This need to make sense of life is an element in the development of sociology which we shall find again.

Both Macaulay and J. S. Mill, however, in different ways, in rejecting the utilitarian theory were reacting against its parochialism: Macaulay by invoking history as a corrective to the simplifications of utilitarian psychology; J. S. Mill by turning to the continental philosophies of history for new sources of inspiration and enlightenment.[1]

But there still remained one element in John Stuart Mill's utilitarian heritage to which he had to assign what he regarded as its proper place on the intellectual map. Much of the appeal of classical Political Economy for utilitarians lay in the fact that it provided in its own sphere what in the psychological sphere proved so difficult to obtain—namely, a means of determining what people want in an exactly measurable way. The price mechanism offered in the objective sphere of social life precisely what the Benthamite calculus failed to do in the subjective and inscrutable area of psychology. The area of observation is shifted from private feelings to public acts—namely, purchases. And

[1] For J. S. Mill and continental ideas, see J. S. Mill's *Autobiography*, esp. ch. v; I. W. Mueller, *J. S. Mill and French Thought* (Univ. of Illinois, 1956).

purchases are automatically given a numerical value relative to each other, by the price which is paid in each case. This was exactly what the utilitarians needed—a numerical index of relative wants.

It is true that this index will only apply to things which are purchasable, but it is at least plausible to assume, as James Mill does in the *Essay on Government*, that only the distribution of economic goods constitutes a problem for government and hence for political theory. It is plausible to assume that the only problems which arise for governments arise over economic goods, since they are by definition the only things which are scarce relative to demand, and hence the only things over which conflict need arise. The argument of James Mill's *Essay on Government* runs: the end is to maximize happiness; the means by which happiness is increased are goods; the production of the maximum amount of goods is ensured by the maximum incentive; therefore the solution to the problem of maximizing happiness is to ensure to each man the maximum of the produce of his labour. To do this is the central task of government. The means by which it is to be achieved must be dictated to us largely by our knowledge of the universal principles of human nature.

It was this last assertion that Macaulay attacked specifically. But J. S. Mill came to disagree with the doctrine on two counts. He objected to the conception of happiness as a commodity on moral and psychological grounds, and he objected to the universal applicability of the theory on historical grounds. The conditions of the system James Mill envisages will be realized only if three conditions are fulfilled—that there is free competition for goods, that men find their happiness only through goods, and that they will act rationally in pursuit of these goods. All these conditions,

J. S. Mill pointed out, were fulfilled by any actual system
only to a limited extent. It was through the teachings of the
Saint-Simonians, he says, 'that my eyes were opened to the
very limited and temporary nature of the old political
economy, which assumes private property and inheritance
as indefeasible facts'.[1]

It is a measure of the prestige of Political Economy in
Benthamite circles in the eighteen-thirties that he found it
necessary to state that 'what is now commonly understood
by the term "Political Economy" is not the science of
speculative politics, but a branch of that science',[2] though
the abstract and hypothetical character of political economy
was not, according to Mill, a defect, but a necessary characteristic of scientific method. 'Political Economy considers
mankind as occupied solely in acquiring and consuming
wealth....Not because any political economist was ever so
absurd as to suppose that mankind are really thus constituted, but because this is the mode in which science must
necessarily proceed.'[3] And he makes the obvious analogy
with the assumption of frictionless engines in mechanics.

But it is not enough merely to appreciate the true character of political economy. The situations it postulates are
rarely realized in fact, because there are what Mill calls
'disturbing causes', akin to friction in mechanics, which
are not included in the economist's assumptions. 'But',
says Mill, 'the disturbing causes are not handed over to be
dealt with by mere conjecture...they have their laws, as
the causes which are thereby disturbed have theirs.'[4] This
last statement is obviously one of mere faith, since no such
laws had yet been discovered, but it was a kind of faith—

[1] J. S. Mill, *Autobiography*, p. 141.
[2] 'On the Definition of Political Economy', *London and Westminster
Review*, XXVIII (October 1836), p. 12.
[3] *Ibid.* pp. 12–13.   [4] *Ibid.* p. 21.

faith in the universality of natural causation—which we shall meet again in other writers and which was to exercise a profound influence on the development of sociological theory. The science of the laws of these disturbing causes J. S. Mill calls 'social economy', being obviously not yet familiar with, or not ready to use, the term sociology—this was in 1836—but it is obviously sociology to which he is referring.

These criticisms were primarily based on a belief in the importance of history and the necessity for an historical perspective. The growth of this conviction is, indeed, the most obvious way in which the parochialism of philosophic radicalism was becoming difficult to maintain.

2. THE EMPIRICAL TEST

There was also another way, however, in which intellectual horizons were being stretched. Its influence was not decisive, and by itself it supplied little to the new movement of ideas but examples. Nevertheless, it provided a testing-ground, as it were, for the theories of philosophic radicalism. Expositions of their failure became part of the intellectual stock-in-trade of the social theorists of the second half of the century. The limits of experience were being widened, and the theories by which it was interpreted were being revised in consequence, not merely temporally, but geographically. Imperial commitments grew; Africa was being opened up. It was a sign of the times when the *Royal Geographical Society* was founded in 1830. Little though the essential parochialism of European culture may have been shaken, it was becoming increasingly necessary to find ethical and social theories which did not ignore the fact that primitive modes of thinking, and widely varying and apparently irrational types of social organization did not merely belong to the past, but made up the everyday experience of Imperial administrators,[1] in whose hands—and this was perhaps their vital point of difference from the explorers, colonists, traders and missionaries of former centuries—the responsibility for the well-being of these societies was placed. Certainly by the middle of the century it was coming to seem no longer sufficient, at least for those actively engaged in Imperial and Colonial administration or legislation, to regard primitive customs and superstitions as merely curious, disgusting, or tedious, or as useful ammunition in religious and political controversy. Irrational and disgusting they might be, but men were prepared to murder and die for them, and seemed to become quite literally demoralized when deprived of them.

Even in India, the tide eventually began to turn against the extreme Westernizers.[2] Sir Henry Maine, in particular, who was both the author of *Ancient Law* and other works on primitive institutions, and Legal Member of the Council in India from 1862 to 1867, was acutely aware of the intellectual challenge offered by primitive modes of thought and behaviour. 'The tone of thought common among us', he wrote, 'would be materially affected, if we had vividly before us the relation of the progressive races to the totality of human life.'[3]

He used Indian examples to telling effect in combating the old legal and economic theories to which his objections were not only theoretical but practical. 'The theory is perfectly defensible as a theory but its practical value... differ(s) greatly in different ages and countries.'[4] In *Popular Government* (1885), he directly criticized the British Govern-

[1] Cf. below, p. 128 n. 2.
[2] See Bearce, *British Attitudes towards India*, esp. ch. IX.
[3] Maine, *Ancient Law* (O.U.P. 1954), p. 18 (1861).
[4] Maine, *Lectures on the Early History of Institutions* (1875), p. 384.

ment of India, on the ground that 'political abstractions, founded exclusively upon English facts, and even here requiring qualification, are applied by the educated minority, and by their newspapers, to a society which, through nine tenths of its structure, belongs to the thirteenth century in the West'.[1]

The intellectual climate of the first half of the century had not been very propitious to understanding the alien and the primitive. The arrogance of conquest, the missionary ardour of Evangelical Christianity, the heat engendered by the Slavery Controversy, the narrowness of utilitarianism and Political Economy, all helped to produce an atmosphere of dogmatism.[2] The discarding of the Social Contract and the State of Nature from political theory had cut away one source of interest in the primitive. Facts about the savage tended to be regarded merely as 'curious' or disgusting, or as useful controversial ammunition, but whether he was regarded as a sub-human or degenerate, or as a man and a brother whose chief need was for a pair of shorts and a Bible, his behaviour was hardly ever regarded as a subject of legitimate human and scientific interest.

Among those English intellectuals who most cherished a belief in the possibility of basing social relations upon a body of scientific propositions—that is to say, the philosophic radicals—irrationality was to be refuted rather than understood. The most popular explanation of myth was probably Condorcet's,[3] in terms of deliberate perversions of known truth by priestly and ruling castes, as it appears, for example,

[1] *Popular Government* (1885), p. 108. Elsewhere he referred to the difficulties experienced by officials attempting to 'discover how the economical phenomena of the East could best be described in the economical language of the West' (*Observation of India*, p. 23).

[2] Stokes, *The English Utilitarians and India*, pp. 30–5.

[3] Condorcet, *Sketch for a Historical Picture of the Progress of the Human Mind* (Library of Ideas edition, 1955), pp. 34–9. See above, p. 9.

in T. R. Edmonds's *Practical, Moral and Political Economy*.[1]
As an example of the change in the intellectual climate by
the end of the century, we may note Huxley's facetious
pretence in 1893 that his audience may 'have become
acquainted with fairyland only through primers of comparative mythology'.[2] There was a tendency, however, to
exaggerate the extent to which there had been a change
since the early years of the century; when an anonymous
writer remarked, reviewing a book in the Master of the Rolls
Series entitled 'Leechdoms, Wortcunning and Starcraft of
Early England', in the eighteen-sixties, 'What would our
grandfathers have said to a book of this sort being published
by the state as a contribution to English History?',[3] he under-
estimated the interest of the generation of the Romantics
in the quaint and primitive, and the enduring influence of
Scottish conjectural history.[4]

Direct contact with the problems raised by alien and
primitive societies helped to give a sense of urgency to the
reinterpretations being undertaken in social theory; it pro-

---

[1] 'The wise, having thus acquired...ascendancy over the minds of the
ignorant, will make some assertions of the truth or falsity of which the
ignorant can have no direct experience; this assertion or relation will probably
be for the advantage of the wise; they will probably establish a religion of
which they will make themselves priests' (T. R. Edmonds, *Practical, Moral
and Political Economy* (1828), p. 192). In other respects Edmonds's work
was quite original, being an attempt to introduce into social thinking the
Lamarckian and (Erasmus) Darwinian idea of adaptation, in support of the
thesis that 'the law of the strongest, or war, is one of the most benevolent
institutions of Nature', in a way which clearly anticipates Spencer. See the
chapter by C. H. Driver, 'Walter Bagehot and the Social Psychologists',
in F. J. L. Hearnshaw (ed.), *Social and Political Ideas of the Victorian Age*
(1933).
[2] *Evolution and Ethics* (Romanes Lecture 1893), reprinted in T. H. Huxley
and Julian Huxley, *Evolution and Ethics, 1893–1943* (1947), p. 60.
[3] *AR*, v (1867), 314.
[4] See, for example, the sympathetic review in the *Edinburgh Review* of
Scott's *Minstrelsy of the Scottish Border* (*ER*, II (1803)). Clive attributes
this review to Brougham (Clive, *Scotch Reviewers*, p. 176 n. 5).

vided data to be used as ammunition against the older views; it did not, itself, initiate.[1] It was not until it could be interpreted in terms of a philosophy of history that the data it provided, the problems it posed, could enter the consciousness of the English intelligentsia. The trains of thought suggested by practical contemporary problems were subsidiary, though complementary, to those arising from increasing contact with the intellectual life of the continent, and particularly from the reawakening of interest in history.

Sociology and social anthropology began to establish themselves in this country as recognizable and at least partially recognized disciplines in, roughly speaking, the third quarter of the nineteenth century.

Of course, any attempts to set limits of this kind must necessarily be somewhat arbitrary, but there are good reasons for isolating this particular period. To take the least significant first, the National Association for the Promotion of Social Science was founded in 1857, the Anthropological Society of London in 1863. The connection of the pursuits of these bodies with sociology and anthropology as understood today is perhaps tenuous and to some extent merely verbal;[2] nevertheless, their foundation was a straw in the wind.

Much more significant was the sudden spate of works, particularly in the eighteen-sixties, by men whom modern sociologists and anthropologists seem agreed to recognize, in some sense, as ancestors. In sociology, a steady increase in interest in the possibility of a social science can be traced from the time of J. S. Mill's *System of Logic* (1843), with

[1] For the case of Maine, see chapter 5.
[2] See Peter R. Senn, 'The Earliest Use of the Term "Social Science"', *Journal of the History of Ideas*, XIX (1958).

its section on the methods of, and need for, a science of society, and from the awakening of English interest in Comte in the eighteen-forties and eighteen-fifties. The third quarter of the century saw the publication of almost all the major works of Herbert Spencer[1] and there followed, in the 'eighties, in a rather different tradition of inquiry, the great survey of the Tower Hamlets conducted by Charles Booth and his assistants.

It was the third quarter of the century which saw a revival, after half a century of relative neglect, of interest in primitive society. It was in the 'sixties of the nineteenth century that a systematic, well-documented comparative social anthropology was born, and an interest in the manners, customs, institutions and beliefs of primitive and oriental peoples ceased to be confined to travellers, antiquarians and satirists, and to take the study of them seriously became no longer merely a proof of eccentricity.[2]

As Herbert Spencer put it, 'Instead of passing over as of no account, or else regarding as purely mischievous, the superstitions of the primitive man, we must inquire what part they play in social evolution.'[3] E. B. Tylor referred to his own generation as one 'among whom there has sprung up a new knowledge of old times, and with it a new sympathy with old thoughts and feelings'.[4] (By 'old' he meant primitive.) Tylor's own *Researches into the Early History of Mankind and the Development of Civilization*, from which

---

[1] *The Principles of Sociology* actually began to come out in 1876.

[2] The older attitude was slow to die out, however, if indeed it has done even now. In the early nineteen hundreds a friend wrote to R. R. Marett, 'A man of your talents seems rather wasted on the habits of backward races' (R. R. Marett, *A Jerseyman at Oxford* (O.U.P. 1941), p. 164).

[3] *The Principles of Sociology* (3 vols., 1876–), vol. II (1882), pp. 230–1.

[4] Tylor, *Researches into the Early History of Mankind and the Development of Civilization* (1865), p. 10.

this quotation comes, appeared in 1865, which also saw the publication of Sir John Lubbock's *Prehistoric Times* and J. F. McLennan's *Primitive Marriage*. Sir Henry Maine's *Ancient Law* had come out four years earlier, and Tylor's second and more ambitious work, *Primitive Culture*, was published in 1871.

It was Tylor in whose person anthropology received the benediction of academic recognition, when he became the first Reader in Anthropology at Oxford in 1884. Sociology had to wait another twelve years, however, until the School of Sociology, later swallowed up in the London School of Economics, was founded in 1903.

To contemporaries it seemed that the study of man and society had at last been put on a truly scientific basis. 'The time has gone by', pronounced Frazer complacently in 1905, 'when dreamers like Rousseau could reconstruct the history of society out of their own minds' (i.e. by deducing it from assumptions about human nature).[1] In other fields also, the same reaction had taken place. 'In the last decade of the nineteenth century', said Pound, 'it was for a time the fashion for every dabbler in jurisprudence to have a fling at Austin',[2] and even Marshall wrote that 'while the earlier economists argued as though man's character and efficiency were to be regarded as a fixed quantity, modern economists keep constantly in mind that it is a product of the circumstances under which he has lived'.[3]

Graham Wallas summed up what was commonly seen as the difference between the social theories of the early and the late nineteenth century when he wrote: 'The only form of study which a political thinker of one or two hundred

[1] J. G. Frazer, *Lectures on the Early History of the Kingship* (1905), p. 7.
[2] Quoted from W. S. Holdsworth, *Some Makers of English Law* (C.U.P. 1938), p. 258.
[3] A. Marshall, *The Principles of Economics* (2 vols. 1898), I, 65.

years ago would now note as missing is any attempt to deal with politics in relation to the nature of Man.'[1]

A sterile and unrealistic a-priorism, so the new orthodoxy ran, had been superseded by patient observation of social facts—a change so profound as to constitute a revolution in social thought. But which facts were to be observed, and why? Such questions could not be avoided, ultimately, even by the heroic, hit-or-miss inductivism of Beatrice Webb's fact-gathering methods,[2] while Frazer's remark, typical of the period, that 'the prime want of the study [i.e. of anthropology] is not so much theories as facts',[3] implies a theory in that it implies the possibility of distinguishing between facts which are interesting and those which are not. In fact, of course, Frazer in 1905 was writing within an evolutionary tradition established some forty years earlier.

3. SOCIAL SCIENCE AND THE PHILOSOPHY OF HISTORY

The demand for an inductive science grew largely out of a perception of the inadequacies of the older political and social theories which claimed to be 'scientific', most notably utilitarian political theory and Political Economy, and a vital part of this perception was a greater sensitivity to the radical changes wrought in men and society in the course of history. It followed that no single generalization about human nature and human wants could be universally valid, and hence able to serve as an axiom in a deductive science of politics and society. It also followed that the institutions presupposed by the most successful kind of social science

---

[1] Wallas, *Human Nature and Politics*, p. 12. Wallas deplored this, but many of his elders would have regarded it as a sign of health.

[2] B. Webb, *My Apprenticeship* (5th ed. 1950), appendix C (1926).

[3] Frazer, *Early History of the Kingship*, p. 5.

up to that time—Political Economy—were not universal and that hence its conclusions also were of merely limited validity. Being based, therefore, in part at least, on an increased respect for history and a perception of the fundamental character of historical change, it is perhaps not surprising, prima facie, that the creation of a social science should have been assumed to be virtually identical with the creation of a science of history—an equation which Alfred Marshall, writing at the end of the century, made quite explicitly: 'Social science, or the reasoned history of man, for the two things are the same...'[1] It is often difficult in the nineteenth century to distinguish between sociology and the philosophy of history and, if the central preoccupation of sociology is with discovering laws of social development, this is not surprising.

But why did the idea of social development come to predominate so overwhelmingly as the central concept of nineteenth-century social theory? It was not as if the conception of the alternative approach, the analysis of working social systems, were altogether lacking among the continental theories which so influenced the development of social theory in England in the middle years of the century. Comte divided sociology into Social Statics and Social Dynamics. J. S. Mill, expounding him, saw the two major tenets of the new approach as, first, its insistence that human nature is historically conditioned, and hence there can be no *direct* deductions from the laws of human nature,[2] and second, its assertion that the different aspects of social life are interrelated, that there is a 'consensus', as Comte called it. J. S. Mill's own version of the idea of functional

[1] 'The Old Generation of Economists and the New', *Quarterly Journal of Economics*, XI (1897), 121.
[2] See J. S. Mill, *August Comte and Positivism*, p. 84.

interdependence, which he christened 'Uniformities of Co-existence', he expounded in his *System of Logic*.[1]

We have, therefore, in the work of the two most eminent propagandists for social science of the first half of the nineteenth century, the conceptual basis for the study of societies as working systems. If the study of society did not proceed along these lines, it was not because the possibility had never been canvassed. At the same time, in Germany, an 'organic' conception of society pointed essentially in the same direction, even if it tended to be explained in terms of a mystical and unanalysable unity rather than the interdependence of functioning institutions.[2] In Germany too, therefore, an historical approach to the study of society was accompanied by an assertion that the coexistence of social facts was not arbitrary.

How then, can we explain, to adopt the Comtist terminology for a moment, the relative neglect, as social science developed, of Social Statics in favour of Social Dynamics? Why does so much attempted social science in the latter half of the nineteenth century have to be classed either as mere empirical fact-finding or as speculative philosophy of history? Why did it seem correct to equate social science with—to use Marshall's phrase—'the reasoned history of man'?

There were, of course, in the first place, a number of purely practical factors in Victorian England which tended to inhibit the study of society, or at least of alien and remote societies, as working social systems.

Let us assume that social anthropology has two possible alternative methods—the arrangement of social institutions in an evolutionary series, and the study of functional relations within a given society. The practical difficulties of the

---

[1] J. S. Mill, *A System of Logic* (2 vols., 9th ed. 1875), II, 509 (1843).
[2] See Forbes, *The Liberal Anglican Idea of History*, p. viii.

two methods are by no means equal. The former can be pursued by the scholar in his study in England, granted only a reasonable amount of data provided by travellers and administrators from various parts of the world. The latter requires money, and the willingness to disrupt one's whole way of life for a considerable period and to work under unusual and possibly dangerous conditions. The association of the evolutionary and the 'functionalist' theories with the Victorian 'armchair' anthropologist and the modern field-worker respectively is not fortuitous. An 'armchair' student would find it very difficult to carry out the modern type of social analysis even if he wished to do so.

The natural sciences in the nineteenth century gained enormously from men of scientific interests travelling to remote parts of the world as ships' doctors or naturalists: Darwin, Huxley, Alexander von Humboldt and A. Bastian, to name four. But such a channel of new information was of little use to the study of society.

In the first place, the men who obtained such posts were more likely, by the nature of their vocation, to be interested in the natural sciences; there were no posts for ships' sociologists or psychologists. Secondly, modern anthropology requires, not the collecting of specimens but long residence and intimate contact. The only way the Victorian anthropologist could have studied primitive societies in the modern manner would have been to go and live with them with that purpose in mind. To have done so would have required an almost superhuman leap of imaginative curiosity. Exploration, administration, missionary work and the collection of specimens were one thing; residence among savages as an equal for the purpose of sociological study was quite another.[1]

[1] Few, even among those whose callings brought them into constant contact with primitive peoples, were capable of imitating the Abbé Dubois, who wrote: 'During the long time that I remained among the natives, I made

Even if anyone had been capable of entertaining such a project, funds would have been a problem. Anthropology was new and unestablished. Huxley, writing to A. C. Haddon in the eighteen-eighties, when the latter was becoming interested in anthropology, warned him of the need to earn a living, adding, 'I do not see any way by which a devotee of anthropology is to come at the bread—let alone the butter.'[1] Haddon himself once bitterly exclaimed: 'Who cares for anthropology? There's no money in it.'[2] But it was he who, though constantly embarrassed by financial limitations, led the first specifically anthropological expedition to the Torres Straits 1898–9.

It would be a mistake, however, to think of the expedition as inspired by functionalist notions. It grew, in fact, out of the zoological expedition to the same area that Haddon had undertaken ten years before. A thorough evolutionist, he became alarmed at the way in which the priceless documents of the past of mankind—the customs, beliefs, institutions, etc., of the natives—were being obliterated by contact with civilization, and of the need to save them for anthropology by recording them before it was too late.[3] This was the stimulus, at least so far as Haddon was concerned, to the second, specifically anthropological expedition. The study of primitive societies as working systems seems to have grown from direct observation and, of course, a changing intellectual climate,[4] not vice versa.

it my constant rule to live as they did, conforming exactly in all things to their manners, to their style of living and clothing, and even to most of their prejudices' (J. Dubois, *Manners and Customs of India* (1817), p. xv).

[1] A. Hingston Quiggin, *Haddon the Head Hunter* (C.U.P. 1942), p. 94.

[2] *Ibid.* p. 114. Andrew Lang once remarked to Marett, 'If I could have made a living out of it, I might have been a great Anthropologist' (Marett, *A Jerseyman at Oxford*, p. 167).

[3] Quiggin, *Haddon the Head Hunter*, pp. 88, 90, 93, 107–8.

[4] See E. R. Leach, 'The Epistemological Background to Malinowski's Empiricism', in Firth, *Man and Culture*.

One class of men, it is true, were brought into close and prolonged contact with alien and primitive peoples—the administrators of empire. Men like Sir Alfred Lyall and Sir Baldwin Spencer deliberately set themselves to collect anthropological material. But they remained, perhaps not surprisingly, within the intellectual framework of the evolutionary comparative method, as did the most distinguished of them all, Sir Henry Maine. Maine made much use of Indian material and insisted that Englishmen must 'recognise that Indian phenomena of ownership, exchange, rent and price are equally natural, equally worthy of scientific observation with those of Western Europe'.[1]

But this 'respect' consisted primarily, not so much of recognizing a viable alternative way of conducting the affairs of a society, but of paying these alien customs the doubtful compliment of regarding them as analogous to those of the Westerner's remote ancestors.[2]

Obviously, lack of experience of other societies was not the only reason for the triumph of the historical approach to anthropology, though we should perhaps remind ourselves, in Maine's case, of the gulf, which Kipling made the basis of a parable, between the Legal Member of the Council in India and the people for whom he legislated.[3] There were other, more compelling, reasons than mere practical difficulties, and it is to these reasons that we now have to turn.

For it may be asked, even if the direct study of the simpler social systems *as* systems was beyond the means and sympathy of the Victorian student of society, what about the society in which he himself lived? And it is true

[1] *The Effects of the Observation of India on Modern European Thought* (Rede Lecture, C.U.P. 1875), p. 24.

[2] See above, p. 13.

[3] R. Kipling, 'Tod's Amendment', *Plain Tales from the Hills* (3rd ed. 1890).

that the case of sociology is rather different from that of anthropology. Here we have to account, not for the lack of systematic direct observation, but for the lack of relation between it and sociological theory.

There was, of course, a large amount of serious social survey work being undertaken during the second half of the nineteenth century. As already mentioned, the National Association for the Promotion of Social Science was founded in 1857. A decade later, in 1869, the Charity Organization Society of London was founded, with the object of basing a distribution of charity on a sound knowledge of where and how it could do most good.[1] And in the eighteen-eighties there came Charles Booth's great survey of the conditions of the poor in East London.

According to Beatrice Webb, who took part in that survey,

detailed descriptions of the life and labour of the people in all its various aspects, sensational or scientific, derived from personal observation or statistical calculation, became a characteristic feature of the publications of this period, whether newspapers or magazines, plays or novels, the reports of philanthropic organisations or the proceedings of learned societies.[2]

The main inspiration for this type of work was charitable, but it was based on the same belief in the insufficiency of deduction from first principles as the other intellectual developments we have tried to trace. 'The *a priori* reasoning of political economy, orthodox and unorthodox alike, fails from want of reality. At its base are a series of assumptions very imperfectly connected with the observed facts of life. We need to begin with a true picture of the modern industrial organism, the interchange of service, the exercise of

[1] C. L. Mowat, *The Charity Organisation Society, 1869–1913* (1961).
[2] B. Webb, *My Apprenticeship*, p. 130.

faculty, the demands and satisfactions of desire.'[1] How apparently inexplicable, therefore, is the almost complete separation between this sort of inquiry and the professedly 'inductive', 'empirical' and 'scientific' methods of sociological theory and social anthropology!

But perhaps no explanation is needed. Do not social theory and social surveys derive from different traditions of inquiry, and do not the divergences still exist today?[2] Is our problem perhaps a pseudo-problem, generated by the over-generosity of the terms sociology, social science, or social studies?

We are perhaps verging here upon an evaluation of what a social science should be; since it is not the purpose of this book to offer prescriptions of this kind, it is worth pointing out at once that the Victorians themselves were worried and hampered by the gap between theory and practice. If the weakness of nineteenth-century theoretical sociology lay in the fact that its evolutionary preoccupations led it all too easily away from structural analysis in the direction of speculative prehistory, 'practical' sociology suffered from the lack of a theoretical framework. Charles Booth's biographers say of him: 'It was his inability to construct a sufficiently elaborate and clearly defined framework of analysis that led him to accumulate vast numbers of facts that, far from "speaking for themselves", obstructed the development of a better understanding of their significance.'[3]

Booth himself seems to have sensed as much, when at the conclusion of his great survey he wrote: 'The dry bones that lie scattered over the long valley that we have traversed together lie before my reader. May some great soul, master

[1] Charles Booth, quoted B. Webb, *ibid*. p. 192.
[2] See, for example, the remarks in C. Wright Mills, *The Sociological Imagination* (New York, 1959), esp. chs. II and III.
[3] Simey, *Charles Booth—Social Scientist*, p. 196.

of a subtler alchemy than mine, disentangle the confused issues, reconcile the apparent contradictions in aim, melt and commingle the various influences for good into one divine uniformity of effort, and make these dry bones live.'[1] Theoretical sociology, for Booth, remained—alchemy.

Contemporaries noticed the dichotomy between theory and practice. W. H. Mallock, for example, contrasted what he regarded as the success of 'speculative' social science and its failure as a practical study.[2] He then attempted to define the distinction, and to specify the phenomena which should be the concern of the 'practical' sociologist: 'Whilst the business of the speculative philosopher is solely with the phenomena that have been unintended, the business of the practical sociologist is with those that have been intended.'[3] The argument with which he attempts to support this distinction is highly curious: 'The meaning of the words "practical science" is a science from which we can draw practical advice; but all advice implies an intended end; and every attempt to solve social problems scientifically must be concerned with results which we may deliberately set ourselves to produce.'[4] This argument is unexceptionable taken by itself. Obviously any 'practical' science cannot be concerned with achieving results which human endeavour is incapable, by definition, of achieving. But read in this way, the argument no longer supports the original statement, which referred, not to phenomena which *can* be intended, but to those which *have* been intended. If Mallock is to be interpreted as meaning what he says, the whole force of the argument depends upon an absolute separation of phenomena which can be intended from those

---

[1] Simey, *Charles Booth—Social Scientist*, p. 160.
[2] W. H. Mallock, *Aristocracy and Evolution* (1898), pp. 10–14.
[3] *Ibid.* p. 106.   [4] *Ibid.*

which cannot, ignoring the possibility that similar phenomena may be the products of intention in one case and of
accident or the operation of an unalterable law in another.

It is possible that Mallock was confused by an ambiguity
in the phrase 'concerned with'; e.g. a bacteriologist is
'concerned with' microbes. He is also, in another sense,
'concerned with' combating disease. Mallock may have un-
consciously thought that, because a practical sociologist was
'concerned with' intended results in the second sense, he
must be 'concerned with' them also in the first.

But the problem also drew discussions from acuter commentators than Mallock.[1] Beatrice Webb, by her contacts
with Herbert Spencer and Charles Booth, had a foot in both
camps. She worked devotedly as a 'social investigator', but
she was convinced that 'the historical method is imperative',
for 'only by watching the *processes* of growth and decay
during a period of time, can we understand even the contemporary facts at whatever may be their stage of development'.[2] She had moods of intellectual ambition as grandiose
as those of any conjectural historian: 'The old dream of a
bird's eye view into the past, and through it a glimpse into
the future—that old dream, now recognised as a dream—
fascinates me still.'[3] It was she who threw at Herbert
Spencer the query which drew from him an exposition of
the difference between his type of sociology and hers. He
bases his argument on two main points:

(*a*) a rational pathology can come into existence only by virtue
of a previously established physiology...until there is an

---

[1] For example, Maitland, who wrote in *The Body Politic* that 'those who
are talking most hopefully about sociology are constantly forgetting the
greatest lesson that Auguste Comte taught...I mean the interdependence
of human affairs' (F. W. Maitland, *Selected Essays* (C.U.P. 1936), p. 247).

[2] B. Webb, *My Apprenticeship*, p. 211. Italics original.

[3] *Ibid.* p. 122.

understanding of the functions in health, there is no understanding of them in disease.

(*b*) Further, when rational pathology has been thus established, the course of treatment indicated by it is the course which aims as far as possible to re-establish the normal functions—does not aim to readjust physiology in such a way as to adopt (*sic*) it to pathological states.[1]

Oddly enough, Spencer is not here defending primarily his theory of progress, but the laws of Political Economy. The two are linked in Spencer's system, however, so the distinction is not here very important.[2]

If we may take Spencer's exposition as being typical of the beliefs of the evolutionary social theorists in general, our question is answered, partially at least. Both the 'speculative' and the 'practical' students of society were ethically inspired, but their ethical attitudes did not coincide. The 'social investigator' was inspired primarily by the fact of contemporary human misery, and the belief that accurate knowledge was a prerequisite of any successful attempt to diminish it; his work may be regarded as an aspect of what Beatrice Webb called 'a new consciousness of sin among men of intellect and men of property'.[3]

Spencer, on the other hand, regarded it as

the business of moral science to deduce, from the laws of life and the conditions of existence, what kinds of action necessarily tend to produce happiness and what kinds to produce unhappiness. Having done this, its deductions are to be recognised as laws of conduct; and are to be conformed to *irrespective of a direct estimation* of happiness or misery.[4]

---

[1] Letter of Herbert Spencer, 2 October 1886. Quoted B. Webb, *My Apprenticeship*, p. 251.   [2] See below, chapter 6.

[3] *Ibid.* p. 154. Charles Booth's biographers say of him, 'His starting-point was the moral dilemma in which he found himself; as a rich man in a world whose prosperity seemed to be unavoidably linked with poverty' (Simey, *Charles Booth—Social Scientist*, p. 3).

[4] H. Spencer, *An Autobiography* (2 vols. 1904), II, 88. Italics mine.

The needs which suggested themselves most forcibly to the evolutionary social theorist were not so much those of immediate social amelioration as of ethical and political theory, and few were, like L. T. Hobhouse and Beatrice Webb, almost equally conscious of both. No account of evolutionary social theory can do it justice which regards it merely as an attempt to apply scientific methods, with the aid of concepts borrowed from the vogue science of the period, to the study of society. It was a response to needs —emotional and intellectual—which no mere analysis of society as it actually existed, whether empirical and fragmentary or theoretically sophisticated, could give.

4. THE ETHICAL DILEMMA

Essentially the needs were for reassurance, for guarantees that all was, ultimately at least, well with the human situation, and for ethical and political certainty, for ethical premises which should not be arbitrary and recommendations which should be more than tentative and piecemeal.

The acuteness of this need can only be understood in terms of the collapse or modification of the certainties, religious, ethical and political, of the earlier part of the nineteenth century, which must be our justification for devoting a chapter to a subject already so well understood as the disintegration of utilitarian political theory. Anarchy— social anarchy as a fear, intellectual anarchy as a fact—is a word which constantly occurs in the work of advocates of a social science—and of many other people, of course—in the eighteen-forties and eighteen-fifties. Hence much of the attraction of Comte for the mid-nineteenth-century English intelligentsia; Comte had also diagnosed anarchy, and offered a solution. Harriet Martineau, in the preface to her translation of Comte, sounded the note of anxiety as well as of triumph:

The supreme dread of everyone who cares for the good of nation or race is that men should be adrift for want of anchorage for their convictions. I believe that no one questions that a very large part of our people are now so adrift.... The moral dangers of such a state of fluctuation...are fearful in the extreme.[1]

G. H. Lewes described his own time as

an age of universal anarchy of thought, with a strong desire for organisation; an age, succeeding one of destruction, anxious to reconstruct—anxious, but as yet impotent. The desire of belief is strong; convictions are wanting; there is neither spiritual nor moral union. In this plight we may hope for the future, but can *cling* only to the past: that alone is secure, well grounded. The past must form the basis of certainty and the materials for speculation.[2]

Lewes's words bring out, not merely the need, but the direction in which satisfaction was to be sought—in a science of history.

In the case of Harriet Martineau, her subsequent remarks make it clear that the background to her words, and to the kind of anarchy she thought she discerned, was the religious doubts and anxieties of the eighteen-forties,[3] and doubtless the religious malaise, the deprivation of the kind of certainties

---

[1] A. Comte, *Positive Philosophy* (freely translated and condensed by Harriet Martineau, 1853, 2 vols.), I, viii. For the same kind of observation made from a very different standpoint, cf. Matthew Arnold: 'In all directions our habitual courses of action seem to be losing efficatiousness, credit and control, both with others and even with ourselves; everywhere we see the beginnings of confusion, and we want a clue to some sound order and authority' (*Culture and Anarchy* (2nd ed. 1875), p. 149 (1869)).

[2] Lewes, 'The State of Historical Sciences in France', p. 73. Italics original.

[3] Harriet Martineau had apparently lost her own unitarian faith as a result of a visit to the Middle East and the reflections on comparative religion it aroused, in 1847 (R. K. Webb, *Harriet Martineau* (1959), p. 287).

and reassurances that it has been the traditional office of religion to supply, was not wholly irrelevant, even in the case of men like Lewes and Spencer, who lost their faith early and apparently painlessly.[1] But earlier in the century such men would probably have found adequate consolation in utilitarianism and the science of mind of Locke and Hartley. This they could no longer do.

Earlier in the chapter we considered some of the objections which were made to the utilitarian analysis of society. These attacks amounted, not so much to a total repudiation of the science of mind on which it was based as to a denial that it provided, by itself, an adequate basis for social understanding. There was also, however, a more radical kind of criticism, represented most notably by Lewes and T. H. Buckle, which amounted almost to total repudiation of the tradition, though even Lewes never went so far in this direction as his master, Comte.

The origin of this kind of criticism was undoubtedly the failure of the English empiricist philosophy of mind, hitherto regarded as the *science* of mind, decisively to rebut the challenge of the Kantian idealist alternative. If it *was* a science, why could it not prove itself to be so? The failure to do this led, in some cases, to a rejection of philosophy and, up to a point, of all introspective psychology—it is difficult, on the old empiricist premisses, to distinguish between them altogether. Lewes announced that 'Philosophy has ceased to form a portion of the national culture',[2] and gave as the reason the apparently insoluble disputes of the various schools of philosophy, though he admits that the Lockean school has made a contribution to scientific psychology. In

---

[1] For Lewes, see A. T. Kitchel, *George Lewes and George Eliot* (New York, 1933), p. 9.
[2] G. H. Lewes, *Biographical History of Philosophy* (2 vols. 1845–6), II, 234.

spite of this qualification, however, the whole trend of the book is away from introspective psychology and towards physiology—Lewes approves the aims, though not the dogmatism, of phrenology[1]—and the study of history.

T. H. Buckle, stigmatizing introspective psychology as metaphysical, and capable of producing only sterile conflicts like those of idealism versus sensationalism,[2] and turning instead to study what he called 'the dynamics of masses',[3] is another example of the same trend.

Even those who could not accept Comte's crude version of pragmatism as a substitute, felt that the English philosophical and psychological tradition faced a crisis. John Grote, cleric, younger brother of the historian, and Professor of Philosophy at Cambridge, wrote in 1865, 'I am myself very much of opinion that the old vein of the Philosophy of the Human Mind...is worked out',[4] and went on to notice 'the tendency of questions and subjects of all kinds at this time to run to history...the study of the history of man is now put before us as that by means of which we are to understand man himself, and know what we ought to do.'[5]

Fitzjames Stephen was another who made the same observation, and again connected it with the discredit into which traditional philosophical methods had fallen.

No one can have watched the course of modern speculation without perceiving how deeply it is affected by a sort of weariness caused by the apparently unfruitful discussions which have so long prevailed upon political and moral subjects...Historical

---

[1] G. H. Lewes, *Biographical History of Philosophy*, II, 233–4.
[2] T. H. Buckle, *History of Civilization in England* (2 vols. 1857–61), I, 144, 149–50.
[3] Quoted in A. H. Huth, *The Life and Writings of Thomas Henry Buckle* (1880), p. 145.
[4] J. Grote, *Exploratio Philosophica* (2 vols. 1865), I, ix.
[5] *Ibid.* I, xvii.

inquiry has been the common resource of those who have shared in this feeling, and have nevertheless recognised the necessity of some wider and more durable results than those which the mere transaction of the current affairs of life can afford.[1]

Both Stephen and Grote pointed to the weakness in this tendency: the need for a definition of progress which must itself be normative if it is to have normative consequences. But both were aware of its attraction, its air of scientific neutrality, and its appearance of providing a moral and political theory grounded not on prejudice but in the nature of things. The search of those who felt the need for a scientific basis for ethics was for some self-evident proposition with ethical implications, and for many it was self-evident that a civilized European was 'better' than Neanderthal Man or an Andaman Islander, in a way that the fundamental assumptions of Christianity or doctrinaire utilitarianism were, for some at least, ceasing to be. The importance of this is hardly reduced by the fact that the reasons why he was regarded as 'better' had a good deal to do with Christian and utilitarian assumptions. The questioned assumptions could be smuggled in, as it were, at a deeper level, hidden beneath the unquestioned truth that modern civilization was superior to past barbarism.

Evolutionary social theory arose, not only from a desire to emulate in the study of society the achievements of biology, geology and philology, but as a reaction against the collapse of systematic utilitarianism and the weakening of traditional religious belief. The wider world of evolutionary biology and uniformitarian geology was making Bible Protestantism look parochial, just as utilitarian psychology and the dogmas of classical economics and analytic jurisprudence

[1] J. Fitzjames Stephen, 'English Jurisprudence', *ER*, CCXXXII (1861), 480–1, attrib. by Leslie Stephen, *The Life and Letters of Sir J. F. Stephen* (1895), p. 205.

began to seem parochial in face of a greater historical sophistication and knowledge of other cultures. In each case the difficulty was to reconcile a traditional system of descriptions and explanations with phenomena outside its range. How to reconcile the Atonement or the universal laws of human nature with Neanderthal Man? How to find an Austinian sovereign in a tribal assembly? How to apply Ricardian economics to a village community?

Grote touched the sensitive nerve when he suggested as a prime need of contemporary ethics 'that it should fully recognise the largeness and variety of human nature'.[1] But what was to prevent recognition of this variety from turning into total relativism? Grote himself admitted that 'the difficulty offered to morals in the view of fact, by the existence of mankind in so many different stages of development, or in something not unlike distinct species, relatively superior and inferior, is very great'.[2] At least since the time of the Stoics, the essential unity of mankind, the possession, that is to say, by all men of some common essence or nature, had been a major postulate of European social and political thought, and because of this it had been thought that ethical principles of universal validity could be asserted, and generalizations made about human motives and behaviour. Was this no longer to be the case?

The specific attraction of evolutionary social theories was that they offered a way of reformulating the essential unity of mankind, while avoiding the current objections to the older theories of a human nature everywhere essentially the same. Mankind was one not because it was everywhere the same, but because the differences represented different stages in the same process. And by agreeing to call the

[1] J. Grote, *An Examination of the Utilitarian Philosophy* (C.U.P. 1870), p. 342.   [2] *Ibid.* p. 319.

process progress one could convert the social theory into a moral and political one. Later Victorian theories of progress were not merely a spontaneous overflow of powerful feelings of self-confidence, they were often also a way of avoiding the unpleasantly relativist implications of a world in which many of the old certainties were disappearing and it was becoming increasingly difficult to be unaware that

The wildest dreams of Kew are the facts of Khatmandhu,
And the crimes of Clapham chaste in Martaban,

or to feel entirely comfortable that it was so.

The crisis described in this chapter has been considered as a consequence of changes in the acceptability of various theories and ideas, particularly in connection with the confrontation of the ideas characteristic of philosophic radicalism with realities and systems of ideas which they were inadequate to comprehend. This concentration on the fate of one set of theories has been justified because the philosophic radicals had, in common with the social evolutionists of the second half of the century, a belief in the possibility of creating a science of social relations.

But beneath the crisis caused by the reassessment of the tenets of philosophic radicalism lay the deeper malaise of the loss of faith and the need to provide some adequate substitute for the sanctions, the consolations and the sense of the meaningfulness of existence which religion had provided, a need recognized even by those whose loss of faith had entailed little anguish.[1]

On another plane again, we have to recognize the malaise of a society transforming itself by industrialization with a speed hitherto unprecedented in the history of the world. The fact of historical change, its speed and its terrible apparent autonomy and indifference to individual human

[1] E.g. Herbert Spencer's preface to *The Principles of Ethics* (2 vols. 1892–3).

desires and actions, was something of which no thoughtful mid-Victorian could remain unaware. It is understandable that men involved in such a transformation should become aware of the impersonal character and immense possibilities, exhilarating and terrifying, of social change, and only natural therefore that they should become preoccupied, not merely with the existence of sociological laws, as distinct from laws of individual human nature, but particularly with the question of social change, as opposed to the less spectacular problem of social stability. They knew that their society was travelling, and they wanted to know the route and destination. It would be beyond the scope of this book to explore this aspect of the problem, but it is worth remembering, if only for a moment, that if the history of ideas is not simply a by-product of social circumstances, and predictable in terms of them, neither does it take place in a vacuum.

There remains, however, one other aspect of the problem which does require detailed treatment. Just as there were powerful factors in the contemporary state of ethical and political theory, and of society itself, tending to produce an equation of the need for social science with the need to discover the laws and course of social development, so there were similar factors in the contemporary state of the sciences themselves, and in the current conceptions of the task and nature of scientific explanation. It is to these that we now have to turn. And in this connection one thing at least is clear. When the cradle of evolutionary social theory was being prepared, Darwin was in his hammock and three thousand miles away.

CHAPTER 4

THE LAWS OF NATURE AND THE
DIVERSITY OF MANKIND

I. THE PROBLEM OF EXPLANATION

The separation of sociological and political theory in nineteenth-century England is largely unreal, though it may be necessary for the sake of clarity. Only Hobhouse, of the sociologists, made any serious attempt to keep them in separate compartments. Evolutionary social theory was an attempt to answer not merely the question 'how does it work?', or perhaps better still, 'how does it happen?', but also 'what shall we do?' Of course, presumably any sociologist hopes that his work may be useful, but the perhaps overconscientious relativism of modern sociology, as well as the conservatism of political theorists, has inhibited contact between discussions of the two aspects of political decision —decision about means and decision about ends. There are, it is true, signs of a desire for a *rapprochement*; on the one hand, criticism of the very possibility of a value-free sociology, with the implication that one's value-judgements had better be made explicit, instead of remaining unrecognized or hidden with spinsterly modesty;[1] and on the other, signs of bridge-building from the social scientists themselves.[2] But these are single swallows; the last non-Marxist[3]

[1] E.g. B. Crick, *The American Science of Politics* (1959).

[2] E.g. D. Bidney, 'The Concept of Value in Modern Anthropology', in *Anthropology Today*, (ed.) A .L. Kroeber (Chicago, 1958), and Ralph Linton, 'The Problems of Universal Values', in *Method and Perspective in Anthropology*, (ed.) R. F. Spencer (Minneapolis, 1954). See also P. Laslett and W. G. Runciman (eds.), *Philosophy, Politics and Society*, 2nd series (1963).

[3] Marxism itself, of course, at least in the hands of Engels, was merely a subspecies of evolutionary positivism.

social theory of consequence to attempt to be equally a sociology and a political theory was evolutionary positivism.

It would be easier to regard the subsequent divergence of sociology and political theory as simply an example of the division of labour inevitably concomitant with intellectual progress if it were clearer which part of the divided empire political theory has inherited. As it is, the separation must be regarded as another aspect of the failure of evolutionary social theory; it was, as it were, another of the deaths it died. Positivism, of which evolutionary social theory was a subspecies, in its moral and political aspect represented the contortions of an intellectual tradition, predominantly secular and hence deprived of transcendental sanction for its values, trying to escape an absolute moral and political relativism. The attempt took the form of trying to exclude certain types of social behaviour and organization and to justify others by grounding them in 'the nature of things' —the latter being conceived of in terms of universal human wants or the inexorable conditions of existence.

The moral and sociological aspects of positivism were complementary, the link between them being the central position occupied in both by the problem of values. For while the relativity of values threatened the conception, dear to the positivist, of a rational ethics and political theory, it also threatened the equally vital conception of a rational understanding of the social order. Indeed, to the positivist the two aspects are not really separate. Hobbes's *Leviathan* is both an explanation of the social order and a justification of it.

Values present a problem to the positivist account of social relations because of the nature of certain basic positivist assumptions. Positivism in social thought is rooted in the nominalist and individualist traditions. Idealist thought of any kind is alien to it. Its fundamental assumption is of a free, rational individual, with certain egoistical wants, contemplating his situation in a scientific manner, and suiting means to ends accordingly. But the ends themselves do not come within the scope of reason. The choice of means may be reasonable or unreasonable, scientific or unscientific (in other words it may proceed from sound logic and observation or it may not), but ends are simply given or, in Talcott Parsons's term, random. As Hume put it,

it is evident our passions, volitions, and actions, are not susceptible of any [such] agreement or disagreement; being original facts and realities, complete in themselves and implying no reference to other passions, volitions, and actions. It is impossible, therefore, they can be pronounced either true or false, and be either contrary or conformable to reason.[1]

This sets the positivist social theorist the problem of explaining how, if ends are outside the scope of reason, and form no intelligible order, there comes to be a social order at all.

One form of solution was some type of contract theory. In order to pursue their ends in safety, men voluntarily agreed to certain restrictions. This view made society a device—a deliberate creation of human will and reason.

But following Hume's and Bentham's criticisms of the Social Contract theory, attempts to explain the origin of the social order in terms of rationally controlled purpose had been largely abandoned. The Benthamites for the most part ignored the question. It was enough to demonstrate the advantages offered by the social order, and to assume that the perception of these advantages played a major part

[1] D. Hume, *A Treatise of Human Nature* (ed. Selby-Bigge, O.U.P. 1888), p. 458.

in maintaining it. But as we have seen in the previous chapter, the Benthamites' own assumptions had been challenged. Men's purposes were not essentially one but many and diverse. The social order was maintained not primarily by men's rational appreciation of the advantages they derived from it, nor simply by coercion, but by the influence of habits and customs, many of them, particularly in the earlier stages of society, apparently irrational. Moreover, men appeared to obey these customs, not for the true reason that they helped maintain social order, but for reasons which often seemed entirely fanciful, or for no reason at all.

This insight is the central core of the emerging sociology of the nineteenth century. There are customs and institutions which do not appear, like the R.S.P.C.A. or a joint-stock company, to have been rationally devised to achieve a readily comprehensible purpose, and are certainly not explained in this way, if at all, by the individuals who maintain them. Yet they cannot be dismissed as simply random and accidental phenomena, or striking examples of human folly and absurdity, to be eradicated as soon as possible by demonstrations of their absurdity, because although they do not contribute to the ostensible purposes which are claimed for them—appeasing the gods, say, or giving comfort to departed ancestors—they do seem to contribute very strikingly to another, recondite purpose, namely, the maintenance of social order. If to see this was the great insight of nineteenth-century sociology, it can be claimed that its failure was that it did not attempt to explore these social functions in detail.

We have already seen, in the last chapter, something of the difficulties raised for moral and political theory by the disintegration of the strict utilitarian theory, and the enlargement of sympathy which both followed and helped to produce that disintegration. What now of the explanatory difficulties?

Granted that a society forms a system of mutually contributing parts, how can we explain the adaptation and dovetailing involved in a working social system, assuming that it has not been rationally designed. The Social Contract theory, considered not so much as part of a political argument but as a concept of social analysis, was an attempt to show that it *had*, or must have, been rationally designed. This being rejected, what were the alternatives? One alternative was the theory of the natural identity of interests. This differed from the Contract theory in that, though it assumed social life to consist of a set of rational actions in pursuit of clearly conceived ends, it did not require that the actors in the social drama, or at any rate their ancestors, should have an overall view of the social system. This was what the Contract theory required. Men had to be rational not merely in seeking their ends in the limited context of their immediate situation; they had to be capable of seeing the implications of their actions for society as a whole, and capable of conceiving of the form of society which would best serve their ultimate ends. The 'natural identity of interests' theory did not require nearly so much of its citizens. In fact it did not require anything of them at all except that they should act rationally in a narrowly selfish context.

Essentially it was the belief that the intelligent pursuit of clearly recognized ends was adequate as a key to understanding society that was breaking down in the mid-nineteenth century. The social functions even of apparently irrational customs and practices were beginning to be recognized, and it was seen that the kind of system to which the enlightened self-interest theory best applied, namely, economic life, took place within, and required, a social context which could not be explained in the same terms. How then could this social context be explained?

Of course, it is possible not to try to explain it in general terms at all, but merely to explore it, at least in the first instance. This is the order in which the social sciences today appear characteristically to work. In the nineteenth century they worked equally characteristically in the opposite direction.

The reasons for this are discussed in some detail in a subsequent chapter,[1] and so a few brief illustrations at this point will have to suffice. For the mid-nineteenth-century sociologist or advocate of sociology, one of its chief attractions was that it seemed to promise to heal the breach between the natural world, over which man seemed progressively to be gaining the mastery, both practical and intellectual, and the puzzling, untidy, disturbing world of human affairs. Harriet Martineau wrote enthusiastically of Comte's *Cours de philosophie positive*:

We find ourselves suddenly living and moving in the midst of the universe—as a part of it, and not as its aim and object. We find ourselves living, not under capricious and arbitrary conditions, unconnected with the constitution and movements of the whole, but under great, general, invariable laws, which operate on us as part of a whole.[2]

The distinction was almost invariably put as a stark antithesis. As Buckle wrote, the crucial question is 'Are the actions of men and therefore of societies, governed by fixed laws, or are they the result either of chance of of supernatural interference?'[3] and there are parallels to this statement in Spencer, Maine and Tylor. This is in effect to ask

---

[1] Chapter 6.
[2] Comte, *The Positive Philosophy* (Martineau's translation), I, xiv.
[3] Buckle, *History of Civilization in England*, I, 8.

whether the actions of men are intelligible or not, with the added condition that if they are it can only be because, like the rest of nature, they can be subsumed under 'fixed laws'.

The belief of many nineteenth-century intellectuals in the universality of natural causation is something which any history of ideas of the period has to reckon with. Spencer became an evolutionist, not because he was convinced by the evidence but because of his faith in the universality of natural causation. If there were some, like J. S. Mill, who were oppressed by the spectre of determinism, there were others who rejoiced, as the quotation above from Harriet Martineau witnesses, and her biographer says of her that 'in the certainties of science she became more and more cheerful'.[1] Spencer, too, obviously found in the notion of cosmic order some substitute for religion.

We have already touched on the relevance of these ethical and emotional consequences to the development of social theory, and will return to them again later. For the moment, it is most relevant that this faith in natural causation, this determination to prove human life part of an ordered universe, led to an impatience with merely partial and limited explanations and explorations of social relations. Sociology was to uncover the laws governing the social life of men, and this meant not merely as it was lived, but as it had come to be lived. As J. S. Mill put it,

the mutual correlation between the different elements of each state of society is...a derivative law, resulting from the laws which regulate the succession between one state of society and another, for the proximate cause of every state of society is the state of society immediately preceding it. The fundamental

---

[1] R. K. Webb, *Harriet Martineau*, p. 303. Harriet Martineau claimed that she frequently wept tears of joy while translating Comte—a feat of sensibility which only those who have read Comte at length can fully appreciate. H. Martineau, *Autobiography* (3 vols. 1877), II, 391.

problem, therefore, of the social science, is to find the laws according to which any state of society produces the state which succeeds it and takes its place. This opens the great and vexed question of the progressiveness of man and society; *an idea involved in every just conception of social phenomena as the subject of a science.*[1]

The result is an emphasis on the detection of laws of social change at the expense of the study of social systems.

2. THE CONTRIBUTION OF THE SCIENCES

The sources of this confidence in the universal operation of natural causation were various, and it is perhaps inaccurate to call them sources, since the extension of scientific methods to new fields was a result as well as a cause of optimism about the possibility of such an extension. There was no one master science from which aspiring social scientists drew inspiration. Statistics, for example, do not usually spring to mind as one of the sources of evolutionary social theory, but both Buckle and Tylor were deeply impressed by statistics, and particularly by the work of the Belgian statistician, de Quetelet,[2] and J. S. Mill, apropos of Buckle's work, referred to statistical regularities as 'a brilliant confirmation of the general theory...that man's actions are subject to law'.[3]

Statistical methods offered encouragement rather than, except in rare cases, a model. The same could not be said so confidently of a number of other sciences which had come, or were coming, to maturity in the first half of the nineteenth century. The list is a long one. Geology, palaeontology, evolutionary biology, comparative philology

---

[1] *A System of Logic*, II, 510. Italics mine.
[2] Buckle, *History of Civilization in England*, I, 20, 23, 25, 30. For Tylor see below, chapter 7.
[3] *A System of Logic*, II, 534.

and prehistoric archaeology[1]—all, be it noted, with the exception of philology, related by their common dependence on geology—were all concerned with the reconstruction of states no longer directly observable, by means of classification into stages and the postulation of laws or sequences of development. It is understandable, therefore, that the intellectual life of the period exhibits many cross-currents, some surprising, and some, probably, untraceable.

Darwin, for example, uses philology to help illustrate the concept of rudimentary organs.[2] In many cases it is difficult or impossible, since we are dealing with a method and an intellectual attitude that was extraordinarily widely diffused and within which a good deal of cross-fertilization took place, to say what was the specific influence in any particular case. The account given by M. T. Hodgen[3] of the sources of Tylor's theory of survivals is largely conjectural. In some cases, it is possible to trace particular influences with relative certainty; Spencer, for example, acknowledges Coleridge, Lamarck, Von Baer, Goethe and Wolff,[4] though his sociological theories as a whole owe more to English utilitarianism and *laissez-faire* doctrines. But when Tylor compares the phenomena of the anthropologist to 'species', when G. L. Gomme suggests that folk-lore may be accounted for 'by some law analogous to Grimm's law in the study of Language',[5] when Max Müller speaks of 'the Stratification of Language' and says that he doubts whether

[1] The two latter are classed here as sciences for convenience rather than with any dogmatic intention.

[2] Charles Darwin, *The Descent of Man* (2nd ed. 1874), pp. 90–1. Cf. Jacob Grimm: 'es bleiben Wörter in dem Verhältnisse der alten Einrichtung stehen; der Strom der Neuerung ist an ihnen vorbeigeflossen'. Quoted H. Pedersen, *Linguistic Science in the Nineteenth Century* (trans. J. W. Spargo, Cambridge, Mass., 1931), p. 262.

[3] M. T. Hogden, *The Doctrine of Survivals* (1936), pp. 40–1.

[4] Spencer, *Autobiography*, I, 176, 384.

[5] G. L. Gomme, *Folk-lore as an Historical Science* (1908), p. 159.

'we should have arrived at a thorough understanding of the real antecedents of language, unless what happened in the study of the stratification of the earth, had happened in the study of language',[1] when Maine says that the evidence for the patriarchal theory 'appeared to me very much of the same kind and strength as that which convinces the comparative philologist that a number of words in different Aryan languages had a common form',[2] and, in *Ancient Law*, says that 'these rudimentary ideas are to the jurist what the crusts of the earth are to the geologist',[3] the situation is far from clear. Are these intended to be merely persuasive analogies, picturesque metaphors, interesting parallels, or clarifying illustrations of the methods of new subjects by reference to better known ones; or do they represent actual, if vague, influences?

It is difficult to answer; though the overall impression one receives is that the subjects which combine to form modern anthropology owed more, methodologically, to geology and comparative philology than to evolutionary biology. It must, in any case, have been both stimulating and encouraging to the evolutionary anthropologist to observe parallel methods in so many disciplines. But specific lines of influence and cross-fertilization are difficult to draw, and should make us wary of any attempt to give any science a key role in the development of evolutionary social theory.

The publication of Lyell's *Principles of Geology*, in 1830, may be taken as a convenient starting-point. Lyell's influence was enormous. The importance of geological uniformitarianism was twofold.

---

[1] F. Max Müller, *The Stratification of Language* (Rede Lecture, 1868), p. 12.
[2] Maine, *Dissertations on Early Law and Custom* (1886), p. 194. See also *Village Communities in the East and West*, p. 6.
[3] Maine, *Ancient Law*, p. 2.

In the first place, it offered a method for the recovery of an unobservable, unrecorded past. Its foundation is the assumption of a continually operating law, whose effects are still observable, and which may be used to infer past processes. The whole theory depends, as Lyell observed, 'on the degree of confidence which we feel in regard to the permanency of the laws of nature'.[1] It postulated, in contrast to the catastrophist doctrine, a gradual process, of which the ordinary laws of nature were a sufficient cause. Catastrophism may be compared to the doctrine of special creation in biology. Both require the whimsical intervention of an incalculable, irregular force. It was the achievement of Lyell and Darwin to provide accounts of how the ordinary laws of nature could be made to yield sufficient causes of even the greatest changes, given a sufficient time scale. They freed the 'historical' natural sciences from finalism and providentialism as physics and chemistry had been freed in the seventeenth century.

The similarity to evolutionary social theory is obvious. Like the uniformitarian geologist and the evolutionary biologist, the conjectural historian was anxious to join present and past by an unbroken chain of natural causation. The uniformitarian's rejection of catastrophism, the Darwinian's of Special Creation, are paralleled by the rejection of the Social Contract, the Great Man theory of history, and the mechanical conception of society as an artifact, transformable almost at will; all the newer theories were concerned to present the relation of past and present as a steady growth, a chain of cause and effect related in accordance with discoverable natural laws.

Maine wrote in *Village Communities*: 'If indeed history be true, it must teach that which every other science teaches

[1] Quoted C. C. Gillispie, *Genesis and Geology* (Harvard, 1951), p. 121.

—continuous sequence, inflexible order, and eternal law.'[1]
Spencer insists as firmly as any orthodox Marxist that stages
cannot be jumped:

As between infancy and maturity there is no short cut by which
may be avoided the tedious process of growth and development
through insensible increments; so there is no way from the lower
forms of social life to the higher, but one passing through small
successive modifications.[2]

Spencer, also, of course, has no doubts of 'the permanency
of the laws of nature'. He writes: 'True interpretations of
all natural processes, organic and inorganic, that have gone
on in past times habitually trace them to causes still in
action. It is thus in Geology: it is thus in Biology: it is thus
in Philology';[3] and draws the moral for sociology. In *Social
Statics*, twenty years earlier, he had written: 'These changes
are brought about by a power far above individual wills.
Men who seem the prime movers, are merely the tools with
which it works; and were they absent it would quickly find
others.'[4]

The second offering of uniformitarian geology to other
sciences was not a method but simply time. Lyell's hypothesis required an enormous time scale, infinitely greater
than the now ludicrously small one allowed by Ussher's
cosmogony. The acceptance of Lyell's theory made his
time scale available to other sciences. The theory of gradual
growth, and the unbroken causal relation of past and present
in every sphere was greatly strengthened. Objections that

[1] P. 266.

[2] Herbert Spencer, *The Study of Sociology* (3rd ed. 1874), p. 402 (1873).
Cf. Max Müller: 'Language, or any other production of nature, admits only of
growth', *Lectures on the Science of Language* (1861), p. 36, and 'Language
cannot be changed or moulded by the taste, the fancy, or genius of Man'
(*ibid.* p. 39).

[3] Spencer, 'The Origin of Animal Worship', *Fortnightly Review* (May
1870), reprinted in *Essays* (3 vols. 1858–74), III, 122–3 (1874).

[4] *Social Statics* (1851), p. 433.

primitive societies were not observed to advance to civilization, arguments that species must be fixed because the animals depicted on ancient Egyptian tombs differed in no important respect from those of the nineteenth century,[1] lost most of their force.

Moreover, geology not only gave an absolutely longer time scale, it provided the means of placing fossils, bones and artifacts in a time sequence, based upon the stratum in which they were discovered, and of roughly dating them. The parallelism between the grading of organisms according to structure, and their chronological sequence as revealed by geology, became one of the major arguments in favour of biological evolution.[2] There were, in fact, three great parallels which influenced the development of the theory of evolution, one static and two dynamic; two have just been referred to. The third was the relation between structural complexity and chronological sequence revealed by embryology. Was it surprising that anthropologists should have postulated a similar relation in their own subject, and attempted to arrange societies according to structure in a developmental series?

But the effects of geological uniformitarianism did not become apparent immediately. Lyell himself continued to believe in the fixity of species, being unable to see an alternative to the vitalism implied by the evolutionary hypothesis, and regarding it as not proven. Moreover, by an odd compromise, the vaster time scale did not yet include man.[3]

On both counts the break-through was thirty years later. Darwin satisfactorily accounted for the mutability of

[1] See C. F. A. Pantin, 'Darwin's Theory and the Causes of its Acceptance' (*School Science Review*, March 1951, p. 201).

[2] T. H. Huxley, 'Geological Contemporaneity' (1862), reprinted in *Lay Sermons* (1871), pp. 204–5.

[3] Gillispie, *Genesis and Geology*, p. 147.

species in non-vitalist terms, supporting his hypothesis by an overwhelming weight of evidence, and the antiquity of man, as well as his kinship with the animals, was firmly established.

Darwin's theory implied three things which were relevant to anthropology; none was entirely new but all were hotly disputed. The history of Darwin's influence on social theory belongs, except in the case of the theory of natural selection, to the history of the diffusion of ideas rather than of their development. In this context, Darwin was undoubtedly important, but it is a type of importance impossible to estimate at all precisely. He was certainly not the father of evolutionary anthropology, but possibly he was its wealthy uncle.

It was easy to see what were the three specific implications of Darwinian theory which were relevant to evolutionary anthropology. The first was that man, by his kinship with the animals, is part of nature, not outside it. The view of all those theorists, from the eighteenth-century materialists to Buckle, who had insisted that human behaviour is susceptible to scientific treatment, was powerfully reinforced. As J. B. Bury put it: 'The prevailing doctrine that man was created *ex abrupto* had placed history in an isolated position, disconnected with the sciences of nature',[1] though this is perhaps slightly misleading, since the same had applied to the whole organic world.

Secondly, Darwinism seemed to justify social theorists in accounting for racial differences in terms of environmental differences over a long period, rather than regarding them as ultimate and unaccountable data.[2]

---

[1] 'Darwinism and History' in A. C. Seward (ed.), *Darwin and Modern Science* (C.U.P. 1909), p. 535.
[2] Note particularly the paper by A. R. Wallace on 'The Origin of the Human Race', in *JAS*, ii (1864). Wallace put forward the idea that after

Finally, there is the question of natural selection. In one sense, the influence of the theory of natural selection on sociology was enormous. It created for a while, in fact, a branch of sociology. It seems now to be felt that the influence on sociology of the doctrine of 'survival of the fittest' was theoretically speaking, unfortunate, chiefly because it seemed to offer an explanatory short cut, and encouraged social theorists to aspire to be Darwins when probably they should have been trying to be Linnaeuses or Cuviers.[1] As Professor MacRae points out,[2] in sociology the principle explains too much. Any state of affairs known to exist or to have existed can be explained by the operation of natural selection. Like Hegel's dialectic and Dr Chasuble's sermon on The Meaning of Manna in the Wilderness, it can be made to suit any situation. However, 'Social Darwinism' was only a subspecies of the intellectual movement we are considering. Neither Maine, nor Tylor, nor McLennan made much use of the theory of natural selection and Spencer used it only as a garnish for a theory he had already developed.

The last important development of the late fifties and the early sixties was the extension of the new geological time scale to the study of man. During the first half of the century a number of discoveries had been made of artifacts and human remains in association with extinct animals in what must be, according to uniformitarian theory, ancient strata. These discoveries, uniformitarianism being granted, could mean only one thing, but they were not accepted.

men had become sociable, natural selection would operate on *societies* rather than on individual physical attributes. This idea Wallace admitted, however, he had drawn very largely from Spencer. One member, describing the idea as entirely new to him, said it constituted 'a new era in anthropology' (*JAS*, II, p. clxxiii). See also *AR*, II, 303, and *MAS*, III (1867–9), 134.

[1] See D. G. MacRae, 'Darwinism in the Social Sciences', in Barnett (ed.), *A Century of Darwin*.

[2] *Ibid.* p. 304.

Men like Boucher de Perthes and MacEnery, who explored Kent's Cavern, could obtain no sympathetic hearing.[1] Adam was harder to defeat than Noah. But, in the late 'fifties, a dramatic change took place. In 1858, a group of British scientists visited de Perthes's excavations, and returned convinced. In 1859 Pengelly's excavations at Brixham, which pointed in the same direction, were completed and Prestwich read his paper on 'The Occurrence of Flint Instruments associated with the Remains of Animals of Extinct Species' to The Royal Society. In 1863 Lyell published his *Geological Evidences of the Antiquity of Man*, and Huxley proclaimed the humanity of the Neanderthal skull which had been discovered in 1856—a point in support of Darwin as well as of the prehistoric archaeologists.

The archaeological evidence for the antiquity of man did more than merely extend to anthropology the advantages which the vaster time scale offered to any theory of gradual, causally determined growth. The demonstration that man, living in the rudest of shelters, had hunted his food, and cooked it, with the most primitive of implements, in Devon and the Dordogne, in the Danish Peninsula and by the shores of the Swiss lakes, just as he did in nineteenth-century Borneo and central Africa, seemed to prove the developmentalists correct in assuming the ancestors of civilized man to have been at least as savage as the most primitive of contemporary savages.[2] From this it seemed to follow that anthropologists would be on the right lines in ascribing the cultural differences between contemporary societies to the achievement of different stages of essentially the same process.

---

[1] Glyn E. Daniel, *A Hundred Years of Archaeology* (1950), p. 34.
[2] E.g. the anniversary address by the Rev. Dunbar Heath, *JAS*, VI (1868), p. xci.

Moreover, one probably should not underestimate, though it is difficult to assess, the challenge to the imagination presented by these dumb relics, the stimulus to the historian-anthropologist to clothe them with some sort of life, and to explain how men so primitive could have been the ancestors of European civilization. And, granted the uninterrupted operation of eternal laws of nature, there seemed no reason why he should not do so. One thing, however, archaeology did not do for evolutionary anthropology which it conceivably might have done. Palaeontology had shown a relation between structural complexity and geological antiquity. Archaeology and evolutionary anthropology might have become similarly associated, so that the chronological classifications of the one were the structural classifications of the other. Categories like stone-age were, in fact (and still are), applied to modern savages where they were appropriate, but there was no real correspondence between archaeological and anthropological classifications.[1] As Glyn Daniel says of L. H. Morgan, his 'stages' are based

not on archaeological evidence but on comparative study of modern primitive peoples, the arrangement of these existing economies and societies into an evolutionary sequence; and the projection of this hypothetical sequence into the historic past.[2]

This was typical. Part of the reason was perhaps that, whereas comparative anatomy had already worked out a satisfactory system of classification before palaeontological evidence began to be studied seriously, a similarly satisfactory system of social categories did not exist; it was natural that men like Morgan should try to work out such

[1] See, however, *JAS*, v (1867), cxcii. Also, in our own times, Gordon Childe, *Social Evolution* (1951).

[2] Daniel, *op. cit.* p. 188.

a system by studying contemporary societies. Secondly, man has been man, biologically speaking, for many thousands of years. No entirely new species has emerged since recorded history began. But the relatively short span of recorded history has seen, even according to the broadest and most economical classification, the emergence of a number of new social types, and about this period archaeology has a good deal less to say. Thus, a greatly enlarged time scale was more vital to evolutionary biology than to evolutionary anthropology, because without it the arguments against biological evolution—the lack of record of any transmutation of species, etc.—were more telling.

3. THE ANTHROPOLOGICAL SOCIETY OF LONDON

The danger of this list of sciences, all in some way pointing the way or smoothing the path for evolutionary social theory, is that it tends to give to its development an air of calm inevitability when in fact the reverse was much more the case. It tends to present a picture, of which the over-emphasis on Darwinism is an aspect, of the growth of social anthropology in the third quarter of the last century as a kind of joyful and conscious imitation of the natural sciences. Of course this *was* an element, but to concentrate on this aspect alone is to present altogether too smooth and simple a picture of intellectual history and to miss the stresses and confusions which were as important to contemporaries as the opportunities. This must not be understood primarily as a reference to the conflict of science and religion, though it is seldom wise to ignore that altogether, but to the difficulties experienced in formulating and readjusting their ideas even by those who were quite happy to forget Adam and the bishop of Oxford.

As a corrective, it may be useful to glance for a moment

at the Anthropological Society of London, founded in 1863. Its members were conscious of great opportunities but were almost totally in the dark about how to take advantage of them.

The society was not, it is true, completely representative of all the impulses which led the mid-Victorians to take an interest in primitive society, and it also gave a hearing to much that now seems quite irrelevant. The evidence it provides is largely negative, and therefore suggestive rather than conclusive. It tells us more about how the foundations of social anthropology were not laid than about how they were. It does little or nothing to support the view that evolutionary social anthropology arose as a result of conscious borrowing from the methods of the natural sciences.

The members of the society set out with high hopes, a set of rules modelled on those of the Geological Society, and the 'nearly perfect' skin of a large male gorilla as the first item of a proposed museum collection. The mood of the founders was one of unbounded confidence in the prospects of a science of anthropology combined with a wide diversity of ideas, and in many cases no ideas at all, about the methods appropriate to such a science.

The society's objects, as announced in its prospectus, were

to study man in all his leading aspects, physical, mental and historical; to investigate the laws of his origin and progress; to ascertain his place in nature and his relations to the inferior forms of life, and to attain these objects by patient investigation, careful induction, and the encouragement of all researches tending to establish a *de facto* science of man.

The choice of name—Anthropological Society of London —was an innovation, since anthropology, though not an entirely new term like sociology, was one whose meaning had hitherto been restricted to, as a definition of the eighteen-fifties put it, 'the determination of the relation of man to the other mammals'.[1]

It is easy to smile at the enormity of its founders' ambitions, but they were justified, at least to this extent: that many of the traditional boundaries between the sciences were breaking down. Did the questions raised by the Neanderthal skull and the Fossil Man of Abbeville belong to the province of the Linnean Society, the Geological Society or the Society of Antiquaries? Obviously to all of them and yet to none exclusively.[2] It seemed reasonable to think, with James Hunt, the President of the Anthropological Society, that 'the time has arrived when it has become absolutely necessary that all the different branches of science relating to man shall no longer be isolated'.[3] Moreover, mention of the Society of Antiquaries is a reminder that subjects which had hitherto indulged an amiable but essentially unadventurous curiosity were now raising profound and deeply disturbing questions about the origin, nature and duration of human life. Inevitably there was tension within the societies between those who welcomed the wider horizons offered and those who wished that things could be as they used to be, with everything in its place and no nonsense about hundreds of thousands of years and ape-men.

It was one such set of stresses which in 1863 led the secretary and a number of leading members of the London Ethnological Society to secede and found the Anthropo-

---

[1] R. G. Latham, *The Natural History of the Varieties of Man* (1850), p. 559. It is perhaps worth noticing that there had been an Anthropological Society from 1837 to 1842 which was eventually merged in The Christian Phrenological Society! (*AR*, vi (1869), 395.)

[2] *JAS*, ii (1864), lxxxvi. It seems curious that the speaker, Hunt, in noting this state of affairs, did not mention the existence of the British Archaeological Association, founded in 1843.

[3] *JAS*, ii (1864), lxxxi.

logical Society. The immediate cause of the secession, the decision of the ethnologists to follow the example of the Royal Geographical Society and admit ladies to its meetings, though not entirely trivial in its implications in mid-Victorian England, was little more than a pretext.[1] The new society differed altogether from its reluctant parent, whose aims were much narrower, being confined to classifying and tracing the history of the various races of mankind, chiefly by philological evidence. It is worth dwelling on this because of a curious misconception in a well-known paper by J. L. Myres.[2] According to Myres, the foundation of the Anthropological Society represented a revolt of those who upheld the unity of mankind against the pro-slavery propaganda of the polygenist Ethnological Society.[3] This is quite untrue. James Hunt,[4] the president and most active member of the new society, was an ardent racialist, and so favourable to slavery as to be suspected of some sinister American or West Indian interest.[5]

The Ethnological Society, on the other hand, was in part an offshoot of the Aborigines Protection Society,[6] and its

---

[1] James Hunt, the leader of the revolt and first president of the Anthropological Society, admitted that he had become dissatisfied with the Ethnological Society as a result of seeing the wider scope permitted by the Société d'Anthropologie de Paris. Failing to persuade the Ethnological Society to remodel itself on similar lines, he seceded and founded the Anthropological Society (*AR*, VI (1868), 464). Elsewhere the Paris Society was referred to as 'our parent society' (*JAS*, II (1864), xcii).

[2] J. L. Myres, 'The Influence of Anthropology on the Course of Political Science'. Given as a paper to the British Association, Winnipeg, 1909, published in *California Publications in History*, vol. IV.

[3] *Ibid.* p. 74.

[4] James Hunt, M.D. (1833–69). Joined the Ethnological Society, 1854; secretary, 1859–62. President of the Anthropological Society, 1863–9.

[5] *JAS*, II (1864), ccxvi. He could hardly complain since, though dissociating himself from the 'horrors' of the slave-trade, he was prepared to assert that 'our mistaken legislature has done the Negro race much injury by their absurd and unwarrantable attempts to prevent Africa from exporting her worthless or surplus population' (*MAS*, I (1863–4), 53).

[6] *AR*, VI (1868), 395.

president at the time of Hunt's secession, Crawfurd,[1] though, like Hunt, he regarded negroes as a distinct species,[2] condemned slavery unequivocally.[3] At a meeting of the British Association in 1863, he told a moving story, according to the *Anthropological Review*, of the conversion of 50,000 natives to Christianity and of one native chief to Free Trade.[4]

It is inevitably difficult to sum up the tone and opinions of a whole society, but, broadly speaking, the aims of the Ethnological Society were both narrower and more clearly defined than those of its undesired offspring. Founded in 1843, it did not begin to publish its proceedings regularly until 1848, when it announced its aims as 'inquiring into the distinguishing characteristics, physical and moral, of the varieties of Mankind which inhabit or have inhabited the Earth; and to ascertain the causes of such characteristics'.[5]

An inquiry into the distinguishing *moral* characteristics of men might well have been a programme for evolutionary sociology, but in this case it was not. The inquiries to which the Ethnological Society devoted itself were for the most part purely classificatory and historical, or even merely descriptive. There was no attempt to detect laws of social or psychological differentiation. On the contrary, a demonstrably historical explanation was looked for, if an explanation was sought at all.[6] The society was, in other words, predominantly diffusionist rather than evolutionist in character. As late as 1869, E. B. Tylor was rebuked by the

---

[1] John Crawfurd (1783–1868), Indian Army doctor who became an orientalist.

[2] See *TES*, new series, III (1865), 60–1; also VI (1868), 49, *passim*.

[3] *TES*, IV (1866), 233.   [4] Reported in *AR*, II (1864), 334.

[5] *JES*, I (1848).

[6] In 1855 the secretary said: 'It is the task of the ethnologist to trace the migration of races and the process of the formation of nations which preceded what is more strictly termed history' (reported in *JAS*, III (1865)).

chairman for a paper he had read on 'The Philosophy of Religion among the Lower Races of Mankind', which he had, of course, treated in an evolutionary manner, on the ground that 'the only scientific method is the historic. We must trace up the history of *known* religions to their sources if we are to generalize on the source of *all* religions.'[1]

The method of tracing origins chiefly in favour in the society was philology—philology used, not as Maine was to use it, as a model for and guarantee of evolutionary social theory, but as a means of tracing actual historical affinities. Its members were concerned with classifications based on historical connection rather than on sociological similarities.[2] Hunt, the President of the Anthropological Society, was chiefly interested in anatomy, but Crawfurd was primarily a philologist, and the proceedings of each society tended to be weighted correspondingly.

Neither anatomy nor philology may seem very promising foundations for social science, but the Anthropological Society was more concerned with the possibility of establishing laws—even if it never succeeded in doing so—than with the more purely historical, classificatory and antiquarian preoccupations of its parent; the tone of the latter was, despite a distinguished membership which included Huxley and Galton, altogether more orthodox. George Eliot's Mr Casaubon, with his key to all mythologies,[3] would have been, surely *was*, a member of the Ethnological Society; he would have been badly out of place among the fiercer spirits

---

[1] *TES*, ii (1869–70), 380. [2] See, e.g. *JES*, i (1848), 19.

[3] Cf. the theory of J. C. Prichard (1786–1848), the most prominent of English ethnologists and a leading member of the Ethnological Society. 'The earliest faith was pure and simple, exhibited comprehensive and exalted conceptions of the Deity, and contained the most awful and impressive sanctions of morality' (J. C. Prichard, *Analysis of Egyptian Mythology* (1819), p. 296).

of the Anthropological Society. In the eighteen-forties, at least, not really surprisingly, the ethnologists breathed easily the atmosphere of the *Bridgewater Treatises*. There is apparent in some of their earlier writing a feeling that, in exploring the varieties of mankind, they were exploring the mind and intentions of the Creator.[1]

For the most part, despite Crawfurd's views on the negro, the Ethnological Society seems to have been heavily under the influence of the monogenist Prichard, while the anthropologists, or at least their leaders, were under that of the racialist anatomist Knox.[2] Prichard, though like Hunt and Crawfurd a doctor by training, had tried to demonstrate the unity of mankind on philological grounds;[3] and to prove 'the cherished unity of mankind' had been put forward by at least one early contributor as one of the main objects of ethnology.[4]

Relations between the two societies were bitter, and the contempt of the ethnologists was a constant stimulus to the anthropologists to define their amorphous and unwieldy subject. The ethnologists denied their right to existence, denied that anthropology was a subject at all. Most irritating of all, they monopolized the subsection of the British Association to which anthropological papers had to be submitted. The anthropologists, baffled, consoled themselves by prophesying the verdict of history.[5]

---

[1] E.g. *JES*, I (1848), 17, 26.   [2] See below, p. 130.

[3] E.g. 'Remarks on the Application of Philological and Physical Researches to the History of the Human Species', *Report of the British Association* (1833), pp. 530 ff.   [4] *JES*, I (1848), 17.

[5] 'Sooner or later it will be learnt that the glory of scientific men will consist in the patient record of observed facts rather than in the fatal facility of being able to attract a crowd of both sexes to listen to equivocal science and still more equivocal pleasantries' (*AR*, II (1864), 299). Anthropology, which does not even appear in the index to the reports of the British Association from 1831 to 1860, became a subsection of section D in 1866.

This challenge to its existence provided a rallying point, a centripetal tendency in a society whose wide interests and lack of clear aims made a central unity of purpose difficult to maintain. It proved easier to announce that 'Anthropology is the science of the whole nature of man' than to know how to set about creating it. A list of papers from a single volume of the society's proceedings gives some idea of the difficulties:

'On the Human Hair as a Race Character.'
'Pott on the Myths of the Origin of Man and Language.'
'Notes on Scalping.'
'Abnormal Distension of the Wrist.'
'Danish Kitchen Middens.'
'Anthropological Documents of the State of New York.' (These are statistics of births, diseases, deaths, etc.)
'The Fossil Man of Abbeville Again.'
'Bain on the Senses and the Intellect.'
'The Gypsies in Egypt.'[1]

A list of the distinguished men among the original members gives a similar impression of heterogeneity. There was the vice-president, Richard Burton, then under the shadow of his dispute with Speke over the source of the Nile, airing his distaste for negroes and rejoicing in the rising value of phallic specimens among European collectors. There were Rajah Sir James Brooke of Sarawak and the notorious Governor Eyre of Jamaica;[2] there were Thirlwall, the historian, ecclesiastic and former tutor of Trinity College, Cambridge, and the future Bishop Selwyn, the prehistorian Pengelly who had excavated Kent's cavern, and Algernon Charles Swinburne. It is only fair, though disappointing, to add that of these Burton was the only active member.

[1] *AR*, II (1864).
[2] Upon whom Hunt pronounced a eulogy when he was under attack by the liberals of the Jamaica committee (*JAS*, IV (1866), lxxviii).

He was later joined by Alfred Wallace and the future Dean Farrar, already the author of *Eric, or Little by Little, St Winifred's or the World of School*, and an *Essay on the Origin of Language*. Both these were active members. The only names subsequently to be distinguished in anthropology as it became a recognized discipline were E. B. Tylor, the future first Professor of Anthropology at Oxford, and Colonel Lane-Fox (later Pitt-Rivers).

A better idea of the composition of the society, however, is given by the fact that among the original members or Founder Fellows, as they were rather grandly called, were sixty-six men with medical degrees—the largest single group; fifty-eight Fellows of the Royal Geographical Society and forty-six of the Geological Society. The Linnaean and Zoological Societies contributed thirty each and the Ethnological Society and the Society of Antiquaries twenty each. There were also twenty brave clergymen. Obviously, except in the case of the medical and clerical, these categories are not mutually exclusive, so the same men appear in several.

Given such a diversity of interests, held together by such very loose terms of reference, not to mention the fluid state of scientific opinion in many fields, it is hardly surprising that, besides providing a platform for genuinely important discussion, the society became a stamping-ground for cranks and exhibitionists of every description. There were men obsessed by statistics and men obsessed by comparative anatomy; men with an eye for phallic symbols determined to prove that the Israelite Ark of the Covenant contained one; clergymen prepared to refer to the biblical account of the Creation as 'the quite baseless traditions of the former barbarous inhabitants of Syria';[1] and laymen who announced themselves 'fully convinced that the entire human

[1] The Rev. Dunbar Heath, *JAS*, VI (1868), xci.

species sprung from the first man Adam, and that the inferiority of race arose from the curse passed on Canaan'.[1] The last were rare, however, and always liable to a presidential rebuke since biblical authority was not admissible evidence in the society.

Of course, divergencies are inherent in any society which is a forum rather than a pressure group, but lack of definition of the subject and agreement about even the most fundamental assumptions made it remarkable that the society held together at all. That it did so was due largely to the efforts of the president, Hunt. When he died in 1869 there was a perceptible loss of vitality, and in 1871, Hunt's old opponent Crawfurd being also dead, the Anthropological and Ethnological Societies were amalgamated on terms which represented at least a verbal victory for the anthropologists in that the new society was called the Anthropological Institute.[2]

Hunt's chief device for holding the society together, apart from hard administrative work, was to issue solemn recommendations, in the name of sound Baconian inductive principles, to allow firmly established facts alone to guide them.[3] *Hypotheses non fingo* may not be a very intelligent recipe for scientific discovery, but that was not its function in the society. Hunt himself was saturated in prejudice and preconception. But it provided a kind of ritual incantation, in applauding which the members could feel again the unity of purpose and assumptions which always seemed to elude them when discussing specific questions.

[1] *MAS*, II (1865–6), 401.
[2] Much to the disgust of its first president, Lubbock, who disliked the word (H. E. Hutchinson, *Life of Sir John Lubbock, Lord Avebury* (2 vols. 1914), I, 118).
[3] E.g. *AR*, I (1863), 13.

4. RACIALISTS AND EVOLUTIONISTS

It is difficult not to give too neat a picture of the society's rather tumultuous life-processes, and it is impossible to convey their flavour and quality by a summary of doctrines. Nevertheless, it is possible to pick out certain very general assumptions about the nature of their problems common to most members of the society. In particular there was a recognition of the difficulty of generalizing about man in a scientific or a moral context in face of the diversity of forms that human nature seemed capable of assuming. As one member put it:

Human nature is, or appears to be, very different in China or America. If the doubt on this point was not shared by almost everyone, would the Anthropological Society exist? Would not a Londoner be quite as good a subject for study as twenty different races, for the purpose of knowing what is and what is not human nature?[1]

It is not an exaggeration to see this as the central inspiration of the society. The common enemy was what they regarded as the *a priori* theories of the utilitarians and the economists, and they made the reasonable inference that if previous attempts to construct moral and political sciences were based on inadequate foundations, their own science must supply new ones. According to Hunt, Political Economy must be based on anthropology.[2] Others emphasized the importance of anthropology to an imperial power.[3] The differences between peoples were the anthropologist's

[1] *AR*, VIII (1870), cxliii.
[2] *JAS*, V (1867), lxiv.
[3] 'It is...the anthropologist by whatever name he now goes, who must be consulted for the future help and guidance in the government of alien races' was a typical pronouncement (*JAS*, VI (1868), lxxxvi). See also *JAS*, II (1864), xciii, xcviii; *AR*, III (1865), 169; *AR*, V (1867), 20; *Anthropologia* (1873), pp. 34, 226, 229.

problem and his opportunity, and most of the members were convinced that these differences were not due to mere accident, as the essentially historical procedures of the Ethnological Society seemed to imply. Man was part of nature, not disconnected from it. 'Religion and philosophies', one member wrote, 'are not accidents but the mormal product, the necessary consequence, of antecedent conditions. They were not made by art, but have grown in obedience to law.'[1]

This is the authentic voice of mid-Victorian positivism, and involved a criticism of Benthamism and the political economists—the older versions of positivism—though it came for the most part from different sources from those more usually considered in this context—Comtism, or some kindred philosophy of history, German historiography, or detailed philosophical analysis. To some extent the society's impatience with what one member called 'the unwarranted application of experiences obtained only from the European race (*sic*), to the whole of humanity...due to the preponderance of abstract ideas over concrete experience',[2] was due simply to the inability of the traditional theories of society to cope with the diversity of facts presented by a wider world. Many of the members of the society had had experience of actual contact with barbarous and primitive peoples, and some doubtless even had a vested interest in denying the unity and essential equality of mankind which was the central postulate of traditional political theory.

But there were other, more strictly scientific reasons put forward for the denial of this postulate, and it was here that a new note was struck. The bias of the society was medical, and the chief source of its interest in the variety of mankind

---

[1] *AR*, IV (1866), 289. Cf. *JAS*, V (1867), lxi.
[2] *AR*, IV (1866), 121.

was comparative anatomy, which offered, of course, the opportunity of classifying the groups of mankind by structure, and also made more plain than ever the gradual shading off, anatomically speaking, of human into animal. The most favoured earlier explanation of human diversity, climate, seemed unable to explain the structural diversities revealed by comparative anatomy. As Farrar said at the British Association in 1864,

There was at one time an impression that the diversities of type and complexion observable in the human race might easily be accounted for from the effects of climate, custom, food and manner of life. This opinion is now entirely abandoned by the majority of scientific men.[1]

Hunt himself had been strongly influenced by Robert Knox, now best known as the Edinburgh anatomist who employed Burke and Hare. Knox, who seems to have been strongly influenced by the German transcendentalists, was an almost hysterical racialist, utterly contemptuous of the empiricist's construct, 'the creature with a soul composed of associations of ideas',[2] as he put it. His book, *The Races of Man*, published in 1850, was an attempt to prove that 'race is everything; literature, science, art—in a word, civilization, depends on it'.[3]

It has been said[4] that the theory of evolution shattered the supposition of the essential unity of mankind by emphasizing the gradual shading off of species into each other. In fact, of course, it was the older science of comparative

---

[1] *AR*, II (1864), 302.

[2] R. Knox, *The Races of Man* (1850), p. 411. Characteristically, he thought that Darwin's theory 'leaves the question precisely where it was left by Goethe, Oken and Geoffroy St. Hilaire' (H. Lonsdale, *Life and Writings of Robert Knox* (1870), p. 386).

[3] *Op. cit.* p. v.

[4] B. Russell, *History of Western Philosophy* (1946), p. 753.

anatomy which threatened to do this by drawing attention to the structural differences between different races.[1] The Anthropological Society was a by-product of the scientific excitement of the early 'sixties, but it would be utterly false to see it as an evolutionist pressure group. Its intellectual roots go back farther than Darwin or even Lamarck, and its starting-point was a question, not a doctrine. The findings of prehistoric archaeology, the proofs of the immense antiquity of man, were pretty generally accepted in the society,[2] but not so Darwin's theory, or even the theory of evolution itself. At least until Wallace joined, Darwin was mentioned seldom and patronizingly, as another evolutionary speculator.[3] Huxley's account of man's place in nature was strongly disputed, and the Neanderthal skull held by Hunt to be that of an idiot.[4] Incidentally, this dispute—missing link or mere degenerate—helps to explain the society's otherwise unaccountable obsession with freaks and monstrosities, its preoccupation with bearded women and microcephalous children.

To say that the society was not Darwinian, or even evolutionist, is not, of course, to say that it was fundamentalist. It is only in retrospect that the issues seem so clear. In fact it had a rather unsavoury reputation for godlessness, which is perhaps why Swinburne thought its membership worth two guineas. Missionary-baiting was common. But its keynote is really confusion; intellectual chaos, the result of a breakdown of the empiricist psychological

[1] Gobineau's *Essai sur l'inégalité des races humaines* began to come out in 1853.

[2] The archaeological record was used by the social evolutionists in the society, of whom there were a few (see below), to prove the original savagery of civilized peoples, and also to demonstrate that all peoples passed through essentially the same stages of development. See *JAS*, v (1867), cxcii.

[3] E.g. *JAS*, II (1864), clxxx.

[4] *Ibid.* p. clxxviii.

tradition, faced with a brave determination to study man scientifically, but almost total indecision about how to start. As Hunt put it: 'We are as yet groping in the dark, and know not yet what to study, or hardly what facts we want to get, to found our science.'[1]

If evolutionary anthropology and sociology had grown smoothly out of the contemporary state of science, one would expect to find them, making due allowance for the inevitable cranks and monomaniacs such a society was bound to attract, strongly foreshadowed in the proceedings of the society. In fact this is not the case. Those members whose ideas were essentially those of evolutionary social anthropology[2] were obviously regarded by Hunt, not without a certain justice, as quaintly old-fashioned. 'So far as he understood them, Mr Wake's[3] views as published in his book were common about a century ago, and the present paper seemed to revive the metaphysical disquisitions of that period.'[4]

This was a palpable hit, but the future lay with Mr Wake's views, not with Hunt's racialism; the English intelligentsia, by and large, continued to regard environment as the ultimate determinant, even while admitting that past theories had been too naïve and parochial in their accounts of its manner of operation. They were assisted in this attitude, of course, by the vast time scale now made available, and by the Darwinian account of the formation of species. Racial

---

[1] *AR*, I (1863), 19.

[2] Apart from Wake (see next note) the most prominent was Hodder M. Westropp (1826–85), an archaeologist and author of *Prehistoric Phases* (1872), *The Cycle of Development* (1881), and *Primitive Symbolism and Phallic Worship* (1895).

[3] C. S. Wake, author of *Chapters on Man* (1868), *The Evolution of Morality* (1878), *Serpent Worship and other Essays* (1888), and *The Development of Marriage and Kinship* (1889). I have been unable to trace his dates.

[4] *AR*, VI (1868), clxx.

differences did not have to be regarded as ultimate data, but could be set in a wider explanatory framework.[1]

What then, is the importance of the society in the history of social theory? Primarily, it is that it represents that most neglected of factors in the history of ideas, the losing side. It reminds us that in science, and in fields close to science, no less than in ethical and political philosophy, this was a period of crisis and confusion as well as of confidence and opportunity. There is, in fact, a considerable parallel, though at different levels of sophistication, between the difficulties experienced by traditional social thought and those encountered by the traditional picture of the natural world, as horizons widened and one by one, with extra-ordinary rapidity, the old boundary posts of thought were uprooted. A member of the Anthropological Society neatly connected the two aspects of the traditional view when he said that 'to them [i.e. the utilitarians and economists], humanity is one from the educational standpoint, as it is also one to the theologians from the creational standpoint'.[2] Early nineteenth-century intellectual life in England was parochial in many ways compared with the intellectual climate of the second half of the century. The world, human and non-human, was, intellectually speaking, a much cosier place than it was later to become. Species were immutable and specially created, and the belief in man's literal kinship with the beasts that perish was confined to a few eccentrics. A few thousand years could still be offered, in all seriousness though perhaps no longer with complete confidence in finding agreement, as the age of the earth. Paley's *Evidences* still traced to most people's satisfaction the hand of the Creator in every work of Nature.

[1] Note the paper by A. R. Wallace on 'The Origin of the Human Race', *JAS*, II (1864). See above, p. 114 n. 2.   [2] *AR*, IV (1866), 114.

It is the intellectual crisis, no less than the excitement, produced by the collapse of this tidy and limited world picture that is reflected in the meetings of the Anthropological Society. The advances of the various sciences had not merely opened up vistas, they had created problems, not only for traditional theology but for the whole structure of thought. And in particular they seemed to reveal as narrow and inadequate the traditional assumptions about the nature of mankind.

It was not only the changing picture of the world offered by the natural sciences and prehistoric archaeology, however, which was making theories of society derived from assumptions about an essential, unchanging human nature appear naïve and unsatisfactory. German jurisprudence, a more subtle historiography, and direct philosophical criticism of the English empiricist epistemology and psychology which had been the backbone of deductive social and political theory were also profoundly important. They found little place, however, in the deliberations of the Anthropological Society,[1] which had its own kind of parochialism. Towards the end of the eighteen-sixties, that is to say *after* the publication of the first major works of Maine, Tylor and Lubbock, Wake lamented that 'the present existence of various families of mankind, exhibiting every stage of the supposed development [i.e. of mankind] appears to have hitherto almost escaped attention'.[2]

It was typical of the society that of its list of honorary fellows, only two, Kingsley (a doubtful case perhaps) and Renan, had any connection with history; the rest were almost all distinguished in some branch of the natural sciences. Occasionally there would be a book review of some

[1] See, however, Hunt's use of John Grote's *Exploratio Philosophica, JAS*, v (1867), ccxvi.   [2] *MAS*, iii (1867–9), 134.

work of history or philosophy—Alexander Bain's *The Senses and the Intellect*, for example. One courageous reviewer even attempted Sterling's *Secret of Hegel*, but, not surprisingly, was able to make nothing at all of 'this ungrammatical German'.[1] J. S. Mill and Spencer were mentioned occasionally, but usually only to be dismissed as upholders of an outworn psychology, with apparently no appreciation of the differences between their approach to the study of society and that of Bentham, with whom they are bracketed. Maine was apparently not even a name.

One of the striking things about the society, in fact, is the absence from its meetings or even its roll of members of a number of the names one would expect. There were reasons for this, of course. Lubbock, easily shockable, was vice-president of the rival Ethnological Society. Maine was out of England for much of the eighteen-sixties, and would in any case have had little in common with the sometimes disorderly rabble at 4 St Martin's Place. Spencer was already a recluse. McLennan is, perhaps, the most surprising absentee. Nevertheless, the interesting fact is that the foundations of evolutionary anthropology were hammered out, not in the eighteen-sixties, in a society dedicated to the task of applying the methods of science to the study of man, but at least partly in the eighteen-fifties, by a number of scholars the sources of whose ideas were juristic and philosophic rather than scientific, and for some of whom, at least, the repudiation of Bentham and Austin was more immediately important than Darwin's vindication of biological evolution, or even the relevation of the antiquity of man, profoundly significant though it was. These, rather than Hunt and his colleagues, were the men who revised the methods of social thought, and in the meetings of the Anthropological Society

[1] *AR*, IV (1866), 43.

we see not so much the foundations of the new discipline as some of the confusions and difficulties which were making revision necessary.

The evolutionary method in social thinking triumphed, not only or perhaps even primarily because it was in tune with that of the vogue sciences of the period, but because it offered a way of coping with new kinds of experience and new methods of interpreting them—methods which had been germinating throughout the earlier part of the century, with, admittedly, a sudden acceleration between 1858 and 1863—with the fewest possible adjustments. The history of this period in anthropology is at once more complex, more interesting, and more intelligible than is suggested by the view which sees the development of theories of social evolution essentially as a leap on to a pre-existing scientific band-wagon. To suppose this is to forget that the Victorians had problems as well as opportunities. The proceedings of the Anthropological Society, during its short life, reveal the impasse reached by mid-nineteenth-century positivism once it had abandoned, for various reasons, the belief that a science of man and society could be deduced from a few cardinal propositions about human nature. The way out of that impasse—in a sense, for the Victorians, the only way— was by some kind of evolutionary theory, but it was not, by and large, those who were most immediately concerned to imitate the methods of particular branches of the natural sciences who led the way. Hints from the natural sciences, and from archaeology, took their places in a whole complex of ideas which lay behind the appearance, in the eighteen-sixties, of the first major works of evolutionary social anthropology.

CHAPTER 5

SIR HENRY MAINE

I. CAREER AND WORKS

Sir Henry James Sumner Maine is an eminent Victorian who escaped the usual posthumous compliment of a two-volume Life and Letters, compiled—the word is usually just—by a devoted friend or dutiful relative. Sir M. E. Grant Duff[1] upon whom, in Maine's case, the duty of commemoration fell, excused himself for being content with a brief Memoir[2] on the ground that although a Life 'of the regulation size' could doubtless be compiled 'by stringing together great numbers of his letters to various official personages at home or in India when he was serving at Calcutta or Simla...it would not be of any general interest'.[3]

This may well be so, but there are a number of questions one would like to ask about Maine's earlier life, and about the early Cambridge period in particular, to which Grant Duff's Memoir provides no answer. Indeed, on this period, which was before his own acquaintance with Maine began,[4] Grant Duff appears to have little information which cannot be found elsewhere. Sir Alfred Lyall, reviewing Grant Duff's book, seems to have spoken justly of the 'somewhat scanty biographical materials'.[5]

[1] Sir M. E. Grant Duff (1829–1906). His best-known work, *Notes from a Diary, 1851–1901* (14 vols. 1897–1905), contains nothing of importance about Maine.

[2] Duff, *Sir Henry Maine, A brief Memoir of his Life*, with speeches etc., ed. by Whitley Stokes (1892).

[3] *Ibid.* p. 1.

[4] He first met Maine in 1853 (*ibid.* p. 13).

[5] *Quarterly Review*, 176 (1893), p. 287. This article is attributed to Lyall in H. M. Durand, *Life of Sir Alfred Lyall* (Edinburgh, 1913), p. 355. According to Maine's grandson, the late Mr Henry Maine, who very kindly

The outline of Maine's career is easily drawn. His father was a doctor, a native of Kelso, and Maine himself was born in 1822. The only unusual circumstance about his childhood was his possession of a future archbishop of Canterbury, Dr Sumner, then bishop of Chester, as a godfather, but this contact with the hierarchy seems to have given Maine little but a middle name and his admission to Christ's Hospital.[1] In 1840 he went up to Pembroke College, Cambridge, as an Exhibitioner. He distinguished himself at Cambridge, becoming a member of the 'Apostles',[2] winning the Chancellor's Medal for English Verse in 1842, and graduating as Senior Classic of his year. There being no vacancy at Pembroke, he accepted a tutorship at Trinity Hall in 1845, but was unable to take up the Fellowship usually associated with it, because it necessitated his being in Holy Orders.

It is tempting to read into this reluctance of Maine's to take the obvious step a hint of early unorthodoxy, but probably no more was involved than the superior attractiveness of the Law. There is no more reason to assume serious religious doubts in Maine on account of this decision than in his friend, Fitzjames Stephen, who took the same decision and left an account of his reasons.[3] Years later, when Darwinism was a commonplace and agnosticism almost respectable, when many, including Fitzjames's younger brother, who at Maine's own college had blithely taken the step that Maine jibbed at, had drifted into unbelief, Maine

gave me every assistance he could, Maine's papers were destroyed after his death by his widow. The most exhaustive account of Maine's life is now to be found in G. A. Feaver, *From Status to Contract. A biographical study of Sir Henry Maine 1822–1888* (1962)—an unpublished thesis deposited at the London School of Economics.

[1] Duff, *Sir Henry Maine*, p. 2.

[2] For the Apostles' Club in the nineteenth century, see F. M. Brookfield, *The Cambridge Apostles* (1906).

[3] L. Stephen, *The Life and Letters of Sir J. F. Stephen*, pp. 114–18.

could say to Fitzjames with an almost naïve note of surprise and injury: 'It is a great shock to find that the world was not made for man.'[1] Maine's *Saturday Review* articles in the eighteen-fifties, however, show traces of anti-clericalism, and he speaks of 'the intolerable and irreligious obligation of taking orders as a condition of holding or retaining a College Fellowship'.[2]

Having decided on the Law, Maine quickly made his mark. He became Regius Professor of Civil Law in 1847; in 1850 he was called to the Bar. He became Reader in Roman Law and Jurisprudence at the Inns of Court in 1852, though he continued to hold his Cambridge chair till 1854. In 1856 he contributed an article on 'Roman Law and Legal Education' to *Cambridge Essays* (1856). He had been contributing articles to the *Saturday Review* since its foundation in 1855. He published *Ancient Law*, the work for which he is chiefly remembered, in 1861. He had already delivered the substance of it, however, in the form of lectures at the Inns of Court and perhaps in Cambridge. One authority for this is Frederic Harrison, who was a private pupil of Maine in 1857, and attended the lectures.[3] Grant Duff, whose acquaintance with Maine began at the Inns of Court in 1853, says of the lectures that they contain the substance of *Ancient Law*, referring to the whole period from 1853. This is sufficient to dispose of the notion that *Ancient Law* owed very much to Darwin's *Origin of Species*, though of course it does not preclude the possibility that Maine, like Spencer, may have been influenced by the ideas

---

[1] J. P. C. Roach, *Sir James Fitzjames Stephen*, unpublished Cambridge Ph.D. thesis (1954), p. 255.

[2] 'Academical Freedom', *Saturday Review*, II (7 June 1856), 119. For the attribution of *Saturday Review* articles see M. M. Bevington, *The Saturday Review* (Columbia, 1941), pp. 358–60.

[3] F. Harrison, *Autobiographic Memoirs* (2 vols. 1911), I, 152, 157; II, 76.

of evolutionary biology. It also refutes Sir Carleton Allen's odd remark that 'it is well known that acquaintance with Indian customary law first inspired Sir Henry Maine to embark upon his researches into the growth of law, and consequently to put a new complexion on the accepted English dogmas on the subject'.[1] This is misleading if by 'acquaintance' he means simply knowledge; *Ancient Law* does contain evidence of such knowledge,[2] but it is difficult to see why this particular element should be singled out unless by 'acquaintance' is meant 'personal experience'. If this is the case, the remark is sufficiently refuted by the fact that *Ancient Law*, which Allen admits contains the germs of almost all Maine's subsequent work,[3] was published in 1861, and Maine did not leave for India until 1862.

But even 1853 is not necessarily the earliest date at which we can discern the origins of *Ancient Law*. Maine had been lecturing on Roman law in Cambridge for six years by then, and a phrase of Pollock's suggests that the substance of *Ancient Law* was given also in his Cambridge lectures, that is, between 1847 and 1854.[4] The germination of *Ancient Law* thus lies somewhere in the decade 1843–53. These, then, the years 1843–53, are the crucial years in the development of Maine as a social theorist. Unfortunately, they are also among the blankest in our knowledge of his life.

In 1862 Maine accepted the post, which he had refused the previous year on health grounds, of Legal Member of the Council in India. During his time in India he served under Lords Elgin, Lawrence and Mayo. A selection of his

---

[1] C. K. Allen, *Law in the Making* (2nd ed. O.U.P. 1930), p. 74.

[2] Maine, *Ancient Law*, pp. 5, 127, 159, 160, 187, 193–4, 216–17, 220, 232–3.   [3] *Ibid*. p. xix.

[4] 'Sir Henry Maine as a Jurist', *ER*, 178 (1893), p. iii. Authorship admitted by Sir Frederick Pollock in *The Pollock–Holmes Letters* (2 vols. C.U.P. 1942), I, 45.

speeches and minutes belonging to this period, edited by Whitley Stokes, was published in the same volume as Grant Duff's Memoir. Returning at the end of his term, Maine took up the Corpus Professorship of Jurisprudence at Oxford in 1869. In 1871 he published *Village Communities of East and West*, a study in the comparative method based on his Indian knowledge and the European researches of various German historians.[1] His next book, *The Early History of Institutions*, was published in 1875. *Dissertations on Early Law and Custom*, based largely on the early Irish Brehon laws, followed in 1883. In 1885 he revised and published under the title *Popular Government* a series of articles on Democracy which had originally appeared in the *Quarterly Review*. In 1887 he became Whewell Professor of International Law at Cambridge. He had been Master of Trinity Hall since 1877. The lectures he gave in this capacity were revised and published after his death under the title *International Law* by Frederic Harrison and Sir Frederick Pollock. Maine died in 1888, leaving a widow and two sons, having married his cousin, Jane Maine, in 1847.

The later years of Maine's life present few problems. They offer the routine story of the publications and honours of a distinguished man. Maine's importance to our subject springs chiefly from the fact that he was the author of *Ancient Law*; most of his subsequent work may be regarded as an amplification of the theories of *Ancient Law*, enriched but not fundamentally altered by his Indian experience. The vital years, therefore, are those to which attention has already been drawn, the years in which the theories

[1] Maine, *Village Communities in the East and West* (3rd ed. 1876) (1871), chapters III and V; see also appendix II. Maine's work on the Indian village community is a counterpart to the work of European scholars on the Teutonic Mark and the Russian *mir*. In Russia this work provided a scholarly basis for Populism. Maine's use of it was very different. See below, pp. 159 ff.

expressed in *Ancient Law* must have been conceived. Even *Popular Government*, which does not fall into quite the same category as Maine's other books, comes as no surprise to anyone who has followed his career. One can, as it were, watch it growing—in his other books, in his *Saturday Review* articles, in his Indian speeches and minutes. But can one watch the growth of *Ancient Law*? Unfortunately not; not, at least, in any detail.

2. HISTORICAL JURISPRUDENCE AND THE COMPARATIVE METHOD

The importance of *Ancient Law* to jurists lies in its introduction to an English audience of the historical method of jurisprudence usually associated with the name of Savigny.[1] We do not know exactly when Maine became acquainted with the work of the German historical school. In fact, as Sir Carleton Allen says,[2] there is not much evidence that Maine was intimately familiar with the writings of Savigny.[3] Allen thinks he was more influenced by the work of another member of the historical school, the *Geist des Römischen Rechts* of Rudolf von Ihering, which appeared in 1858. Kantorowicz puts Allen's point more strongly when he says that 'to call Henry Sumner Maine a representative of the historical school is true only in the sense that he was in sympathy with the so called 'younger' school led by Ihering'.[4] These views seem difficult to reconcile with the knowledge that the substance of *Ancient Law* had existed

[1] See the *Pollock–Holmes Letters*, II, 112. Also Sir Frederick Pollock, *Oxford Lectures* (1890), pp. 158–9. For a discussion of Savigny, see the article by H. Kantorowicz, 'Savigny and the Historical School of Law', *Law Quarterly Review*, LIII (1937).

[2] In his introduction to *Ancient Law* (O.U.P. 1954), p. xiii.

[3] He is mentioned twice in *Ancient Law* as an authority on the Roman Law of Property (pp. 211, 241).

[4] *Ibid.* p. 333.

in the form of lectures since 1853 and probably earlier. Sir Paul Vinogradoff calls Maine 'the English disciple of Savigny', and says that 'the special disquisitions of *Ancient Law* on testament, contract, possession etc. leave no doubt as to his close dependence upon Savigny and Puchta's writings'.[1]

The opinions of lawyers have been extensively quoted, because in such a case, depending as it does almost entirely on internal evidence, and somewhat technical evidence at that, a lawyer's opinion is more valuable than that of an historian. It seems fairly clear that Maine's historical approach to law was influenced by the writings of the German historical school, though there is some doubt as to whether he was directly indebted to Savigny. Perhaps the best summary is in the elastic phraseology of Pollock, when he says that Maine 'began his work in the mighty and still present shadow of Savigny'.[2] Our dating of the origin of *Ancient Law* makes it probable that Maine had come under the influence of the German school by 1853 and perhaps before. Maine's Cambridge contemporary and friend, Franklin Lushington, says in a letter he contributed to Grant Duff's Memoir that Maine's appointment to the Regius Professorship of Civil Law in 1847 'may rightly be looked on as the first definitive call to that great study to which he gave, in one phase or another, so much of his mind and so many years of his life'.[3]

This may be merely rhetoric, but it does help to establish a credible picture. A young middle-class don, of great ability and ambition,[4] but possessing, so far as we know,

---

[1] Sir P. Vinogradoff, *The Teaching of Sir Henry Maine* (O.U.P. 1904), p. 9.
[2] Pollock, *Oxford Lectures*, p. 153.
[3] Grant Duff, *Sir Henry Maine*.
[4] Lushington emphasizes his ambition (*loc. cit.*).

no private means, and suffering much ill health,[1] might naturally look to make a name for himself in academic law, rather than in legal practice. His work as Regius Professor would bring him into close touch with the only field of law, apart from International Law, with which it is closely linked, studied by both continental and English scholars— the very field in which Savigny had worked and the German historical school, paradoxically in view of its nationalism, was strongest. Maine's marriage in 1847 caused him to swerve for a time from the obvious course and to read for the Bar,[2] but it must soon have become apparent that he would not be strong enough for practice. The Readership at the Inns of Court, again in the field of Roman Law, would help to recall him to the path of academic law. Taking these circumstances together and allowing for exceptional ability, the publication in the early eighteen-sixties of an English work treating jurisprudence historically seems a natural enough outcome.

But so far we have considered *Ancient Law* simply as an event in the history of jurisprudence. What was it that gave the publication of *Ancient Law* a wider importance, particularly for the development of sociology and anthropology? One can understand perhaps that it might help to stimulate the development of these subjects to regard law not merely as a technical specialism, an abstract system of rules, but as a developing body of norms, forming part of, and incomprehensible apart from, the total life of the society to which they apply. But what has this specifically to do with the Comparative Method? The German historical school of

---

[1] According to Grant Duff his frequent ill health 'would have made anything like the work of a fully employed lawyer quite out of the question for him' (Grant Duff, *op. cit.* p. 14). All the contemporary accounts of Maine refer to his ill health.

[2] *Ibid.* p. 10.

jurisprudence was strongly Romantic and nationalistic, inclined to assert the unique and ineffable character of the entities it dealt with, particularly the nation. Such a doctrine might well encourage detailed historical research, as in fact it did, but if rigidly held it would make the classification of, and generalization from, elements from many different social traditions, which was the essence of the comparative method, impossible.

There is, in fact, another element in Maine's thought; for some of the characteristic doctrines of German historical jurisprudence, had he accepted them in their entirety, would have made nonsense of most of his work. The other element was a scientific bent, an urge to classify, order, abstract and generalize. He accepted the historical bias of the German school with its emphasis on the organic character of law, but he ignored its epistemology. For all his conservatism, there is nothing of the mystic in Maine, and, his detractors would have said, little of the precise scholar either. Vinogradoff seems to have been the only lawyer who noticed the conflict, and the break with the German tradition which it involves.

Maine brings into the field of enquiry a new element, the element of *science* in the English sense of the word, that is of exact knowledge based on observation and aiming at the formulation of laws. The fact is that Maine did not only stand under the influence of the preceding generation, which had given such an extraordinary impulse to historical research, but also under the sign of his own time with its craving for a scientific treatment of the problems of social life.[1]

Maine himself made the same point when he wrote: 'During the last five-and-twenty years German enquirers have been busy with the early history and gradual developments of

[1] Vinogradoff, *The Teaching of Sir Henry Maine*, pp. 10-11. Italics original.

European ownership, ownership, that is to say, of land. But the Historical Method in their hands has not been quickened and corrected by the Comparative Method.'[1]

This presents a new problem. How and when did this scientific element, so alien to the tradition of jurisprudence whose influence on Maine we have tried to trace, become a distinctive part of his thinking? It is perhaps worth remembering at this point that Maine's father was a doctor. Maine was thus not born into an atmosphere of high politics or administration but was, like Spencer, the son of a middle-class man of science, and we know how much influence his father's scientific turn of mind had on Spencer.[2] The question of the origin of Maine's scientific outlook is vital because, although without it he might still have introduced historical jurisprudence into England, he would certainly not have written a work which, as Pollock said, 'at one masterstroke... forged a new and lasting bond between law, history and anthropology'.[3] We already know that for our purpose the crucial period in Maine's intellectual development probably occurred some time before 1853-4. It is to Cambridge, therefore, the Cambridge of the eighteen-forties, that we must turn.[4]

What information is provided by Maine's Cambridge contemporaries and pupils? Perhaps the fullest description of Maine at this period is by one of his pupils, C. A. Bristed, in his *Five Years at an English University*.[5] But though interesting on points of character and appearance, it offers no account of his intellectual development. Among the

[1] Maine, *Observation of India*, pp. 23-4.
[2] See below, p. 184.
[3] Pollock, *Oxford Lectures*, p. 159.
[4] Note Leslie Stephen on the influence of J. S. Mill in Cambridge during this period, e.g. in the *D.N.B.* article on William Whewell.
[5] C. A. Bristed, *Five Years at an English University* (New York, 1852).

members of the 'Apostles', that most exclusive and intellectually distinguished of undergraduate societies, in Maine's time (he seems to have continued to attend after he graduated) were Fitzjames Stephen, H. F. Hallam, a brief memoir of whom Maine wrote in collaboration with Franklin Lushington, E. H. Stanley (afterwards Lord Derby), Vernon Harcourt[1] and Julian Fane. W. H. Thompson, the Trinity tutor and lecturer on Plato, sometimes attended meetings. Some of these contribute a little to our knowledge of Maine, but nothing very relevant. Thus we know from Leslie Stephen's *Life of Fitzjames Stephen* that Maine opposed the motion (which Fitzjames supported) that Carlyle is a philosophic historian—it would be interesting to know why—and the motion that no reconstruction of society is necessary.[2]

The most important of Maine's writings before the publication of *Ancient Law* are his *Saturday Review* articles and his contribution to *Cambridge Essays* (1856) on 'Roman Law and Legal Education'. The latter is an interesting forerunner of *Ancient Law* in its emphasis on the historical approach to the study of law, but it contains nothing very relevant to our present concern. There is a cryptic statement that 'it is not because our own jurisprudence and that of Rome were *once* alike that they ought to be studied together —it is because they *will be alike*. It is because all laws, however dissimilar in their infancy, tend to resemble each other in their maturity';[3] but it is difficult to place this remark in the context of Maine's later theories.

In Maine's later work there is ample evidence of his knowledge of other sciences, and his appreciation of the parallels they offer to the task he has set himself. But of

---

[1] Maine is mentioned in A. G. Gardiner, *The Life of Sir William Vernon Harcourt* (1923), I, 39, 40, 86, 194, 259, 344. Maine contributed to R. Lytton, *Julian Fane, a Memoir* (1871), pp. 54-7.

[2] *Op. cit.* p. 104.   [3] *Cambridge Essays* (1856), p. 2.

course, to notice a parallel, though it proves knowledge, does not necessarily indicate that it has influenced one's thinking; one might merely have used it to make a point more effectively.

On the second page of *Ancient Law* we come across a geological analogy. Maine goes on to say that 'the Inquiries of the jurist are in truth prosecuted much as inquiry in physics and physiology was prosecuted before observation had taken the place of assumption'.[1] This embodies the assumption that jurisprudence is capable of being treated as a science. Later we find Maine asserting that his methods 'are as little objectionable as those which have led to such surprising results in comparative philology'[2]—an analogy to which he frequently returns in subsequent works.

There is, in fact, a far greater number of references to comparative philology (sometimes bracketed with comparative mythology) in Maine's works than to any physical science.[3] Often he seems not merely to be pointing to comparative philology as an interesting analogy, but actually to be using it as a justification of his own method.[4] In *Early Law and Custom* he wrote: 'The evidence for it [i.e. the patriarchal theory] appeared to me very much of the same kind and strength as that which convinces the comparative philologist that a number of words in different Aryan languages had a common form in a now unknown ancestral mother tongue.'[5] He made the same point in his article on the patriarchal theory in the *Quarterly Review*,[6] protesting

[1] *Ancient Law*, pp. 2–3.   [2] *Ibid.* p. 19.

[3] *Village Communities*, pp. 6, 8; 'Address to the University of Calcutta' (1865), reprinted in *Village Communities*, pp. 267 ff; *Early History of Institutions*, ch. II *Observation*; *of India*, pp. 8–10.

[4] E.g. *Observation of India*, pp. 20, 25, 30.

[5] *Early Law and Custom*, p. 194.

[6] *Quarterly Review*, no. 162 (1886), attrib. Maine in Grant Duff, *Sir Henry Maine*, p. 67.

that the rigidity with which the brothers McLennan applied the Comparative Method would make comparative philology impossible. He even asserted that J. F. McLennan did not practise the Comparative Method at all, but 'that of the biologist', namely the reconstruction of parts from rudimentary traces. Maine seems here to identify biology with palaeontology, and the justice of his attempt to make a distinction on these grounds between McLennan's method and his own is questionable—we shall come to this later— but it does show that Maine thought there was a difference between the method of evolutionary biology and the method he himself followed. His remark bears out what one would guess in any case from the rest of his writings, that the most powerful parallel to his own method seemed to him to be that of comparative philology.

Comparative philology was becoming fashionable in England in the early eighteen-sixties. Though it sprang originally from the work on Sanskrit of an Englishman, Sir William Jones (1746–94), it had become largely the preserve of German scholarship, and as such was first popularized in England in two series of lectures at the Royal Institution, in 1861 and 1863, by F. Max Müller.[1]

But the dating of *Ancient Law* and its importance relative to Maine's other writings make it certain that, if comparative philology was of any fundamental importance to this thinking, he cannot have become acquainted with it for the first time through Max Müller's Royal Institution lectures. This is not conclusive evidence, however, that he

[1] Subsequently published under the title *Lectures on the Science of Language*. For the development of comparative philology in the first half of the century, see particularly Pedersen, *Linguistic Science in the Nineteenth Century*; also O. Jespersen, *Language. Its Nature, Development and Origin* (1922), and W. Haas, 'Of Living Things', *German Life and Letters*, x (1956–7). I am indebted for the latter reference to Professor W. S. Allen.

was not influenced by Max Müller, though the lectures were the first popular presentation of the methods of comparative philology to an English audience. Max Müller, who had studied under the founder of comparative linguistics, Franz Bopp, had come to England under the patronage of the Prussian Ambassador, Baron Bunsen, himself a philologist, in 1846. At that time his chief interest was in Sanskrit, a subject already known in England, and indeed first introduced to Europe by Sir William Jones. Max Müller's editions of the *Rig-Veda* began to appear in 1849, and remained his chief interest until his failure to obtain the chair of Sanskrit at Oxford in 1860. This disappointment led him to turn to comparative philology, and a Chair in this subject was founded in Oxford on his behalf in 1868, a post which he held till his death. Despite the fact that Sanskrit was his chief interest from 1846 to 1860, however, he had published a number of papers on linguistics during that period, from any one of which an interested reader could easily have derived the essentials of the method of comparative philology, and also the theory of an Aryan race, of which Maine subsequently made considerable use.

Max Müller's first paper to be published in England was read to the British Association in 1847.[1] It was on the relation of Bengali to the Aryan and aboriginal languages of India, and gave considerable space to a discussion of the principles of comparative philology. Bunsen, incidentally, gave a paper on similar lines at the same session.[2] Other references to, and explanations of, the Comparative Method occur in Max Müller's papers on the *Veda* and the *Zend-*

---

[1] *Report of the British Association*, no. 17 (1848).

[2] For Bunsen, see J. W. Burrow, 'The Uses of Philology in Victorian England' in R. Robson (ed) *Ideas and Institutions of Victorian Britain* (1967).

Avesta (1853),[1] and in his essay on Comparative Mythology in *Oxford Essays* (1856). His *History of Ancient Sanscrit Literature* (1859) contains an introductory section on the Aryan 'race' and the methods of comparative philology.[2]

Nor, despite the claim in the article on Max Müller in the *Dictionary of National Biography* that 'nothing was known about comparative philology in England when he came over to this country',[3] was Max Müller the only source from which Maine could have derived a knowledge of the principles of the subject, even leaving aside the possibility that he may have gone directly to the works of German pioneers themselves. We have already noticed the interest taken in comparative philology by the members of the Ethnological Society.[4]

It is true that their interest in it was of a different kind from Maine's. They did not adopt it as a model for the study of society; for them, tracing racial affiliations by means of comparative philology[5] was an end in itself. But this does not, of course, affect their testimony to the use and knowledge, in England in the early eighteen-sixties, of comparative philology. Nor must the contrast of Maine with the ethnologists be allowed to suggest that he was a thorough sociologist. His belief in the validity of his comparisons was not the consequence of a confidence that similar social structures imply similar social functions, race and history

---

[1] Reprinted in F. Max Müller, *Chips from a German Workshop* (2 vols., 2nd ed. 1868), I, 62–4, 81.

[2] F. Max Müller, *History of Ancient Sanscrit Literature* (1859), pp. 1–17.

[3] By Prof. A. A. Macdonnel. Cf. *Life and Letters of Max Müller* (ed. by his wife, 1902, 2 vols.), I, 242, 248.

[4] See above, p. 123. For other examples of the use of comparative philology in England, and of the theory of an Aryan 'race' to which it gave rise, see Burrow, *op. cit.*

[5] To which, incidentally, Max Müller objected, *Lectures*, p. 314.

being largely irrelevant. On the contrary, his assumptions and practice are perfectly summed up by a recent definition of comparative philology: 'Comparative philology may be defined as the comparison of languages (through comparison of items within them) that are, or are assumed to be, *genetically related*, with the object of establishing such relationships and *reconstructing original forms*, from which derivation may be made.'[1] When this definition is compared with Maine's use of the Comparative Method, the impression that comparative philology was, after historical jurisprudence, the chief influence upon him, is further strengthened.

Even if this were the case, however, we still do not know exactly how he became interested in it. Was he drawn to Sanskrit by an interest in Hindu law, of which we know, from *Ancient Law* and his *Saturday Review* articles, he had some knowledge, and then from Sanskrit to comparative philology? Or was it, though this is perhaps less probable, the other way round: was it comparative philology which, by analogy, taught him to take an interest in Hindu law?

If we assume that philology *was* an influence on Maine then we have to agree that the scientific element in his thought, as well as the historical, came largely from Germany, and Vinogradoff's remark, correct though he is in his main contention, about 'science in the English sense' is misleading. But this is perhaps to be too fastidious. Maine must have been influenced by the general English intellectual climate, as well as, possibly, by a particular branch of learning practised in Germany. Whatever view one takes, however, it is at least clear that it is utterly false to regard Maine's work as a conscious imitation of evolutionary biology. His career is another example of the impossibility

[1] J. F. Ellis, 'General Linguistics and Comparative Philology', *Lingua*, VII (1957–8), 2. Italics mine.

of interpreting every piece of evolutionary thinking in the years following 1859 into an effect of the influence of Darwin.[1]

3. MAINE AS A SOCIAL THEORIST

We have traced, as far as possible, the influence reflected in Maine's writings, and can now attempt an estimate of the place of his work in the history of social thought. There are two distinct schools of thought about Maine. To the older school, composed for the most part of men who knew him, Maine's importance lay in his historical outlook, his revolutionary impact on English jurisprudence, and the way he illuminated Imperial problems by historical parallels. These were the men who wrote the obituaries in the learned journals when Maine died, and provided what might be called the first generation of posthumous commentary. Enthusiasm was, it is true, sometimes qualified by unfavourable remarks about the patriarchal theory, and by deprecating comment on Maine's sweeping generalizations and inaccuracy in detail. Pollock even found it necessary to write an elaborate preface to *Ancient Law* as an antidote. But these were technical objections to the substance of Maine's work, not attacks on his fundamental assumptions. His contemporaries and near-contemporaries seem to have been content to accept Maine as the arch-enemy and destroyer of *a priori* theorizing in juristic and political thinking, and as such, whatever his minor flaws, a great liberator and pioneer.

For them his importance was that he had introduced inductive methods into the study of jurisprudence and politics,[2]

---

[1] Maine's references to Darwin, and to evolutionary biology are few and not very important, though he is quoted in support of the patriarchal theory (*Early Law and Custom*, ch. VII).

[2] Fitzjames Stephen, *ER*, 232, VII (1861), Vinogradoff, *The Teaching o, Sir Henry Maine*, and Pollock, *ER*, 365, V (1893) and *Oxford Lectures*.

and had shown that past and present legal conceptions were intelligibly linked. Moreover, he had used the Comparative Method to make intelligible the alien problems of that 'chaos of survivals', the Indian empire, as well as using his Indian knowledge in compiling the comparative history of legal institutions.[1] He also attempted in *Popular Government* to draw political lessons from his historical generalizations, but these, being more controversial, were more coolly received.[2]

This assessment of Maine's work by his contemporaries corresponds very closely with his own view, as expressed in his writings, of what he was trying to do. His works are full of attacks on the Social Contract school for their unhistoricality.[3] *Ancient Law* and *Popular Government*, standing as they do respectively at the beginning and end of Maine's literary career, are both directed against the Contractarian and Natural Law doctrines of society. Elsewhere he wrote: 'The undertaking that I have followed in the work just mentioned [*Ancient Law*], and in others, has been to trace the real, as opposed to the imaginary, or the arbitrarily assumed, history of the institutions of civilized men.'[4] Bentham and Austin he also attacked, though not so bitterly, for trying to give a universal application to theories appropriate to one phase of legal history.[5] On the same grounds, he attacked Political Economy, using Indian examples in an attempt to show the inapplicability of some of its leading concepts to societies fundamentally different from those of western Europe.[6] Maine employed his wide historical know-

---

[1] Lyall, in *Quarterly Review*, 176 (1893) and in *Law Quarterly Review*, IV (1888).   [2] E.g. Pollock, *Oxford Lectures*, p. 160.

[3] E.g. *Ancient Law*, pp. 2–3, 71, 74; *Popular Government*, pp. vii, 152, 157–9.   [4] *Early Law and Custom*, p. 192.

[5] *Ancient Law*, p. 98; *Early History of Institutions*, pp. 346–7, 356–7, 360–1, 380–2, 393; *Early Law and Custom*, p. 361.

[6] *Observation of India*, pp. 23–4, 27, 33; *Early Law and Custom*, p. 347; Duff, *Sir Henry Maine*, pp. 406–7.

ledge and Indian experience to deprive the economists of their claims to final truth and fell back on the Comparative Method to save himself from total relativism. This is not meant to imply that, psychologically speaking, Maine felt in any danger of falling into relativism but merely that this was the logical function of his method. Psychologically speaking, he seems to have regarded the Comparative Method as the foundation of a great new science rather than as a last resort. The alien conceptions and institutions, at least if they are of Aryan origin, are merely the germs out of which have evolved the systems studied by analytic jurisprudence and Political Economy. When the relation between them is properly understood, we shall be able not merely to understand and deal with 'survivals' of earlier stages but to understand better the civilization of modern Europe. 'We are perhaps apt to consider ourselves as exclusively children of the age of free trade and scientific discovery.'[1]

It is ironical that the newer estimate of Maine is based largely on the belief that he himself was too exclusively a child of the age of free trade and scientific discovery—that though emancipated from some of the assumptions of an earlier time he was not emancipated enough. It is obvious that this view represents a shift of emphasis rather than a flat denial of the older view. It does not deny, indeed the evidence is so overwhelming that it would be absurd to do so, that Maine did try to do what he claimed to be doing, and what the older view regarded as his achievement. It accepts that he attempted to substitute historical and comparative study of beliefs and institutions for deduction from first principles, but it depreciates the importance of this by pointing to a persisting framework of ideas within which the change took place. It is not the facts that are in

[1] *Observation of India*, p. 31.

dispute, but the interpretation of them in the light of the general history of social thought.

In 1928 K. B. Smellie fired the first shot from this direction when he pointed out that 'Maine accepted the Ricardian economic man as the goal of progress. It is the Ricardian economic man who is freed from the *patria potestas*, and who enters on a boundless economic and moral progress as status gives place to contract.'[1] Lord Annan has, in a recent lecture,[2] pointed to Maine as one of the Victorians who 'appear to be forerunners of the revolution in sociology', but finds him, in the last resort, disappointing. But how just is the criticism? Was Maine a positivist, and if so of what type? To answer this we shall also have to answer a more general question: is it possible to see in Maine's work a coherent theory of history and society, and if so what was it?

Maine was not a comprehensive or systematic thinker in the manner of James Mill or Herbert Spencer. He wrote no treatise on ethics or scientific method. Our knowledge of his opinions on these subjects must be gathered piecemeal from his various writings. His views were, in fact, something of a rag-bag; an avowedly empiricist epistemology, a rather vaguely utilitarian and liberal approach to ethics, a strong belief in the value of scientific method—all these were specifically English elements in his thought.

Combined with them was a typically conservative conviction of the precariousness and complexity of civilization, from which sprang his distrust of democracy and his insistence on an historical approach to the study of society. In these beliefs, as also, perhaps, in the particular kind of

[1] K. B. Smellie, 'Sir Henry Maine', *Economica*, nos. 22–4 (1928), 77.
[2] N. G. Annan, *The Curious Strength of Positivism in English Political Thought* (L. T. Hobhouse Memorial Trust Lecture, no. 28, O.U.P. 1959), p. 13.

historical study he advocated, there is obviously some German influence, as well as the influence of his own official experience. But Maine was no uncritical adherent of *Historismus*. He did not belong to that class of nineteenth-century Englishmen, of which Coleridge and Carlyle are the outstanding examples in the first half of the century and T. H. Green and F. H. Bradley in the second, whose acquaintance with German thought turned them against the empiricist tradition in ethics and epistemology. Maine would never have called utilitarianism 'pig philosophy',[1] or doubted that inductive science was the way for men to make sense of their society and its history.

Maine thus represents a combination of the sociological and historical insights of German Romanticism with the scientific categories of the Enlightenment. His starting-point, in a sense, is the same as that of Max Weber. Was he, however, merely an eclectic, in whom the different elements of his thinking were never properly reconciled? To what extent does his insistence on an historical approach really represent a break out of the positivist framework?

It is impossible to give an immediate answer, because, if Maine was not an historicist of the German kind, neither was he an evolutionary determinist. We have already noted his slowness and reluctance to accept the implications of nineteenth-century science for nineteenth-century religion. He was not a Social Darwinist and we have seen how scanty is the evidence for Darwinian influence upon him. He did not, like Spencer, believe in a single formula as the key to all change throughout the universe. He approached the study of society, not as a professional scientist, or a man with a formula, but as a classical scholar, a legal historian and, after 1862, a man with experience in governing a

[1] See, for example, his remarks in *Observation of India*, p. 31.

country in which the governors belonged to an alien culture and the governed presented bewildering varieties among themselves. Here, surely, if anywhere in the eighteen-sixties and eighteen-seventies, was an Englishman respectful of scientific method but capable of stepping outside the mental world of positivism, of seeing the values of different societies not as merely irrational and absurd, not as the inevitable outcome of a few highly general laws of development, but as intelligible systems, providing men with models of conduct, and related in intelligible ways to customs and institutions. But did he? Or why did he not?

There is a passage in John Stuart Mill's essay *On Liberty* which seems closer to the spirit of much of Maine's work than any in the writings of the evolutionists with whom he is generally classed. It runs:

Despotism is a legitimate mode of government in dealing with barbarians, provided the end be their improvement, and the means justified by actually effecting that end...But as soon as mankind have attained the capacity of being guided to their own improvement by conviction or persuasion (a period long since reached in all nations with whom we need here concern ourselves)...[1]

The conclusion of Mill's argument does not matter—it is the distinction on which it is based that is relevant here. Mill recognizes, as the evolutionists did, that 'barbarians' are improvable, though he doubts their capacity for spontaneous improvement save in exceptional circumstances ('the early difficulties in the way of spontaneous improvement are so great', etc.). He appreciates, of course, that civilized peoples have a barbarous past ('have attained')— the presupposition of all Maine's writings. He even seems to imply a 'natural' course of growth (e.g. the metaphor

[1] J. S. Mill, *On Liberty* (Basil Blackwell, Oxford, 1946), p. 9.

from human life: 'the race itself may be considered as in its nonage'). But the whole force of his argument rests on a rigid distinction between 'barbarism' and civilization.

It is precisely this distinction, quite as much as the evolutionary element which is also apparent, that underlies much of Maine's social thought. When he wants to emphasize the fact of continuity, the similarity between 'barbaric' institutions and those of the European past or even present, Maine speaks in an evolutionary, 'gradualist' manner. But almost equally often he speaks in terms of a straight dichotomy—status and contract, progressive and non-progressive, barbarous and civilized:

> ...it is most difficult for a citizen of Western Europe to bring thoroughly home to himself the truth that the civilization which surrounds him is a rare exception in the history of the world. The tone of thought common among us, all our hopes, fears, and speculations, would be materially affected if we had vividly before us the relation of the progressive races to the totality of human life.[1]

Elsewhere he says that to confine our observations of human nature to western Europe is justified 'when we are occupied with the investigation of the laws of Progress...But the primitive condition of the progressive societies is best ascertained from the observable condition of those which are non-progressive.'[2]

A similar outlook is reflected in perhaps his most famous dictum: 'Except the blind forces of Nature, nothing moves in this world which is not Greek in origin.'[3] There could not be a more outspokenly 'diffusionist' statement. Civilization, for Maine, was something which, like the Incarnation to a believer, set a sharp dividing line through both history

---

[1] *Ancient Law*, p. 18.
[2] *Early History of Institutions*, pp. 225–6.
[3] *Observation of India*, p. 38.

and contemporary society. His interesting essay on India in *The Reign of Queen Victoria* edited by Humphrey Ward ends with a vivid description of India as an amalgam of the Present and the Past—the use of capital letters is significant —the Present represented by the tiny educated minority, the Past, corresponding to virtually every stage of the European past, by the mass of the people.[1] In *Popular Government* he wrote, 'The natural condition of mankind (if that word "natural" is used) is not the progressive condition. It is the condition not of changeableness but of unchangeableness. The immobility of society is the rule; its mobility is the exception.'[2]

The dichotomy of the Open and the Closed Society is implicit in much of Maine's thought, and his own admiration was reserved for the former. In this sense Maine was a liberal, though not a democrat, but he had none of James Mill's confidence in deduction from first principles, nor Spencer's deterministic optimism. The Open Society had been achieved by a succession of near miracles; to maintain it was a complex task, demanding much respect for history, experience and the *status quo*. We shall discuss this further when we consider Maine's *explanations* of social change. For the moment it is most important to note that the narrow limits within which Maine was prepared to recognize the fact of progress led to, or justified, his concentration on a particular field of inquiry. A sceptic might say that it was oddly fortunate that this field turned out to be the one with which Maine had most acquaintance.[3] It is reasonable enough, in one's search for the causes and conditions of

---

[1] *The Reign of Queen Victoria*, ed. Humphrey Ward (2 vols. 1887), I, 527.
[2] *Op. cit.* p. 170.
[3] Maine recognized this: 'Every man is under a temptation to overrate the importance of the subjects which have more than others occupied his own mind, but...' (*Village Communities*, p. 22).

progress, to concentrate on the history of Europe, but was it not rather factitious to extend the field to India, on no other grounds than the detection of certain analogies and the fact that comparative philology had revealed a common source of the languages of both Europe and India? 'Modern philology has suggested a grouping of peoples quite unlike anything that has been thought of before.'[1]

Factitious or not, Maine held that the proof of linguistic affinity permitted the recognition of a cultural area hitherto unrecognized—the Aryan. And within this area everything of importance for 'progress' and 'civilization' had occurred: 'Civilization is nothing more than a name for the old order of the Aryan world, dissolved but perpetually reconstituting itself under a vast variety of solvent influences.'[2]

The theory of an 'Aryan' past, including both India and Europe, had some curious, but for Maine highly convenient, results. It permitted him to make, within its limits, the dashing comparisons, the equation of the past institutions of one society with the present ones of another so characteristic of the Comparative Method and of his own writing. India, he affirmed, 'includes a whole world of Aryan institutions, Aryan customs, Aryan laws, Aryan ideas, Aryan beliefs, in a far earlier stage of growth and development than any which survived beyond its borders'.[3]

At the same time the Aryan concept allowed him to reprove, as if he were the soberest of traditional historians, the wild speculations of those, like the McLennans, who practised the Comparative Method in a wider context. Maine was very meticulous about making his position clear on this point. When, as he occasionally did, he drew examples from outside the magic Aryan circle, he was careful to say that he regarded the comparison as more speculative

[1] *Observation of India*, p. 9.   [2] *Ibid.* p. 30.   [3] *Ibid.* p. 2.

than usual: 'The passage which I am about to read to you [it turns out to be about the Zulus] may serve to illustrate what probably took place, though there is *nothing except common humanity* to connect the tribes of whose customs it speaks with the primitive Teutons and Celts.'[1]

The phrase I have italicized indicates very clearly how deep was the gulf between Maine and the true evolutionist. An outsider might well wonder, however, whether there was much difference between inferring past traits of one society from the present of another on the basis of common humanity and on that of a common racial origin suggested by linguistic affinity. The evolutionists, treating the matter in terms of causality, of similar causes producing similar effects, may have been mistaken, but they were surely on firmer logical ground than Maine with his purely *historical* assumption of a common origin for all 'Aryan' institutions. The evolutionist who asserted that development took place as a result of certain laws was entitled to assume that it followed essentially the same course everywhere and had merely been arrested at different stages. But Maine, except in so far as he held a theory of development according to fixed laws, had no guarantee that, once the different branches of his 'Aryans' had lost actual cultural contact with each other, their institutions would develop at all in parallel fashion.

He had to assume, in fact, to justify his inferences from East to West, which he professed were based primarily on the assumption of a common origin, that the Indian village community had virtually no history, at least since the original race had divided into its present oriental and occidental branches. Once again the dichotomy of static-progressive appears as a more fundamental concept in Maine than the notion of parallel development. Yet it contrasts

---

[1] *Early History of Institutions*, pp. 142–3. My italics.

oddly with his strictures on the wider use of the Comparative Method. In his *Quarterly Review* article on the patriarchal theory, he asserts that savage tribes have themselves had a past, and may have been acted upon by all sorts of foreign influences. And of the construction of 'a theoretical series of institutions, one growing out of the other', by the Comparative Method he says that 'there may be no real connection between these practices; some may belong to the yesterday of time; others may be a morbid growth of isolation among a few score of families left to themselves for centuries'.[1]

It is interesting that Max Müller, the evangelist of comparative philology, made much the same objection.[2] But if this applies to the savages of Africa, America and the Antipodes, why did it not apply to the Indian village community, surely comparable in primitiveness? As for the question of isolation, it is not at all clear where Maine stands on this. On the one hand he regards the findings of the Comparative Method as liable to be falsified because the tribes it studies may have been subjected to 'foreign influences', on the other hand he refers to the 'morbid growth of isolation'. To the social evolutionist, isolation was a guarantee of purity; Maine, caught between diffusionism and evolutionism, does not know what to make of it.[3]

There are thus two sides to Maine's theories. On the one hand, there was the emphasis on the uniqueness of civilization, the tendency to think in terms of a dichotomy of progressive and unprogressive. Maine was not a determinist

---

[1] *Quarterly Review*, no. 162, p. 201.

[2] F. Max Müller, *My Autobiography. A Fragment* (1901), p. 86.

[3] His whole argument seems at variance with the statement in *Ancient Law* that, 'if the customs and institutions of barbarians have one characteristic more striking than another, it is their extreme uniformity' (p. 305).

evolutionist. He was free, as the determinists were not, to explore without any overriding methodological commitments the irrational beliefs and practices with which his historical and Indian knowledge brought him into contact, and which his distrust of democracy taught him to look for in his own society. But the freedom from positivist methodological commitments was, in part at least, only apparent. The historical method which Maine practised required for its logical validation the typically positivist assumption of general laws of social development. The Aryan hypothesis was a façade hiding from Maine and his opponents the requirements of his method. There was thus a constant tendency in Maine's thought, especially likely to become apparent when he was not under attack and hence was able to forget about the Aryans, towards general explanations of social change.

Because Maine was not a systematic thinker, and because he never fully recognized the conflict between the historical and scientific elements in his intellectual equipment, it would be possible, by selective quotation, to make out a convincing case for either view of him—that he was a legal historian with perhaps too great a fondness for cross-comparison and 'brilliant' generalization, or that he was a rigid evolutionary determinist. The only way to give a picture of his work that approaches accuracy is to try to give due weight to both aspects without pretending that they are wholly compatible.

Consider, for example, an extreme positivist assertion:

It is now affirmed, and was felt long before it was affirmed, that the truth of history, if it exists, cannot differ in any other form of truth. If it be truth at all, it must be scientific truth. There can be no essential difference between the truths of the Astronomer, of the Physiologist, and of the historian. The great principle which underlies all our knowledge of the physical world, that Nature is ever consistent with herself, must also be true of human nature and of human society which is made up of human nature. It is not indeed meant that there are no truths except of the external world, but that all truth, of whatever character, must conform to the same conditions, so that if indeed history be true, it must teach that which every other science teaches, continuous sequence, inflexible order, and eternal law.[1]

The context leaves no doubt that Maine associates himself with this view. It might be Spencer writing, or Lyell on geology. Compare with this the tentativeness and piecemeal character of his own approach to early history. Compare, for example, the assertion that 'no universal theory, attempting to account for all social forms by supposing an evolution from within, can possibly be true'.[2] This proposition is derived from an essentially 'diffusionist' account of social change in terms of the formation of dominant types and their spread by imitation. This theory of imitation, incidentally, forms no fundamental part of Maine's writings, and may well have been borrowed for the occasion, as it were, from Bagehot.

Again, consider Smellie's dictum that 'Maine saw civilization as the result of a lucky legal mutation—the occurrence of the juristic science created by Rome'.[3] In fact, Smellie considerably overstates the clarity of Maine's views on the subject. His account is presumably based on Maine's statement that 'after the epoch of the codes the distinction between the stationary and progressive societies begins to make itself felt'.[4] The Roman code was not the only one, but, 'except in a small section of the world there has been nothing like the gradual amelioration of the legal system. There has been material civilization, but instead of the

[1] Maine, 'Address to the University of Calcutta' (1865), in *Village Communities*, pp. 205–6.
[2] *Early Law and Custom*, p. 285.
[3] Smellie, 'Sir Henry Maine', p. 67. [4] *Ancient Law*, p. 18.

civilization expanding the law, the law has limited the civilization.'[1] So the relation between law and civilization is not so simple as Smellie suggests. In any case, what made the Roman code different from the others? Maine offers suggestions only, for 'the difference between the stationary and progressive societies is, however, one of the great secrets which enquiry has yet to penetrate'. Nevertheless: 'Among partial explanations of it I venture to place the considerations urged at the end of the last chapter.'[2] It could hardly be more tentative.

What was this partial explanation which Maine ventured to urge? It is a theory of legal degradation from a state of original 'fitness of things' which reminds one oddly of the traditional doctrine of the idyllic state of nature, which Maine so fiercely attacked. His own theory is hardly less hypothetical, and if it can be defended on heuristic grounds, so, for that matter, can the hypothesis of a state of nature. According to Maine,

the usages which a particular community is found to have adopted in its infancy and in its primitive seats are generally those which are on the whole best suited to promote its physical and moral well-being; and if they are retained in their integrity until new social wants have taught new practices, the upward march of society is certain.[3]

This, though vague and almost entirely conjectural, is interesting; it suggests the rudiments of a theory of functional interrelationships. But it is true to say that some such 'functionalism' is implicit in all evolutionary social theory,[4]

---

[1] *Ancient Law*, p. 19.   [2] *Ibid.*   [3] *Ibid.* p. 15.
[4] Cf. Spencer: 'Ceasing then to regard heathen theologies from the personal point of view, and considering them solely with reference to the function they fulfil where they are indigenous, we must recognise them, in common with all theologies, as good for their time and places' ('The Use of Anthropomorphism' (1854) repr. *Essays*, I, 435). Cf. *Principles of Sociology*, II, 230–1.

though the evolutionists were prevented from following up this line of inquiry by their preoccupation with progress, and with establishing a general pattern of development.

Maine fully shared the evolutionists' preoccupation with progress, its causes and the hindrances to it. In fact, the passage just quoted is merely a prelude to an account of how these early, 'suitable' practices generate others which form obstacles to progress. The early 'state of nature' theorists had to account for the end of the idyll in terms of sin; the serpent in Maine's Eden was called Superstition. 'There is a law of development which ever threatens to operate upon unwritten usage.' The threat proceeds from the fact that the multitudes who observe customs 'are incapable of understanding the true ground of their expediency...and are therefore left inevitably to invent superstitious reasons for their permanence'.[1]

This is the typical positivist account of the formation of superstition and the arresting of progress. The actors misunderstand their situation; they are regarded as if they were scientists, objectively observing their circumstances, but misunderstanding them through lack of knowledge. In this respect, though it is vague, and has the merit of being regarded in a social context, Maine's attitude to superstition is essentially the same as Frazer's. Frazer's primitive man has been called an incompetent scientist; Maine's is an incompetent sociologist. One might ask why, in view of this, the original usages were wholesome. Why did man begin as a sound positivist, or was Nature perhaps his guide? 'A process then commences which may be shortly described by saying that usage which is reasonable generates usage which is unreasonable.'[2] Having explained wrongly, primitive man now goes on to classify wrongly.

[1] *Ancient Law*, p. 16.   [2] *Ibid.*

Analogy, the most valuable of instruments in the maturity of jurisprudence, is the most dangerous of snares in its infancy. Prohibitions and ordinances, originally confined, for good reasons, to a single description of acts, are made to apply to all acts of the same class, because a man menaced with the anger of the gods for doing one thing, feels a natural terror in doing any other thing which is remotely like it.[1]

But, and this is the point to which the argument is leading, 'from these corruptions the Romans were protected by their code. It was compiled while usage was still wholesome, and a hundred years afterwards it might have been too late.'[2] This is the justification of Smellie's dictum, though it does not do full justice to the tentativeness and complexity of Maine's argument. The break is decisive: 'When primitive law has once been embodied in the code, there is an end of what may be called its spontaneous development. Henceforward the changes effected by it, *if effected at all*, are effected deliberately and from without.'[3] In other words, a code does not guarantee progress; 'material civilization' may even be possible without it; but it is a condition of conscious progress.

The most noticeable element of this scheme, which is Maine's nearest approach to a philosophy of history, is the idea of rational understanding. Leaving aside the suggestion of a primitive harmony of institutions and way of life, which, though methodologically interesting, is not explained, and plays little part in Maine's writing, we pass on to the period of degeneration. Degeneration occurs because the actors misunderstand their situation; their laws, though such as a rational man would have prescribed for them, are obeyed and justified by them in terms of superstitious fear. Misunderstanding the ground of their laws, they proceed to classify wrongly in applying and extending them, and

[1] *Ancient Law*, p. 16. [2] *Ibid*. p. 17. [3] *Ibid*. Italics mine.

the period of degeneration has begun. The chance of salvation occurs with the codification of law as a consequence of the acquisition of the art of writing, but it is a chance only, because if degeneration has proceeded too far, the code will merely petrify the degenerate state already reached.

Only the Romans appear to have produced their code at the crucial moment, and by doing so, paved the way for conscious legal improvement based on rational calculation, though initially such devices as legal fictions and a metaphysical 'Law of Nature' may have been necessary to overcome the natural resistance to innovation. Original, inexplicable state of harmony apart, the whole scheme is in terms of understanding and misunderstanding. Maine emerges as what Talcott Parsons would call an 'intellectualist positivist', of the type of Buckle or Condorcet, though less systematic (rigid, if a pejorative term is preferred) than either. If this is the case, Maine, far from being one of the leaders of evolutionary thought, is rather behind the times—thinking in terms of conscious adaptation to circumstances rather than the mechanical, involuntary adaptation of Spencer and the neo-Darwinists.

A glance at Maine's other writings confirms the impression of an 'intellectualist' bias, of a tendency to regard primitive man as an observer of his situation, assessing it successfully (in which case progress results) or, more often, unsuccessfully. Thus, in his second address to the University of Calcutta (1865), speaking of the means of progress, he says, 'If the mind of man had been so constituted as to be capable of discovering only moral truths, I should have despaired of its making any permanent conquest of falsehood.'[1] But 'happily for the human race, some fragment of

---

[1] *Village Communities*, p. 270. Cf. Buckle's insistence that there is no moral, only intellectual, progress.

physical speculation has been built into every false system. Here is the weak point. Its inevitable destruction leaves a breach in the whole fabric, and through that breach the armies of truth march in.'[1] And, even more picturesquely: 'All Nature witnesses to her own laws and is a witness that can never be silenced. The stars in their courses fight for truth...'[2] It is characteristic that Maine should suggest that the classificatory system of kinship may have its explanation 'in an imperfection of mental grasp on the part of savages',[3] and that it is 'nothing more than a rude and incomplete attempt at the mental contemplation of a tolerably numerous tribal body'.[4] Equally typical is the wording of his account of what he concludes must have been a revolution in the status of aged men—the change, namely, from being regarded as useless, and killed or eaten, to being highly honoured for their wisdom. The latter 'stage' was reached because 'the individual life is always the original source of experience and at some time or other *it must have been perceived*, that the more the individual life was prolonged, the larger was its contribution to the general stock'.[5]

Though of course it is always possible that Maine's explanations may be something like the correct ones, this 'intellectualist' bias really disables him from doing what in other respects he was admirably qualified to do—to probe the great problem of non-rational action and non-utilitarian codes of conduct. It is not a sufficient answer to these problems to refer simply to the baleful influences of superstition, to purely intellectual failures, failures of classification, understandable enough when one considers the defective knowledge and poor 'mental grasp' of savages.

---

[1] *Village Communities*, pp. 270–1.   [2] *Ibid.* p. 272.
[3] *Early Law and Custom*, p. 284.   [4] *Ibid.* p. 290.
[5] *Ibid.* p. 24. Italics mine.

But Maine's rationalist bias, the difficulty he found in forgetting, when dealing with non-rational conduct, that it was erroneous, is due to more than, to use his own phrase, 'a defect of mental grasp'. It is arguable that he was not even interested in the problem; that his overriding concern was with 'progress' and its conditions, and that he was interested in primitive societies only in so far as they might provide clues as to the origins of Progress and, incidentally, help progressive men to govern unprogressive ones. There are many passages in his work to support such a view.[1] Indeed the whole of his writing has a professedly historical aim; the Comparative Method is placed at the service of history. He had a keen eye for non-rational beliefs and behaviour, but his concern with them was always to establish their historical relation to the present. India is of interest because it is 'the great repository of verifiable phenomena of ancient usage and ancient judicial thought'.[2]

He was aware, too, of the problem of non-rational conduct in the present, but was content simply to classify it in terms of survivals:

Political economists often complain of the vague moral sentiments which obstruct the complete reception of their principles. It seems to me that the half-conscious repugnance which men feel to doctrines which they do not deny might often be examined with more profit than is usually supposed. They will sometimes be found to be the reflection of an older order of ideas.[3]

The explanation is historical, not analytic. Indeed, Maine is really more parochial than the bolder practitioners of the Comparative Method; for them, at least, all mankind was useful data as a basis for historical generalization, while Maine, with his interest focused on 'the communities which

---

[1] E.g. *Ancient Law*, pp. 19, 98; *Village Communities*, pp. 6–7, 269; *Observation of India*, pp. 11, 20 *passim*.

[2] *Village Communities*, p. 22.   [3] *Ibid.* p. 195.

were destined to civilization',[1] was sceptical of the value of non-'Aryan' data, being prepared to concede to them only 'interest'.[2] This is virtually to regress to the view of primitive practices which regarded them as 'curious'.

Of course, Maine's interest in the primitive and the irrational is not purely historical. He is concerned to point out the modifications of classical economics and analytic jurisprudence which he considers it makes necessary. He also thinks that the study of it has a practical value for administrators.[3] This interest produces his nearest approach to an empirical and objective analysis of primitive customs and beliefs. Some of the most admirable and intellectually distinguished parts of the whole body of his work are contained in his *Speeches and Minutes* as Legal Member of the Council of India.[4] He was equally free of the rashness and over-confidence of the evangelical and utilitarian improvers, and from the sentimentality of those who wished merely to provide a framework of law and order within which native life could continue as before. Maine, while fully appreciating the difficulty and delicacy of the task of governing India, saw also that the mere fact of enforcing law and order was giving to native usage a rigidity which might result in grave injustice if not checked by legislation.[5]

But if his direct acquaintance with Indian legal problems produced some of Maine's most sociologically perceptive though inevitably fragmentary remarks, almost the exact opposite can be said of his other 'practical' interest. He had suggested as one of the advantages of the study he was advocating that 'we of Western Europe might come to

[1] *Early Law and Custom*, p. 281.   [2] *Ibid.* p. 232.
[3] *Observation of India*, pp. 36–9.
[4] Ed. Whitley Stokes, published in Duff, *Sir Henry Maine*.
[5] See Stokes, *The English Utilitarians and India*, pp. 271–3, 313; Grant Duff, *op. cit.* pp. 51, 234, 288.

understand ourselves better'. Unfortunately, when he did turn his attention to western Europe, understanding took a poor second place to polemic.

Again, it is his overriding concern with progress that prevents Maine from attempting to understand, rather than isolate and condemn, the irrational, traditional, popular elements in his own society. The result is that *Popular Government* is, as it is generally agreed to be, his most disappointing book. There is a natural tendency to regard *Popular Government* as the culmination of Maine's work. It was published only three years before his death, and it is much more general in scope than any of his other books, except the first, *Ancient Law*.

In a way, this judgement is unfair. *Popular Government* was a deliberately polemical work, which originally appeared in the *Quarterly Review*.[1] Had Maine lived ten years longer, he might possibly have written something of equally wide scope, but with greater objectivity. We might have had a general comparative discussion of the relation of institutions and customs to codes and beliefs—a new *Esprit des Lois*, with the added historical sophistication which was the characteristic virtue of nineteenth-century thought, and which Maine criticized Montesquieu for lacking.[2] If something more like this had been written, and certainly Maine more than any other Englishman in the eighteen-eighties was the man to write it, we should not now regard *Popular Government* as the tawdry crown of his achievement. Nevertheless, it remains its author's only major essay in political thought, and as such it must be judged.

---

[1] The date (1884–5) is significant. Maine was deeply disturbed by the Third Reform Bill, and the prospect of universal suffrage. He even toyed with the idea that Britain needed a written Constitution as a safeguard. See *Henry Sidgwick, a Memoir*, by A.S. and E.M.S., p. 393.

[2] *Ancient Law*, p. 96.

In *Popular Government* Maine gives us not so much the
legal historian's mature judgement as the irritable official's
conviction that politics can, and should, be reduced to administration. He does not actually *derive* his values from
the study of processes; he seems to regard all the important
functions of government as being obvious and indisputable:
'Democracy... has exactly the same functions to satisfy as
Monarchy, it has the same functions to discharge; security,
stability, national dignity, maintenance of law, and reforming
legislation... an indispensable, though in the long run, a very
subordinate province of good government.'[1] The last is the
only hint so far that political disagreement may be concerned with the *direction* a society should move in, rather
than with, in James Mill's phrase, 'the adaptation of means
to an end'.[2] For the most part, however, Maine is concerned
with the merits of constitutional forms considered as means.

Summarizing the difference between Maine and the
earlier theory, one might say that Maine and James Mill are
both agreed that the ends of government are readily deter-
minable, and that the problem of the political theorist is to
determine the means. They are agreed, on the whole, as to
the nature of those ends, though James Mill takes the
trouble to try to deduce them from a theory of human
nature, while Maine seems to regard them as self-evident.
They disagree, however, on the method of determining the
means and on what the best means actually are. Mill deduced
them, as he professed to deduce the ends, from human
nature, and came to a democratic conclusion. Maine allows
himself the occasional inference from human nature, but he
does not base his entire case on it. Nor does he, except
occasionally, deduce political recommendations from in-

[1] *Popular Government*, p. 65.
[2] James Mill, *Essay on Government*, p. 1.

flexible biological laws, like the Social Darwinists. Instead, he argues, not by deduction, but by random examples. Democracy and aristocracy are examined and awarded marks, reckless of the niceties of classification and the complexities of historical periods, on their records. And on this basis Maine comes to the conclusion that 'the progress of mankind has hitherto been effected by the rise and fall of aristocracies'.[1] And that 'from that form of political and social ascendancy all improvement has hitherto sprung'.[2]

Maine's conservatism was not of the type that is generally dignified by the term 'philosophical'. Smellie says that Maine attempted to overcome the 'crude experimenters by a picture borrowed largely from Germany of the technical complexity of civilization'.[3] This is misleading if it suggests a picture of Maine catching from the dark forests of German thought a whisper of an ineffable mystery, hidden from shallow empiricists and only to be comprehended by special intuition. 'Technical' is the key word. Maine shared to the full the Benthamite and Malthusian contempt for vagueness and sentimentality. His sharpest words were not for the philosophic radicals but for Rousseau and the upholders of a metaphysical law of nature. But he combined a belief in scientific method with a recognition of the importance of historical conditioning and the extreme difficulty and complexity of social problems.

His approach to them, however, was not at all Burkean. He had no reverence for the historical process as such; he merely insisted that it should be taken into account. At its best this led to an attitude towards alien cultures which, if still essentially parochial, was cautious and respectful. At its worst, it led to the use of the past as an ammunition

---

[1] *Popular Government*, p. 42.   [2] *Ibid.* p. 189.
[3] Smellie, 'Sir Henry Maine', p. 64.

dump for use against views with which he disagreed. But it never led him to flirt with the *Volksgeist* or the 'ancient permanent sense of mankind'.[1] He never doubted that rational thought was a better guide than blind tradition or untutored sentiment; the wisdom he appreciated was emphatically of the head, not the belly. He criticized the classical economists and the analytic jurists, not for attempting to analyse society scientifically, but for relying too exclusively on deduction and building on too narrow a basis of observation, with the result that they oversimplified the problems and claimed for their generalizations a universality they did not possess.

This insistence on the importance of induction and historical perspective was not peculiar to Maine. One has only to think of Buckle, or of Spencer. He was less systematic than they, and more cautious, but he would almost certainly have rejected the suggestion that he was less scientifically minded. It was as an expert, not a mystic, that he rebuked the bungling short-sightedness of amateurs in government and political thought. When he attacked the legal and economic pundits he did so, not in the ragging, contemptuous manner of Carlyle, but as a fellow expert, of a later date and a wider horizon.

The clue to Maine's conservatism is that he had the mentality and some of the experience of an expert administrator at a time when the delicate arts of government seemed to be being handed over to amateurs. Dr Roach has suggested that this attitude to politics at home is related to the experience of despotic government in India, and quotes J. F. Stephen on India as 'the best corrective in existence

---

[1] Burke, *Reflections on the Revolution in France* (O.U.P. 1950), p. 181. Fitzjames Stephen might think Carlyle 'a philosophic historian', but not Maine.

to the fundamental fallacies of Liberalism'.[1] Dr Stokes claims that India infused an authoritarian counter-current into the liberalism of the English middle class.[2] But in Maine's case one can see exactly the same temperament at work in the clever young graduate of the *Saturday Review* as in the experienced Indian official. The contempt for popular clamour and popular opinion, for sentimentality, religious fanaticism and the arrogance of the demagogue who criticizes the professional—all are there in the early files of the *Saturday Review*. Thus we find him deploring 'the immense growth of newspaper influence in England',[3] and condemning irresponsible attacks on the Civil Service.[4] In the same article he pours scorn on 'the theory that the business habits of merchants are a sovereign remedy for all public disasters' and warns, in terms which recall Burke and are probably meant to, against 'turning Her Majesty's Government into what tradesmen call a "concern"'. Popular prejudices are laughed at, particularly those of the Evangelical Sabbatarians.[5] But despite the bias towards the professional and against his popular critic, there is no defence of anomaly simply as anomaly, no sentimentalism of tradition.[6]

Virtually, all his adult life, if one may judge from these articles, Maine seems to have belonged to a type one

---

[1] J. P. C. Roach, 'Liberalism and the Victorian Intelligensia', *Cambridge Historical Journal*, XIII (1957), 64. Cf. Maine, 'The truth is, India and the India Office make one judge public men by standards which have little to do with public opinion', quoted Grant Duff, *Sir Henry Maine*, pp. 74–5.

[2] Stokes, *The English Utilitarians and India*, p. xi.

[3] 'Laid up in Lavender', *Saturday Review*, (17 November 1855) I, 47.

[4] 'A Burst Bladder' (*ibid.*), 1 December 1855. Cf. also 'Head & Tail' (*ibid.*), 14 June 1856.

[5] *Saturday Review* (1 March 1856), I, 334; *ibid.* II, 119, 349.

[6] See the article on the Inns of Court, *Saturday Review*, 1 December 1855 (though F. J. Stephen's list does not agree with Bevington's attribution of this article), and 'Silly Billy' (19 April 1856) I, 487.

associates with the Civil Service rather than with politics—cool, unsentimental, honest and just, but tending always to identify with authority, and lacking in sympathy with the feelings and aspirations of the mass of mankind. It is true that these qualities were characteristic of the tone of the *Saturday Review* as a whole.[1] Nevertheless, in Maine's case one may feel entitled to guess that he found adaptation to it easy or even unnecessary. He, after all, was one of the earliest contributors, one of those who set the tone. And, as Grant Duff remarks, 'he had as little of the *frondeur* in him as any man as I have ever known'.[2] He might have been a more important thinker if he had had more. Of course, Maine was generally right, but that is irrelevant. The question is whether an attitude of cocksure rationalism (in the loose, not the strict philosophical sense) and contempt for the prejudices of the herd is the best equipment for a student of society.

Maine was heir to two traditions: the Baconian-scientific and the Romantic-historical. If a science of society was to be possible at all, both traditions had a part to play in its creation. But it was not Maine who succeeded in reconciling them. The method of comparative philology proved a blind alley; historical explanations continued to do duty for analytic ones, while Maine's emphasis on common racial origins narrowed his horizon without validating his method.

[1] Leslie Stephen has told us how quickly he, at least, adapted himself to the tone (L. Stephen, *Some Early Impressions* (1924), p. 155).

[2] Duff, *Sir Henry Maine*, p. 23. Cf. Henry Sidgwick: 'His intellect has always seemed to me a very cool, disengaged one' (*Henry Sidgwick, a Memoir*, p. 393).

CHAPTER 6

HERBERT SPENCER

I. THE ORIGINS
OF THE 'SYNTHETIC PHILOSOPHY'

George Eliot once prophesied that in the biographical dictionaries of the future it would be said of Herbert Spencer that 'the life of this philosopher, like that of the great Kant, offers little material for the narrator'.[1]

On the whole she was right. Herbert Spencer's life offers little inducement to microscopic scholarship. Even a précis of the Synthetic Philosophy has been rendered unnecessary by the numerous expositions of Spencer which appeared in the days of his popularity, and there have even been a few since; there are abridgements to suit all stomachs, from Collins's *Epitome* to a few pages by Sir Ernest Barker.[2] It is not proposed to add to them here, nor to debate, for example, whether Spencer's sociology is legitimately deduced from the initial assumptions of the persistence of force and the indestructibility of matter, although it does tell one something about the intellectual climate of the period that Spencer should have attempted the deduction.

David Duncan's *Life and Letters*,[3] and Spencer's own *Autobiography*—as cerebral a document as J. S. Mill's and much more massive—provide an account of the origins of

---

[1] J. W. Cross, *Life and Letters of George Eliot* (3 vols. Edinburgh, 1885), I, 325.

[2] F. H. Collins, *An Epitome of the Synthetic Philosophy of Herbert Spencer* (4 vols. 1897); E. Barker, *Political Thought in England, 1848–1914* (O.U.P 1915). See also the bibliography at the end of J. Rumney, *Herbert Spencer's Sociology* (1934).

[3] D. Duncan, *Life and Letters of Herbert Spencer* (1908).

his thought. His almost pathological touchiness about his claims to originality, irritating though they must have been to his contemporaries, has had the fortunate result of providing us with detailed accounts of the chronology and genesis of his ideas.

His inability to read a book by an author he disagreed with,[1] insulating him from new and possibly disturbing influences, and the subjection of all his major works after *Social Statics* to a single grand design meant that, whatever inconsistencies there may be, Spencer's intellectual career followed a singularity rigid and predictable course. The ideas which had influenced him as a young man remained the major influence in his life, because he admitted no others. Having found a set of ideas congenial to him, and organized them in such a way as to make them universally applicable, he could not make any significant shift of his intellectual ground without shattering his life's work. As Beatrice Webb put it, having invented a universal system, he was compelled to spend the rest of his life practising casuistry.[2]

Spencer's name was for his contemporaries almost synonymous with the brand of deterministic positivism which dominated social theory in the second half of the nineteenth century and was supposed to have superseded the old, narrow utilitarianism by calling in the aid of comparative documentation and the theory of evolution. Even today Spencer symbolizes this aspect of the period all the more satisfactorily because of the subsequent repudiation of him. Darwin's name cannot be used in this way as a 'period' label, because his influence is still alive. Among Spencer's contemporaries, to the professional Durkheim as

[1] Duncan, *Life and Letters of Herbert Spencer*, p. 538.
[2] B. Webb, *My Apprenticeship*, p. 23.

to the layman Kipling,[1] Comte and Spencer are the twin pillars of positivist sociology.

About the importance of Spencer's contribution to the intellectual atmosphere of his time there can be no doubt. His enthusiastic following extended from Russia to the United States. But his influence on his fellow authors would probably be as easy to exaggerate as Darwin's. Goldenweiser attributes the rise of evolutionary anthropology to Darwin and Spencer, and is as wrong on the one count as on the other.[2] Leslie Stephen acknowledged a debt to him.[3] Pitt-Rivers, less interested in society than in artifacts, invoked his name,[4] and was perhaps glad to receive philosophical reassurance that he was on the right track; but his inspiration lay elsewhere. The most original minds among his contemporaries, Maine, Tylor, McLennan, went their ways with a few glances at the Synthetic Philosophy. Huxley, as it is well known, repudiated the political inferences Spencer drew from his sociology. Spencer, a prophet to so many, suffered among his intellectual equals from his scrappy education and the enormous field his work attempted to cover. Professionals like Maine and Huxley, specialists in their fields, could never accept Spencer as their leader. And the claims of the Synthetic Philosophy were such that one could not enter into any close intellectual relationship with Spencer on any other terms. The

[1] E. Durkheim, *The Rules of Sociological Method* (trans. S. A. Solovay and J. H. Mueller, Chicago, 1938), *passim*. Kipling wrote of Comte and Spencer that they 'deal with people's insides from the point of view of men who have no stomachs' (*Plain Tales from the Hills*, p. 97)—a criticism which anticipates, in popular terms, very much the kind of objection Graham Wallas was to make in *Human Nature and Politics*. For a discussion of Kipling in this connection, see N. G. Annan, 'Kipling's place in the History of Ideas', *Victorian Studies*, III, no. 4 (1960).
[2] A. A. Goldenweiser, *Anthropology* (New York, 1937), p. 496.
[3] L. Stephen, *The Science of Ethics* (1882), Preface.
[4] A. Pitt-Rivers, *The Evolution of Culture* (1906), pp. 7–8.

pretension to omniscience makes partnership impossible; it allows only opposition or discipleship.

Spencer's personality did not help. His visit to America was a triumph,[1] but his fellow authors in England, constantly reminded of the enormous claims of his system and of his morbid touchiness about anything which seemed to reflect on his originality as a thinker, were on the whole less enchanted. George Eliot liked him and there were rumours of the possibility of a marriage. Darwin, in a moment of enthusiasm, said that Spencer's *Principles of Biology* made him feel 'that he is about a dozen times my superior', and thought that Spencer might one day be regarded as the equal of Descartes and Leibniz, rather spoiling the effect by adding 'about whom, however, I know very little'. Nevertheless, he did not like him very much, thinking him extremely egotistical.[2] Tylor, probably irritated by their undignified squabble over their respective claims to priority in the use of the concept of animism, professed to dislike him both as a man and as a writer.[3] Even Tyndall thought 'he'd be a much nicer fellow if he'd have a good swear now and again'.[4] The pedantry and passion for offering polysyllabic advice even on the smallest topics, the laborious honesty, self-importance and self-righteousness which made his autobiography a masterpiece of unconscious humour cannot have helped him to make friends and influence people.

But if Spencer was the symbol rather than the inspiration of evolutionary social theory, his career is nevertheless im-

---

[1] Spencer, *Autobiography*, II, ch. LXII.
[2] Darwin, *Autobiography* (revised ed. 1958), pp. 108–9.
[3] Duncan, *Life and Letters of Herbert Spencer*, pp. 451–2; also 'Letters from Edward B. Tylor and Alfred Wallace to Edward Westermarck', ed. K. Rob. V. Wickman, *Acta Academica Aboensis, Humaniora*, XIII (1940).
[4] Duncan, *op. cit.* p. 510.

possible to ignore. For one thing, Spencer comes nearest, among the writers we are concerned with, to justifying the orthodox explanation of the development of the new sociology as a consequence of evolutionary biology. He was not, of course, a Darwinian; he had published a number of highly characteristic works before 1859, while the concept of Natural Selection, which he adopted and tendentiously rechristened 'the survival of the fittest', had, in a sense, already been implicit in his sociological work, derived as Darwin derived it, from Malthus.[1] He did not, however, attempt to apply the theory to the biological problem of species, being satisfied with the Lamarckian account. But even Spencer's intellectual heritage was not merely biological. There was also a strong dash of *laissez-faire* economics, and even a dose of German philosophy, all set against the background of a firm belief in science.

Spencer was born in Derby in 1820;[2] he was thus two years older than Maine and more than a decade senior to Tylor. He came of that Evangelical stock one has grown to expect, almost to require, of a Victorian unbeliever, though in Spencer's case it was adulterated with Wesleyanism. There was even a touch of the Quaker background, shared by another Victorian social scientist, E. B. Tylor, for Spencer's father, an eccentric and an anti-clerical, had Quaker sympathies, though he had never formally joined the Society of Friends. Nonconformity, as Spencer boasts, seems to have been the family characteristic.

His clerical uncle, with whom he lived from 1833 to 1836, was orthodox in his Evangelical Christianity; the family nonconformism (of which Spencer was obviously proud)

[1] See 'A Theory of Population deduced from the General Law of Animal Fertility', *Westminster Review*, new series, I (1852).

[2] The sources for Spencer's early life, drawn on for this account, are Duncan, *Life and Letters of Herbert Spencer*, and his own *Autobiography*.

came out in his politics. He was an extreme *laissez-faire* radical and Malthusian, holding lack of success to be a sign of lack of virtue, at least until he lost his money by an unwise investment, an event which, according to Spencer, greatly improved his preaching. He was an opponent of the Corn Laws—according to his nephew, the only member of the clergy to speak out against them, at least in the eighteen-twenties—and a Chartist sympathizer, being actually a member of Sturge's Complete Suffrage Union.[1] But if he was a Philosophic Radical in his political views, he obviously shared to the full the Evangelical's distrust of pleasure. On one occasion, being at a ball with his nephew, and the hostess inquiring why the boy was not dancing, the Rev. Thomas intervened with the superb remark, 'No Spencer ever dances.'[2]

If Spencer got his first glimpse of *laissez-faire* doctrines through his clerical uncle, it was from his father that he received his grounding in science, and his introduction to the scientific attitude. His father, after failing in business, had become a schoolmaster in scientific subjects. Spencer received his education chiefly at home, and it was therefore unusual for his time, in that it had a strong scientific bias. He never became even a moderately good linguist. But his father was more than a mere imparter of knowledge. His inclination, confronted with any phenomenon, was always to ask 'What is the cause?', meaning what is the explanation in natural terms. Spencer himself makes an explicit connection between this habit of his father's and his own subsequent attitude to the species 'question'.[3]

Spencer's father carried the family nonconformism to the point of eccentricity. His dislike of outward forms, titles and ceremonies was such that he even refused to call his

---

[1] *Autobiography*, I, 30.　　　[2] *Ibid.* I, 28.　　　[3] *Ibid.* I, 89.

acquaintances 'Mr'. This attitude is worth remembering when we come to discuss Spencer's own attitude to the role of ceremonies and titles in social life.[1]

Spencer's early environment, therefore, all the more powerful since he had no regular schooling, was one of strict Puritanism—Anglican, Wesleyan and Quaker—and the driest and most rigid kind of *laissez-faire*, Malthusian radicalism. Both were apparent in his later works, though his Puritanism lost its Christian underpinnings, and became a theoretical utilitarianism. The most interesting ingredients of his intellectual heritage, however, were a dash of eccentricity and the scientific bias which he received, probably by heredity and certainly by education, from his father. It was this last which was to destroy in him, as in so many others, the Christian background to his thought, though not its side-effects, and was to lead him to his major import into the family corpus of dogmas—evolutionism. It was with the evolutionary doctrine he derived from his own reading that he attempted to round off his Utilitarianism and secure the *laissez-faire* and Malthusian articles of his faith.

In 1837 Spencer joined the staff of the London and Birmingham Railway as an engineer.[2] From the first he showed more than a routine interest in the work, corresponding with his father about it and the physical principles involved, in great detail,[3] and inventing several gadgets. He had already written, in 1836, his first articles for

[1] In the early eighteen-forties Spencer was apparently in favour of 'abolishing the forms of baptism, the sacrament, ordination, etc. etc. as being unsuited to the times we live in now' (Duncan, *Life and Letters of Herbert Spencer*, p. 35). Cf. Tylor, below, pp. 245, 256.

[2] It is interesting that Sorel and Pareto also began their careers as engineers.

[3] Duncan, *op. cit.* pp. 23–4.

publication. It is characteristic that the first should be on crystallization and the second on the Poor Laws.[1] During the next few years he published a number of articles on engineering,[2] but from 1842 onwards he began to turn more to political and sociological subjects, beginning with a series of letters to the *Nonconformist* on 'The Proper Sphere of Government'. He also wrote some articles on phrenology, in which he had been interested since he had attended Spurzheim's lectures at the age of eleven.[3]

An enormous diversity of problems, practical and speculative, drew his interest. The titles of these early articles range from 'The Form of the Earth no proof of Original Fluidity'[4] to 'A Solution of the Water Question'.[5]

But it is really his article on 'The Development Hypothesis'[6] which marks the beginning of his career as the philosopher of evolution. How did this come about?

From 1841 Spencer had become increasingly involved in radical politics, in which his father and uncle were already active. There was some suggestion of his helping to bring out a new periodical as the mouthpiece of the Complete Suffrage Union.[7] He did in fact become a secretary of the Derby branch of the Complete Suffrage Union, and was sent as a delegate to the Birmingham Conference of 1842. He struggled on the fringes of radical journalism, but in 1845 was forced to return to engineering. He even thought of emigration to New Zealand, but in 1848 he found a safe berth in journalism as sub-editor of the *Economist*.

---

[1] Both for the *Bath and West of England Magazine* (January and March 1836).

[2] Duncan, *Life and Letters of Herbert Spencer*, p. 578.

[3] Duncan, *op. cit.* p. 10.

[4] *Philosophical Magazine* (March 1847).

[5] *Economist* (20 December 1851), repr. *Various Fragments* (1894).

[6] *Leader* (20 March 1852), repr. *Essays* (1858), vol. 1.

[7] Duncan, *op. cit.* p. 36.

Spencer's connection with the *Economist*, which lasted till 1853, lent no particular distinction to either party. The one name does not connote the other, as it does with Bagehot. Its chief value was that it provided him with an assured income and a foothold in the London literary and scientific world. He was also helped in this by the publication of his first book, *Social Statics*, in 1851. It was during these years that he became friendly with G. H. Lewes, George Eliot, Huxley and Tyndall. From the time of his resignation from the *Economist*, Spencer's autobiography, always a highly intellectual one, became largely a record of publications marking the stages of his thought.

The major distinction between the positivism of the later nineteenth century and the utilitarianism of the earlier is the former's gradualism, its insistence on progress as a process passing through inevitable stages according to inflexible laws. This gradualism appears early in Spencer's thought. In 1843 he wrote to a friend:

I look upon despotism, aristocracies, priestcrafts, and all other evils that afflict humanity, as the necessary agents for the training of the human mind, and I believe that every people must pass through the various phases between absolutism and democracy before they are fitted to become *permanently* free, and if a nation liberates itself by physical force, and attains the goal without passing through these *moral ordeals*, I do not think its freedom will be lasting.[1]

He had come across the theory of biological evolution by a reading of Lyell's *Principles of Geology* in 1840. Lyell expounded the Lamarckian theory in order to refute it, but Spencer found himself more impressed by the theory than the refutation, chiefly, he says, because of the inclination he shared with his father to look for explanations always in

[1] Duncan, *op. cit.* p. 41. Italics original.

terms of natural causation.[1] Spencer, incidentally, never went through one of those agonizing crises of religious doubt which shattered so many of his contemporaries. Religion never seems to have meant anything to him emotionally, and he shed it quietly and imperceptibly, finding in the idea of progress a substitute for the promises of Christianity.

Having accepted the ideas of continuity and natural causation, Spencer began to apply them to the various fields to which his wide interests drew him, refining and elaborating his conception of evolution as he did so. In *Social Statics*, on which he began to work in 1847 and which was published in 1850, there are already the ideas of the necessary gradualness of social change and the comparison of society with an organism. But it was really during the eighteen-fifties that Spencer's evolutionary ideas developed and were embodied in a number of articles, both general and specific. In 'The Development Hypothesis', he proclaimed his adherence to the doctrine of evolution in its Lamarckian form. 'A Theory of Population', in the same year, made the Malthusian doctrine yield an optimistic conclusion by making progress the result of population pressure by means of what was, in fact, though not yet in name, natural selection among human beings.[2] In 'The Use of Anthropomorphism' and 'Manners and Fashion', the evolutionary approach was applied to human history, while in 'Progress, its Law and Cause', Spencer attempted to give a general explanation of the evolutionary process.[3]

Spencer does not seem entirely clear whence he derived the elaboration of the idea of evolution as a development from homogeneity to heterogeneity, though it is worth

---

[1] *Autobiography*, I, 176.   [2] See above, p. 183 n. 1.
[3] *Leader* (5 November 1853); *Westminster Review* (April 1854); *Westminster Review* (April 1852). All repr. *Essays*, vol. I.

noticing that he mentions, among the chief influences disposing him in that direction at the beginning of the eighteen-fifties, Coleridge's exposition, in his essay on the Idea of Life, of Schelling's idea of life as the tendency to individuation, and Von Baer's formula that development is from the homogeneous to heterogeneous.[1] Spencer, like many others at this time who were coming to regard the idea of development as the key to understanding, did not, for all his positivism, escape the influence of Germany.

He was already, however, a Lamarckian, already convinced that true political principles, which for him meant *laissez-faire* radicalism, must be demonstrated from the nature of things, and it was perhaps inevitable that sooner or later he should put the two convictions together. He was already thoroughly imbued both with the ideas of growth and continuity which implied the rejection of the notion of society as an artifact, and with the determination to treat all phenomena, which of course included social institutions, as explicable by natural causes. Spencer would have been an evolutionary sociologist, though perhaps with a slightly different terminology, had no German ever written a word. One cannot say the same of, for example, Maine.

The same applies to Spencer's relations with Comte; it infuriated him to be regarded as a disciple of Comte. Spencer first learned of his work through Lewes, whom he had met in the winter of 1850–1.[2] In 1852, at George Eliot's instigation, he read the Introduction to the *Cours de*

---

[1] *Autobiography*, I, 176, 384. Duncan, *Life and Letters of Herbert Spencer*, pp. 541, 546. Spencer also acknowledged a debt to Goethe (*Essays*, I, 2). For Goethe's ideas in this context see Haas, 'Of Living Things'. For the German transcendental biologists generally, see G. S. Carter, *A Hundred Years of Evolution* (1958), and E. S. Russell, *Form and Function* (1916).

[2] Duncan, *op. cit.* pp. 418, 545. Spencer apparently read Lewes's *History of Philosophy* and Mill's *Logic* in 1852 (Duncan, *loc. cit.*).

philosophie positive and in 1854 read Harriet Martineau's translation.[1]

If these dates are correct, Spencer's claims to originality are established, though it seems likely that his interest in sociology was encouraged, if only in a very general way, by such contacts with Comtism. He himself admitted something of the kind when he said that he owed Comte 'the benefits of an antagonism which cleared and developed my own views, while assigning reasons for dissenting from his'.[2]

Spencer became convinced in the course of the eighteen-fifties, of the universal applicability of the law of development from simplicity to complexity. In 1858 he thought he had found for this universal tendency a deductive explanation, in the principle of the Persistence of Force.[3] Out of this belief that he had found a single scientific explanation for the various types of development in which he was interested came the first programme of the subsequent Synthetic Philosophy.[4] The fundamentals of Spencer's intellectual position were settled. It merely remained for him to work out the details. Since we are not concerned with the Synthetic Philosophy as a whole, Spencer's intellectual history can be left at this point.

2. 'SUPER-ORGANIC EVOLUTION'

Spencer's sociology is a paradox. He is at once the most modern and the most dated of the Victorian social theorists. On the one hand he is the most prominent and most rigidly deterministic of evolutionists, a positivist whose enormous works form a suitable mausoleum for an antiquated conception of science; on the other hand he is being increasingly

---

[1] Sketchily, it seems, for which he was later rebuked by J. S. Mill (Duncan, *Life and Letters of Herbert Spencer*, p. 114).   [2] *Ibid.* p. 545.
[3] I.e. the conservation of energy. *Ibid.* p. 551.   [4] *Ibid.*

hailed as one of the chief precursors of a social theory dominated by the basic concepts of structure and function, concepts which he was the first to attempt to define at all rigorously and to use for the analysis of society. Thus Talcott Parsons, taking the first view, opens his account of the rise of modern social theory with the rhetorical query, Who now reads Spencer?, while Evans-Pritchard claims him as an important precursor, saying that his biological analogy 'did much to further the use of the concepts of structure and function in social anthropology'.[1]

Obviously we badly need to make a distinction here; it will not do simply to continue talking in terms of 'modern' and 'antiquated'. For there is no necessary contradiction between the two views just quoted. The fact, however, that they can both be asserted suggests at least that Spencer is a figure of unusual interest, exhibiting within a single body of writings the tension, to be found in much nineteenth-century sociology, between the hope of constructing a social series developing according to ascertainable laws and the approach to societies as systems of complex functional relations.

There is no necessary contradiction between Parsons and Evans-Pritchard. Parsons, in *The Structure of Social Action*, is concerned primarily with the understanding of individual unit acts, of 'action from the point of view of the actor'; Evans-Pritchard with explaining how the study of societies as systems came to replace the conjectural history of institutions as the characteristic occupation of social anthropologists. But the study of societies as working systems need not necessarily involve a repudiation of positivist assumptions. Mr Leach has called Malinowski, the arch-enemy of

---

[1] Evans-Pritchard, *Social Anthropology*, p. 51. Cf. Donald MacRae, *Ideology and Society* (1961), pp. 20, 33.

evolutionism, a positivist, because his theory of needs was essentially a biological one.[1] Are the two attacks, on positivism as a set of assumptions, and on evolutionism as a method, essentially separate, and are we simply confusing two different debates? In fact, even if there are no strict logical relations of entailment or exclusion, there are very strong tendencies of association. It may be possible to be a positivist functionalist, but the conjunction of positivism and evolutionism was not due simply to an historical coincidence. Positivism supplied, as it were, one of the chief motives for evolutionism.[2]

But what of Spencer? Positivist or not—we shall come to that later—how was it possible for him to be both the most rigid of evolutionists and a forerunner of functionalist social theories? In fact there is nothing at all surprising about this. His view of societies as systems was an integral part of his evolutionism. It is significant here that Spencer's main exploits in conjectural history, his attempts to trace the development of domestic, political, economic and religious institutions, were published, not as separate books, with appropriate titles, but as successive parts of his *Principles of Sociology*. It was types of societies, not the history of isolated institutions or culture traits, which interested him. In this sense he was a thorough sociologist, not a historian, and still less an antiquarian. But neither should it be forgotten that *The Principles of Sociology* is part of the 'Synthetic Philosophy', and that sociology is approached by Spencer as 'Super-Organic Evolution'. If it is impossible to dismiss him as a mere conjectural historian, it is equally false to regard him as a functionalist *manqué*, if this is taken

---

[1] E. R. Leach, 'The Epistemological Background to Malinowski's Empiricism'.

[2] See above, pp. 102-8.

to imply that the evolutionary scheme in which his sociology is set was simply an accidental aberration. To Spencer evolutionism and the notion that societies are systems, or to use his own terms, analogous to organisms, were inseparable.

But why should this have been so? What link was there between the evolutionism which so frequently led to constructing series of cultural traits wrenched from their social context and a belief in society as a kind of organism? To some extent the idea of a social system was implicit in even the wilder conjectural histories. The very notion of a dysfunctional 'survival', on which so much was built, implies its opposite, a functioning institution; this, indeed, was one of the reasons why Malinowski hated the concept of 'survivals', because it diverted attention from the functional aspect of institutions. But what distinguished Spencer from most of his contemporaries was that instead of merely paying lipservice to the notion of social cohesion and then adopting a method which utterly ignored it, he devoted almost as much attention to structural/functional relations as to social evolution. This, of course, makes him puzzling if one approaches him in terms of a simple dichotomy—structural/functional *versus* evolutionary—but to Spencer himself it seemed entirely natural.

Oddly enough, a good place to begin a study of Spencer's sociology is with Leslie Stephen's essay on Buckle.[1] Buckle, in Stephen's view, made the expiring effort of the older theory of society before the intellectual revolution of the eighteen-sixties made it antiquated almost as soon as it was published. Buckle's *History of Civilization* was an attempt of the old individualism to come to terms with sociology

[1] 'An Attempted Philosophy of History', *Fortnightly Review*, new series, XXVII (1880).

and it failed because it lacked the essential guiding concept. It lacked, according to Stephen, in common with all pre-evolutionary social theories, the idea of social structure. Consequently, the social regularities Buckle detected seemed, because not related to the structure of society, mysterious, and due to the operation of some external fate, instead of to 'the fixed conditions inherent in the social structure'.[1]

It is beside the point here whether Stephen's attack on Buckle was justified;[2] what is important is that Stephen regards the idea of social structure as the chief contribution of evolutionism to social thought. He names Spencer as one of the chief exponents of the new evolutionary sociology.[3] How far are Stephen's remarks borne out by a look at Spencer's work?

Spencer's 'Synthetic Philosophy', of which *The Principles of Sociology* is a part, was an attempt to apply a formula of evolution[4] whose central idea was the development from simple to complex, purporting to be derived from the fundamental laws of matter and motion, to every kind of phenomenon throughout the universe. This has an important bearing on Spencer's interest in social structure and functions. Few writers have subordinated their work in so many

[1] Stephen, *loc. cit.* p. 692.

[2] Many of the points made in this book in connection with Maine, Spencer and Tylor could have been illustrated also from Buckle. Buckle seemed less rewarding because his work is much more obviously analogous to the intellectualist eighteenth-century philosophies of history discussed in the Introduction. Buckle assumes an innate, self-improving tendency in the human mind, and then discusses the history of progress in terms of the factors which have hindered it—like Condorcet.

[3] *Ibid.* p. 672.

[4] Spencer's complete formula of evolution ran: 'Evolution is an integration of matter and concomitant dissipation of motion; during which the matter passes from an indefinite, incoherent homogeneity to a definite, coherent heterogeneity; and during which the retained motion undergoes a parallel transformation.'

different fields to a single idea so thoroughly as Spencer. His use of structural/functional concepts is not an interesting divergence from the main obsolete evolutionary theme; it is an essential subordinate part of that theme. How could social life be made to yield examples of development from simple to complex if simple and complex were not to be understood and illustrated as qualities of social structures? He could not be satisfied with the antiquarian pursuit of the 'origins' of particular cultural traits, though he was prepared to use them as part of a larger study. But only some kind of integrated unit could yield the sort of classifications he needed: 'Structural traits...distinguish lower and higher types of societies from one another: and distinguish the earlier stages of each society from the later.'[1] The whole biological background to Spencer's thought would dispose him to look for proofs of an evolutionary process defined in terms of changing structure.

The same biological tradition of thought taught him to look for the necessary relations between structure and life processes.[2] Lamarck's whole theory had been based on the possibility of changing activities producing structural changes. Spencer had also been struck by Milne-Edwards' phrase 'the physiological division of labour',[3] and had reimported the notion into social theory. 'Mutual dependence of parts is that which initiates and guides organisation of every kind.'[4] And again: 'Evolution establishes in them both [i.e. societies and organisms] not differences simply...but differences such that each makes the other possible...the changes in the parts are mutually

[1] *The Study of Sociology* (2nd ed. 1874), p. 331 (1873).
[2] Note the parallel to his social theory in *The Principles of Biology* (2 vols. 1864–7), sections 37, 40 *passim*.
[3] Duncan, *Life and Letters of Herbert Spencer*, p. 542.
[4] *S of S*, p. 331.

determined, and the changed actions of the parts are mutually dependent.'[1]

Spencer's works are studded with such remarks. Darwin was accused of failing to take sufficient account of physiological and anatomical co-ordination.[2] The same could hardly be said of Spencer. This mutual dependence of parts, he asserts, is the whole point of his constant and much criticized comparisons of society to a physical organism: 'There exist no analogies between the body politic and a living body, save those necessitated by the mutual dependence of parts which they display in common.' The comparisons have been made only because structure and functions in the human body furnish the most familiar illustrations of structures and functions in general.[3] These mutual dependences are one of Spencer's chief reasons for believing in the possibility of sociology: 'The relations of ...structures to the surrounding conditions and the dominant forms of social activities entailed; and...the metamorphoses of types caused by changes in the activities[4] are sufficient to show that there is a general order of coexistence and sequence.'[5]

But of course Victorian sociology was full of assertions of the unity of society, even if they were not expressed in such precise terms, by men whose lines of research were a direct negation of the idea. How did Spencer use the ideas of structure and function he derived from evolutionary and transcendental biology? The answer is, quite extensively, though always subordinately to the master concept of evolution. Structure and Function form two of the primary classifications of the *Descriptive Sociology* which was to be

---

[1] *The Principles of Sociology* (3 vols. 1876), I, 469.
[2] E. S. Russell, *Form and Function*, pp. 232, 238–41.
[3] *P of S*, I, 616.
[4] Note the Lamarckianism here.   [5] *P of S*, I, 618.

an arsenal of facts for the new science. Part II of the *Principles of Sociology* is almost entirely concerned with the relations of social structures and functions, and it ought to have been almost impossible for a reader of Spencer to dip into his sociological writings—except perhaps the early essays—at any point without being impressed with the primary importance of these two concepts. A modern sociologist would probably want to reclassify Spencer's main division of functions—regulative, sustaining, etc., and tidy up his terminology, and might take exception to the poverty of illustration, but Spencer's book was intended, after all, chiefly to inculcate 'principles'.

But though his treatment of societies as systems earned him marks from Durkheim,[1] and subsequently from modern sociologists, it is impossible for long in writing about Spencer to get away from evolution. The plan of *The Principles of Sociology* is unintelligible unless one bears in mind that the whole purpose of the exercise was, for its author, to find out how social structures were enabled, compelled in fact, by their environment, to modify themselves, and how this modification sometimes—not always—took the form of greater complexity.

Part II of the *Principles of Sociology* from which we have been quoting, is preceded by a section on the mental processes of savages, and followed by one on the evolution of the family, which are pure conjectural history. Seen in an evolutionary context, the structural/functional correspondences discussed in Part II fall into place. *The Principles of Sociology* begins with an analysis of the various factors, internal and external, original and derivative, which determine 'Super-Organic Evolution'; then the two original factors, the natural environment and the mind of primitive

[1] Durkheim, *The Rules of Sociological Method*, p. 21.

man, are discussed, followed by the classification of various types of social structures and institutions, and their inter-relations. The rest of the book is devoted to a largely con-jectural account of the evolution of these separate institutions and their various subdivisions.

If the average reader, therefore, could hardly have failed to derive from Spencer an idea of the importance of regarding societies as integrated systems, he would find much of his practice an incitement to concentrate on recon-structing the history of individual institutions and ordering them in an evolutionary series. Even his functionalist state-ments are full of evolutionary terms ('Societies in different stages', etc.) and the correlation of structure and function is made explicitly for the purpose of understanding 'how an organisation originated and developed'.[1] His recognition of the social functions of irrational institutions is limited by his projection of them into the past. Spencer writes: 'Instead of passing over as of no account or else regarding as purely mischievous, the superstitions of primitive man, we must inquire what part they play in social evolution.'[2] Not, be it noted, merely what part they play in social life.

Admitting, then, that Spencer was always essentially an evolutionist, what, according to him, are the mechanisms of social evolution? At first it looks as if he may be going to derive social development directly from human intelligence or human instincts, in the manner of the eighteenth-century philosophers of history. He even commended Ferguson for seeing 'the way in which social phenomena arise out of the phenomena of individual human nature'.[3] In 1852 he wrote to a friend, 'Until you have got a true theory of humanity, you cannot interpret history, and when you have got a true

---

[1] *P of S*, III, 1.   [2] *S of S*, p. 328.
[3] *P of S*, II, 230–1.

theory of humanity *you do not want history.*'[1] It is not surprising that Beatrice Webb came to the conclusion that Spencer had no historical sense.[2]

Spencer began all his three major sociological works, *Social Statics* (1851), *The Study of Sociology* (1873) and *The Principles of Sociology* (1876), with displays of atomistic preconceptions which would not come amiss in, say, Bentham: 'There is no way of coming at a true theory of society, but by inquiry into the nature of its component individuals...every phenomenon exhibited by an aggregation of men originates in some quality of man himself.'[3] In *The Study of Sociology* this proposition is given as the *reason* for asserting the possibility of a Social Science: 'Setting out then, with this general principle, that the properties of the units determine the properties of the aggregate, we conclude that there must be a Social Science expressing the relations between the two.'[4] In the *Principles of Sociology*, he again begins by asserting that 'be it rudimentary or be it advanced, every society displays phenomena that are ascribable to the characters of its units and to the conditions under which they exist'.[5] He passes easily, and apparently without any sense of the enormous jump he is making, from a description of the behaviour of single inanimate objects, and groups of them, to 'aggregates of men' and finally, without any warning, to 'Society'.

But all this, though perhaps unfortunately worded, is not so naïve as it seems. To begin with, it is not quite clear what is meant by 'determined'. Thus, after saying that 'the character of the aggregate is determined by the character of the units',[6] he later goes on to say merely, 'By the characters

[1] Duncan, *Life and Letters of Herbert Spencer*, p. 62. Italics original.
[2] B. Webb, *My Apprenticeship*, p. 251.
[3] *Social Statics* (1851), p. 16.
[4] *S of S*, p. 52.
[5] *P of S*, I, 9.
[6] *S of S*, p. 48.

of the units are necessitated certain limits within which the characters of the aggregates must fall',[1] a much milder statement with which it would be difficult to disagree, only to follow it with a virtual repetition of the first statement.[2] But what are the characters of the units?

In *Social Statics*, the statements quoted above are immediately followed by a violent attack on what he called 'this prevalent belief that human nature is uniform'.[3] In fact, 'man himself obeys the law of indefinite variation. His circumstances are ever altering and he is ever adapting himself to them.'[4] We are now left merely with the statement that 'no phenomenon can be presented by a corporate body, but what there is a pre-existing capacity in its individual members for producing'.[5] But obviously since these capacities are capable of absolutely 'indefinite variation', the proposition affords no grounds for anything beyond a series of tautologies: if man had not possessed the potentiality of social life, social life could not have risen among men, etc. Nevertheless, Spencer's position does not become completely empty. It still has a methodological importance as a denial that there are unanalysable social *Gestalten*. It affirms that the study of individual human nature *in an evolutionary manner* is essential to understanding society. Social laws, in other words, are not *sui generis*; not primary but derivative. For Spencer, the ultimate unit of study in sociology is not institutions but individuals; individuals studied not simply as data for statements about institutions, but as sources of explanations, facts from which facts about social institutions will be derivative.[6]

---

[1] *S of S*, p. 50.
[2] *Ibid.* p. 51.
[3] *SS*, p. 33.
[4] *Loc. cit.*
[5] *Ibid.* p. 17.
[6] Essentially the same belief, in fact, as that put forward in J. S. Mill's *System of Logic*.

Obviously we are on the verge of a circular argument here, and it may be advisable to try to take stock. It is obvious from the foregoing that Spencer was not what Professor Popper would call a 'methodological essentialist'. Was he then a 'methodological individualist'—of whom Professor Popper approves? Or was he a 'psychologist'— of whom Professor Popper disapproves? The distinction must be a fine one, and at least one critic has professed himself unable to see any difference at all,[1] while Mr Watkins, who agrees with Professor Popper, suggests as a criterion of 'individualism' the reference to dispositions *in a social situation*[2] which would surely include the 'Ethology' of J. S. Mill, whom Popper attacks as a 'psychologist'.

One criteron, however, emerges from Popper's attack on J. S. Mill. Popper claims that the 'psychologist's'

> stress on the psychological origin of social rules or institutions can only mean that they can be traced back to a state when their introduction was dependent solely upon psychological factors, or more precisely, when it was independent of any established social institutions. Psychologism is thus forced, whether it likes it or not, to operate with the idea of a *beginning of society*, and with the idea of a human nature and human psychology as they existed prior to society.[3]

Whether Popper's 'methodological individualism' is saved from this fate by a simple act of abnegation or by some logical distinction is not clear to the present writer, but the application of the criticism to Spencer is undoubted. His account of social evolution opens with an attempt, which he admits will be only partially successful, to reconstruct the

[1] Ernest Gellner, 'A reply to Mr Watkins', in P. Gardiner (ed.), *Theories of History* (Univ. of Illinois, 1959), pp. 514–15.

[2] J. W. N. Watkins, 'Historical Explanation in the Social Sciences', *ibid.* pp. 509–10, n. 6.

[3] Karl Popper, *The Open Society and its Enemies* (revised ed. 1952), II, 92–3. Italics original.

mentality of primitive man. 'The accumulated knowledge and the mental habits slowly acquired during education must be suppressed.'[1] The echo of Hobbes and Rousseau is amusing.

Is Spencer, then, a 'psychologist'? In a sense, clearly yes, but in another sense, no. Psychological factors, together with the physical environment, are primary facts in his sociology, but they are not primary in his philosophy as a whole, being themselves derivative from the laws of life, which are in turn derivative from the ultimate laws of matter and motion.[2] He is, in fact, an environmental determinist. He holds that all changes come about through the action of changes in the action of the environment on the subject of the change. 'Any fresh force brought to bear on an aggregate in a state of moving equilibrium must do one of two things: it must either overthrow the moving equilibrium altogether, or it must alter without overthrowing it; and the alteration must end in the establishment of a new moving equilibrium.'[3]

He recognized two kinds of 'equilibration': direct (i.e. by adaptation), and indirect (by natural selection or the 'survival of the fittest'). Together, given the existence of matter and motion, they formed the motive force of all changes. But there might be any number of intermediate links in the causal chain. In *The Principles of Sociology*, Spencer readily acknowledged that men changed their environment, and that the influence of the physical environment grew less as society advanced.[4] This, indeed, was one of the criteria of progress.[5]

Granted the original assumption that they are all ultimately derivative from physical laws, some more ultimately

---

[1] *P of S*, I, 110.

[2] It is beside the point whether Spencer in fact took these logical hurdles successfully. We are concerned here rather with what he was trying to do than with whether he succeeded.   [3] *P of B* (1864), no. 150.

[4] Cf. Buckle, *History of Civilization*, I, ch. II.   [5] *P of S*, I, 11–12.

than others, Spencer allows for a great multiplicity of factors of social evolution. At the beginning of the *Principles of Sociology* he lists first the basic factors: the physical environment and the pre-social nature of men; and then the derivative factors, which social evolution itself brings into play, including the changes wrought in the environment by men, the reciprocal influence of the society on its units, the super-organic environment (i.e. other societies), and the accumulation of artifacts, means of communication, all the things usually summed up as 'culture'.

The common-sense reaction to the admission of this multiplicity of factors, none of them fixed, all of them variable, as they act and re-act on each other, the whole system increasing in complexity as the factors are twisted more and more out of their original shape, would be to give up the whole business as a bad job and go home, or to accept the necessity of concentrating in a more modest way on some, at least theoretically, isolable system within the gigantic totality.

This Spencer does not—for reasons we shall consider later, cannot—do. Instead he classifies the systems he is considering, as more or less advanced, according to his prior formula of evolution, and 'explains' the respective advances by whatever seems most likely or most appropriate, happy in the assurance that whatever factor he picks on will have been shown in an earlier work to be in its turn derivative from the ultimate laws of matter. He was helped, of course, by the fact that he did not need to show that every set of circumstances produced evolution, but only that some set of circumstances would do so given sufficient time. In fact he held that retrogression and breakdown had been more common than social evolution.[1]

---

[1] *P of S*, I, 106–7.

In explaining the development of social institutions, Spencer adopted explanations readily intelligible to a nineteenth-century Englishman. Thus, religion was explained as a combination of fear and a mistake—a misclassification of phenomena natural to an ignorant savage; political authority grew out of propitiation by the weak and acquisitiveness by the strong; the economic division of labour out of a rational appreciation of its advantages.

Spencer thought that one of the major tasks of sociology was to trace back proximate causes to remote ones.[1] In one sense, a sense which Spencer certainly intended, this agrees well enough with what Professor Popper, for example, sees as the function of social science: 'the discovery and explanation of the less obvious dependences within the social sphere'.[2] But there is another sense, which Popper and most modern sociologists would regard as vicious, in which it involves tracing social phenomena back to their ultimate origins in a pre-social state. We have just seen the difficulties and absurdities to which this latter view led Spencer; why then could he not abandon it? One answer is to say that he was engaged on an attempt to apply a formula to the universe, including, of course, the activities of men. But this is only to push the question a stage further back. The Synthetic Philosophy is very much a document of its time, and intelligible only in terms of a particular prevailing view of the nature of science and its possibilities. Our concern is not with the Synthetic Philosophy as a whole, but only with Spencer's social theory, nor is the present writer qualified to deal adequately with the philosophy of science in the nineteenth century. Nevertheless, it is impossible to avoid all mention of it, at least as Spencer understood it, for it had an important bearing on the overriding claims of

[1] *S of S*, p. 22.　　　　　[2] Popper, *The Open Society*, II, 94.

evolution on his sociology; claims which in the long run
stifled the other, more 'modern' elements in it. The two
major strands in Spencer's education were a belief in the
universality of natural causation and certain strongly held
political opinions which he wished to place on a scientific
basis. Both, in the long run, pointed to evolutionism rather
than to the more detailed study of individual social systems.
The materialism[1] of most nineteenth-century philosophizing
about science led to puzzles about the relation between
mind and matter, and raised the bogey of determinism.[2]
Given the current beliefs about the nature of science,
Spencer's acceptance of the belief that all phenomena must
be capable of scientific treatment could only result in determinism. Two basic conceptions made this inescapable:
first, the idea sometimes expressed by the popular phrase
that science was just 'generalized common sense'—that the
world described by science was all that could be known of
'reality', or, as Parsons puts it, the phenomena to which a
scientific theory is applicable are held to be exclusively
understandable in terms of the theory. And secondly, a conception of scientific explanation, derived from the deterministic paradigm of classical mechanics, as the analysis of
phenomena in terms of general causal laws, scientific progress being seen as the subsumption of more and more kinds
of phenomena under laws of greater and greater generality.

Spencer's belief in the universality of natural causation was, together with his *laissez-faire* political creed, the

[1] For non-technical discussions of nineteenth-century science and attitudes to science, see H. Dingle, 'The Scientific Outlook in 1851 and in
1951', *British Journal for the Philosophy of Science*, II (1951), and the essays
by Dingle, A. J. Ayer and N. F. Mott in *Ideas and Beliefs of the Victorians*
(1949).
[2] Works of the period on the possibility of a social science are often
introduced by a discussion of determinism, as in Buckle's *History of Civilization* and Bagehot's *Physics and Politics* (1869).

bedrock of his thinking. It was this belief, more than any-thing else, that led him to reject Christianity, long before the great conflict of the eighteen-sixties.[1] Moreover, it was his belief in natural causation that led him to embrace the theory of evolution, not vice versa.[2]

'The doctrine of the universality of natural causation, has for its inevitable corollary the doctrine that the universe and all things in it have reached their present forms through successive stages physically necessitated.'[3]

His faith was so strong that it did not wait on scientific proof. Spencer became an ardent evolutionist at a time when a cautious scientist would have been justified at least in suspending judgement. Moreover, had he been merely a gradualist, revolting against the break with the natural order involved in the idea of the special creation of species, he might have found refuge in some teleological half-way house. He owed a good deal to the Germans, Schelling and Von Baer, for some of the fundamental categories of his formula of evolution, but he was too much a nineteenth-century Englishman and a Newtonian to adopt them as part of a teleological scheme.[4] To imagine Spencer as a teleological evolutionist, one would have to reverse the whole order of his ideas; for him the belief in natural causation was primary, the theory of evolution derivative. Even his master Lamarck had to be reinterpreted, to eliminate the apparently teleological implications of his theory of adaptation, by deriving it from physical first principles.[5]

Suspicion of teleology, as well as excitement over the question of the origin of species, and the prestige given by Darwin to the idea of evolution, may help to account for

---

[1] Spencer, *Autobiography*, I, 265.   [2] *Ibid*. I, 76.   [3] *Ibid*. II, 6.
[4] See 'Progress, Its Law and Cause', *Essays*, I, 2.   [5] *P of B*, no. 147.

the relative neglect of questions of correlation within systems by contemporary social theorists. Just as history had once been relatively neglected by the utilitarians, partly because it seemed to be on the side of the traditionalists, so now the study of internal correlations was associated with teleology, with dry systematizing and classification, with Special Creation. The wonderfully integrated, mutually supporting elements of the social system could only be relieved of the suspicion of being teleologically directed, and hence contrary to all sound physical principles, by being explained as the product of the system's relations with the environment.[1] And since the idea that types of societies were directly determined by their present environments was one which, despite the fact that Buckle was (falsely) accused of holding it, social theory had long outgrown, the alternative could only be some kind of evolutionary theory. And it was precisely in pursuit of the remoter ramifications of social evolution that Spencer's sociology went stamping out into the forests of prehistory and there, among the all too numerous variables, died.

Spencer was forced into this pursuit of unascertainable first causes because it followed from his conception of science and of the purpose of the Synthetic Philosophy that if he could not explain social phenomena *ultimately*—the qualification is important—in terms of physical causation, he could not explain them satisfactorily at all. There would be a gap in the causal chain.

---

[1] Cf.: 'The Theory of Natural Selection was invented to account for the evolution of specific differences and of ecological adaptations; it was not primarily intended as an explanation of the more wonderful and more mysterious facts of the *convenance de parties* and the interaction of structure and function. Perhaps Darwin did not realise the inner aspects of adaptation quite so vividly as he did the more superficial adaptation of organisms to their environment' (E. S. Russell, *Form and Function*, p. 232).

Only when it is seen that the transformations passed through during the growth, maturity, and decay of a society, conform to the same principles as do the transformations passed through by aggregates of all orders, inorganic and organic—or when it is seen that the process is in all cases similarly determined by forces, and is not scientifically interpreted until it is expressed in terms of those forces;—only then is there reached the conception of Sociology as a science in the full meaning of the word.[1]

And at the end of *The Study of Sociology* he confesses that he has been obliged to represent the study of sociology as the study of social evolution.[2] This is merely an amplification of what he had already said in *Social Statics*: 'There is no alternative. Either society has laws, or it has not. If it has not, there can be no order, no certainty, no system in its phenomena. If it has, then are they like the other laws of the universe—sure, inflexible, ever active, and having no exceptions?'[3]

'Then are they like the other laws of the universe...'— there is no mistaking the note of triumph. One thinks of Maine's very similar pronouncement,[4] and of Huxley's 'The Universe is one and the same throughout'.[5] But most clearly one sees the dilemma of the Victorian intellectual invited to choose between determinism and obscurantism. For Spencer, understanding social relations *meant* giving them a causal explanation.[6] If they were not so explicable then they were unintelligible, and this could surely not be the case. As Parsons puts it, the positivist consistently tries 'to make his causal analysis cover all intellectually appre-

---

[1] *S of S*, p. 329.   [2] *Ibid*. pp. 384–5.
[3] *SS*, p. 42. Cf. Buckle, p. 106 above.   [4] See above, p. 165.
[5] L. Huxley, *Life and Letters of T. H. Huxley* (3 vols. 1900), I, 314.
[6] Cf. Leslie Stephen, 'Causation, as J. S. Mill is profoundly convinced, always means a beginning. It is only, as we have seen, concerned with changes, not with persistence...He cannot recognise a reciprocal relation' (*The English Utilitarians*, III, 129).

hensible relationships'.[1] Even logical relations were to be interpreted, in the extreme positivist view, in psychological terms; in terms, that is to say, open to causal explanation.

The symbolism of language is not, according to the extreme empiricist view, arbitrary; names become attached to particular impressions originally by a kind of reflex action; Spencer thought that the origin of language was mimetic.[2] Moreover, he seems to have regarded the truth or falsehood even of propositions stating mathematical relationships as a psychological matter.[3] This emphasis on the causal rather than the logical aspect of language led in Spencer's case to the obliteration of any strict line between logical and empirical propositions; the nearest Spencer comes to such a distinction is when he distinguishes between what he calls the temporarily absolute conjunction of subject and predicate and their permanently absolute conjunction.[4]

The wording is peculiar, but the distinction he is aiming at is a distinction between the kind of certainty of a proposition about one's sensations (which is *temporarily* absolute, e.g. the statement 'I have a pain' is true when I have a pain, but not when I have not) and the kind of certainty we have in a purely analytic statement, which, if valid, is always valid. But the fact that Spencer should make *this* distinction the fundamental one shows that he is ignoring the fundamental distinction between two modes of speech—that he is regarding both as statements of *fact*.[5] The consequence of this conflation of logical and empirical propositions is that the

---

[1] Talcott Parsons, *The Structure of Social Action* (New York, 1937), p. 486.

[2] *The Principles of Psychology* (3rd ed., 2 vols. 1881), II, 123–4.

[3] Spencer thought that mathematics should be taught as a factual science; *P of S*, I, 110.

[4] *P of P*, II, 402–4.

[5] For J. S. Mill on the principle of contradiction as a generalization from experience, see Leslie Stephen, *The English Utilitarians*, III, 99.

ultimate test of truth, even of purely logical propositions,
becomes a psychological matter. The test of a necessarily
true statement becomes not the logical test that its denial
must be self-contradictory, self-contradiction being understood as a formal relation between terms or propositions,
but that the truth of its negation should be inconceivable,
inconceivability being understood as a psychological fact.[1]
As an instance of such a cognition Spencer offered the
inconceivability of thinking, when gazing at the sun, that
one was not perceiving light.[2] J. S. Mill denied this.[3]
Spencer, in his reply, invoked the opinions of three friends
(unnamed) who agreed with him, and presumably thought
he had won, 4–1.

Of course, to try to found an empiricist epistemology on
the presumed incorrigibility of statements about one's
sensations is a common enough procedure, but in Spencer's
case this is combined with a refusal to distinguish between
logical and empirical modes of speech.

A proposition may be claimed to be a necessary one
either:

(*a*) because it is analytic, or

(*b*) because it is one of the ultimate metaphysical pre-
suppositions of a universe of discourse.

Spencer ignores the first. He claims not only that there are
synthetic *a priori* propositions (not his phrase) but that all
a priori propositions are synthetic.

Believing that there are such synthetic *a priori* propositions, one may either merely admit that it is a contingent
matter that there are men who inhabit such a universe of
discourse, or one may regard this fact as a causally necessary
consequence of the truth of other synthetic propositions.

---

[1] *P of P*, II, 407 *passim*.   [2] *Ibid.* II, 403.
[3] Duncan, *Life and Letters of Herbert Spencer*, pp. 121–2.

This is the step which Spencer takes. He attempts to provide an evolutionary explanation of *a priori* knowledge; it is that part of our knowledge of the working of the universe which has become, as it were, instinctive, and hence known *a priori* —a kind of biologically conditioned Collective Conscious.[1]

But this *a priori* knowledge is contingent upon the universe working in certain—uniform—ways. What, then, is the logical status of statements of the natural laws of the universe? Clearly they, too, cannot be synthetic *a priori* propositions in sense (*b*) above, for this would make the argument circular; to claim 'necessity' for them could therefore only mean that one was entering the realm of religious utterance, as in the case of those believers who, while claiming the existence of God to be a fact, and not merely a tautology or an ultimate presupposition of human thought, would nevertheless deny that it was in any sense contingent.

Much in nineteenth-century thought can be interpreted on the assumption that the Uniformity of Nature had acquired for many intellectuals a logical status and a numinous aura which made it a substitute for the idea of God. Ostensibly Spencer does not take this road, at least in *First Principles*. All our knowledge, including knowledge of the laws of nature, is said to be 'relative'.[2] 'Absolute reality' is 'The Unknowable' of which we can assert only that it is. But once stated, in *First Principles*, this part of Spencer's system is, not unnaturally, made no further use of, and, if one looks at his life and work as a whole, it is

[1] 'Lest he should not have observed it, the reader must be warned that the terms "*a priori* truth" and "necessary truth", as used in this work, are to be interpreted not in the old sense, as implying cognitions wholly independent of experiences, but as implying cognitions that have been rendered organic by immense accumulations of experiences, received partly by the individual, but mainly by all ancestral individuals whose nervous system he inherits' (*First Principles* (6th ed. 1904), p. 139 n.).

[2] E.g. *ibid.* p. 109.

evident that for Spencer the idea of the uniformity of nature, rather than a vacuous Unknowable, took the place of religion. It did more: possession of it became the outward and visible sign of Grace. 'The progress from deepest ignorance to highest enlightenment, is a progress from entire unconsciousness of law, to the conviction that law is universal and inevitable.'[1]

The distinction between logical and empirical statements being thus blurred, the tendency was to annex the now vague notion of 'necessity' for all the most certain-seeming propositions, most notably the established 'laws of nature'. Durkheim noted the connection in positivist thinking between 'natural' and logical:

Pour qu'on put dire de certains faits qu'ils sont surnaturels, il fallait avoir déjà le sentiment qu'il existe un ordre naturel des choses, c'est-à-dire que les phénomènes de l'univers sont liés entre eux suivant des rapports nécessaires, appelés lois. Une fois ce principe acquis, tout ce qui déroge à ces lois devait nécessairement apparaître comme en dehors de la nature et, par suite, *de la raison*: car ce qui est naturel en ce sens *est aussi rationnel*, ces relations nécessaires ne faisant qu'exprimer la manière dont les choses s'enchaînent logiquement.[2]

This seems to mean that exceptions to natural laws would be regarded as unintelligible in the way that self-contradictions are unintelligible—'outside reason'. But if man is a part of nature, as Spencer was confident he was, then his actions must either be explicable in terms of the laws of nature, or be unintelligible, as violations of those laws. Social behaviour must be intelligible in terms of natural causation or not at all. And a complete causal explanation meant, for Spencer, an evolutionary one.

[1] *SS*, p. 39.
[2] E. Durkheim, *Les formes élémentaires de la vie religieuse* (Paris, 1912), p. 36. Italics mine.

There is, in fact, a striking parallel here. Empiricist epistemology of the kind discussed here tends, by reason of its psychological and causal approach to meaning, and its attempts to break down complex ideas into their simple component impressions, to be drawn into a kind of conjectural history of language[1] and of the formation of complex ideas. By contrast, to look for the meaning of a symbol in its use draws attention to the relations of the symbol to other parts of the system—though philosophers of this persuasion seem to prefer the phrase 'language game'. The twentieth-century revolution in social anthropology might be crudely described in the same terms.

But to return to Spencer. His attempt to write sociology as the history of social evolution was not due simply to overconfidence—though he was never diffident—but arose naturally from his conception of the nature and scope of science. To him, the alternative would have seemed the rejection of any attempt by the human intellect to grasp the social life of man, and its abandonment to randomness and arbitrariness, to Tories and theologians. This would have wounded his pride in the possibilities of science and his faith in the Uniformity of Nature; it would also have ended his dream of a scientific ethics and politics. It is to the latter that we must now turn, for it was the other main factor involved in turning his sociology in an evolutionary direction.

[1] As in, for example, Horne Tooke, *The Diversions of Purley* (2 vols. 1786). Tooke thought that Locke's *Essay concerning Human Understanding* should really have been called 'A Grammatical Essay, or a Treatise on Words, or on Language' (*op. cit.* I, 42 n.).

3. EVOLUTION AND PROGRESS

Nothing shows more vividly the close kinship of the philosophic radicalism of the early nineteenth century with its
parent, the eighteenth-century Enlightenment, than some
of Spencer's early pronouncements. True, it is now a sobered
Enlightenment, harsher and more priggish, having lost wit
and the taste for indecency and acquired Malthus and
Ricardo. But there is still the same sense of a new dawn for
humanity—and the cliché is perhaps a more accurate ren-
dering of the state of mind than a fresher metaphor would
be. Man, freed at last from unreflecting subservience to
immemorial customs and institutions, is about to take his
future into his own hands and shape it, guided and instructed by science, in the image of rationality and justice.
The taboos are broken, nothing is unquestionable. Obviously
men born into a generation on the threshold of such achievements bear a heavy responsibility, and the young Spencer
was fully aware of it.

In what seems to have been a manifesto for a projected
periodical, he wrote, in a passage which is worth quoting at
length:

The signs of the times are indicating the near approach of that
era of civilization when men shall have shaken off the soul-
debasing shackles of prejudice...The long acknowledged
rationality of man and the obvious corollary that he is to be
guided by his reason rather than by his feelings is at length
obtaining a practical recognition...Respect for precedent is on
the wane, and that veneration heretofore bestowed upon un-
meaning custom is now being rapidly transferred to objects more
worthy of its regard. These objects are TRUTH and PRINCIPLES.[1]

The discovery of TRUTH and PRINCIPLES becomes a para-
mount task. It is not sufficient simply to destroy abuses with

[1] Duncan, *Life and Letters of Herbert Spencer*, p. 46.

piecemeal criticism; the right path must be shown, the way of salvation made known. The man who regarded himself as the new Newton[1] could hardly do less than cast himself for the part of that long-awaited hero, the Newton of the moral sciences. Indeed, assuming that the theory of the new Newton would encompass mankind also, as part of nature, did not the former role include the latter?[2]

Thirty-five years after the manifesto just quoted, Spencer wrote: 'The establishment of rules of right conduct as a scientific basis is a pressing need. Now that moral injunctions are losing the authority given by their supposed sacred origin, the secularisation of morals is becoming imperative.'[3] The final volume of the Synthetic Philosophy was *The Principles of Ethics* and at the beginning of it he wrote: 'This last part of the task it is to which I regard all the preceding parts as subsidiary...my ultimate purpose, lying behind all proximate purposes, has been that of finding for the principles of right and wrong in conduct at large a scientific basis.'[4]

All these pronouncements on the need for rationality in conduct and social organization, and the hope of a scientifically based ethics, might have come from an orthodox utilitarian. And in a sense Spencer was a utilitarian: 'I conceive it to be the business of moral science to deduce, from the laws of life and the conditions of existence, what kinds of action necessarily tend to produce happiness, and what kinds to produce unhappiness.'[5] The ultimate ethical standard

---

[1] Spencer to his father, Duncan, *op. cit.* p. 75.

[2] If there was some confusion here, it did not bother Spencer. When he faced the question why man should strive to alter his society if its changes were predetermined, he answered in terms that echo the Marxist's 'easing the birth pangs of the new society' (*S of S*, p. 401).

[3] *The Data of Ethics*, preface, p. iv.   [4] *P of E*, p. vii.

[5] *Autobiography*, II, 88. Cf. *The Data of Ethics*, p. 30, 'The good is universally the pleasurable'.

was the same but it went with a different conception of the exigencies of scientific method.

It would perhaps be overstating the case to say that Spencer found it necessary to write a number of large volumes as a prelude to ethics where Bentham and James Mill found a sentence or two of psychological assumption sufficient. Nevertheless, the place that Spencer gives his *Principles of Ethics* at the end of a series of enormous volumes, the final consummation, as it were, of the project cryptically foreshadowed in his first book, *Social Statics*, is an indication of the change which had come over advanced ethical and political thought in the mid-nineteenth century. It is not unduly stretching the phrase to call Spencer a philosophic radical, but he was emphatically a man of the mid-century. To him the earlier utilitarianism was 'empirical', incomplete because, lacking a sociology, it could consider only the proximate causes of conduct.[1] The principle of utility is 'no rule at all...but rather an enunciation of the problem to be solved'[2]—a statement which neatly gives the measure of both Spencer's agreement and disagreement with orthodox utilitarianism. Without a sociology the principle of utility is no more than a statement of good intentions. We do not know what means to adopt to achieve the desired ends. The statute book is 'a record of unhappy guesses'.[3]

The basis of Spencer's attack on earlier utilitarianism[4] was, of course, the theory of evolution, which shattered the dogma of a universal human nature on which deductive

---

[1] *Autobiography*, II, 89.   [2] *SS*, pp. 1–2.   [3] *SS*, p. 10.
[4] With which, incidentally, he seems to have had only a very sketchy acquaintance. He confessed to Leslie Stephen that when he wrote *Social Statics* he had never read Locke or Paley, and knew of Bentham only that he had enunciated the greatest happiness principle (Duncan, *Life and Letters of Herbert Spencer*, p. 418).

utilitarianism was founded. Man's circumstances are constantly changing and he is constantly adapting himself to them.[1] 'And if humanity *is* indefinitely variable, it cannot be used as a gauge for testing moral truth.'[2] Instructed by the theory of evolution, Spencer saw, as J. S. Mill had seen, that once you go behind the basic utilitarian generalization of ends and ask *what* things have pleasure and pain attached to them, the appearance of a factual generalization vanishes leaving only a verbal façade. 'The standard of happiness', as Spencer put it, 'is infinitely variable.'[3] The attempt to get around the problem of ends by assuming them to be essentially the same for all, thereby making it possible to convert categorical moral imperatives into hypothetical scientific ones, is at an end. We are left with the original chaos of absolutely random ends, outside the scope of intellectual comprehension, and must begin again. Utilitarianism had virtually admitted this in asserting that each man must be presumed the best judge of his own interest, but this could not satisfy men who wanted a science of morals and society, though it continued to play a part in their thinking.

The belief in the variability of man implied political relativism, at least of a qualified kind. Spencer admitted that he had not always thought in this way.

In my youth my constitutional repugnance to coercion, and consequent hatred of despotic forms of rule, had involved a belief like that expressed in the American Declaration of Independence...the belief that free forms of government would ensure social welfare...Along with this went an unhesitating assumption that all superstitions are as mischievous as they are erroneous.[4]

The doctrine of evolution modified all this into a kind of rudimentary functionalism.

[1] *SS*, p. 33.
[2] *SS*, p. 37. Italics original.
[3] *SS*, p. 3.
[4] Duncan, *op. cit.* p. 569.

When there has been grasped the truth that societies are products of evolution, assuming, in their various times and places, the various modifications of structure and function; there follows the conviction that what, relative to our thoughts and sentiments, were arrangements of extreme badness, had fitness to conditions which made better arrangements impracticable.[1]

Again one can see the parallel though independent intellectual development of Spencer and J. S. Mill, though Spencer, younger and further from the centre of utilitarian orthodoxy, had much the easier passage.

With the statement quoted above we seem to have arrived at a mental climate of relativism in which the study of the social functions and interrelations of institutions might have been expected to flourish. But it was only a strictly qualified relativism—absolute moral and political relativism was something the mid-Victorian historian or sociologist could not live with, even in his professional activities. To rest at this point would have been, for Spencer, a repudiation of the whole purpose of the exercise. Could this be the final resting-place of the splendid science of morality and politics—the passive acceptance of everything as good for its time and place? Fortunately, however, there was no need to rest here. The doctrine of evolution which had brought social science to the verge of being the study of the social functions of beliefs and institutions, also drew it away again, in the interests of ethical and political theory. Spencer inferred from his theory of social evolution 'the inevitability of gradualness' and the intractability of social material—his strictures on utilitarian utopianism match those of Marx on the utopian socialists—but no more than Marx did did he give up the belief in a scientific ethics and politics.

[1] *S of S*, p. 394.

Did Spencer then equate evolution with progress? J. S. Mill had seen that the way out lay in some theory of progress. One could then base one's political beliefs on the answer to that question: What great improvement lies next in the sequence? But suppose one can detect the mechanism by which social progress was produced. Does it not then become obligatory to allow this benevolent mechanism the maximum freedom of operation? Both Buckle and the Social Darwinists, in their different ways, answered this question affirmatively, and so, emphatically, did Spencer.

His arguments depended upon an identification of social evolution with progress. His justification for this step, however, is not always clear. His general theory of evolution, of course, embraced dissolution as well as development, though almost all his attention and all his emotional commitment were to the latter. The thought of the development of humanity was the only one which brought him any comfort in his last illness;[1] but, even regarding evolution essentially as the development from the simple to the complex, it is not true that for Spencer increasing complexity implied progress, though it was certainly a prerequisite of it; he had to invoke another principle to explain his disapproval of the kind of complexity represented by the 'Militant' type of society.

This is not the place to say what is wrong with Spencer's ethics—not, in any case, a task likely to enhance one's reputation. But his distinction between the military and industrial types of society, hackneyed though it has become in the work of his commentators, has an important bearing on his whole attitude to the social order and the ways it is maintained.

There were a number of ways, in early and mid-

[1] B. Webb, *My Apprenticeship*, pp. 30–1.

nineteenth century England, in which emancipation from the narrower doctrines of old-fashioned philosophic radicalism could come. J. S. Mill's chief allies, as he fought his lonely battle with his father, were Comte and those Teutonized Englishmen, the Coleridgeans. For Maine, as we have seen, it came through German jurisprudence and historiography, and was given a factual basis by his experience of India. For Spencer, however, it came from the theory of evolution, originally in its purely biological form, as he derived it from French and German sources. In the case of Maine there had been some conflict between the scientific cast of his aspirations and the historical elements in the tradition of thought on which he drew—a conflict which he resolved, to his own satisfaction, by the theory of an Aryan race. Spencer, drawing largely on a different tradition, itself scientific in purpose and methods, met no such difficulty. As with Maine, however, we still have to ask: how complete was his emancipation from the mental habits typical of philosophic radicalism?

Certainly it brought a sharper awareness of the social conditioning of habits and beliefs;[1] a decline in the narrow parochialism of the old utilitarianism; a greater recognition of the diversity of mankind and the variety of his social arrangements. 'If, going beyond our own society and our own time, we observe what has happened among other races, and among the earlier generations of our own, we meet...workings-out of human nature utterly unlike those we assume when making political forecasts.'[2] And there was not merely a recognition of such diversities, but a determination to understand the irrational practices of men instead of regarding them merely as anomalous or disgusting.[3] There is

---

[1] E.g. *S of S*, p. 17.　　　　[2] *S of S*, p. 14.
[3] E.g. *Essays*, I, 435.

nothing particularly new about this—it is an attitude which goes back at least to Turgot, but it was an aspect of eighteenth-century thought which had been neglected by the philosophical radicals. We have already seen, however, how in Spencer this 'functionalist' attitude to institutions was qualified and, as it were, smothered, by the claims of a positivist attitude to the scope and nature of science. Similarly, we can now see it severely qualified by an essentially positivist picture of society, and by particular ethical requirements.

In the first place, there is a crudity, apparent even to the sociological amateur, in Spencer's conception of social functions, in his lack of the concept of social role, and hence his tendency to identify social roles with actual people. In his anxiety to show the mutual dependence which differentiation of functions entails, he ignores the many-sidedness of the social personality, the multiplicity of roles which one individual may play in the social system.[1] He may have been misled here by the organic analogy; body cells do not move from one organ to another. But it seems more likely that he was misled by the phrase 'physiological division of labour', and by his generally utilitarian, economic attitude to social relations. He thinks of social relations essentially in terms of an economic model, as exchanges of services.

A member of a primitive society cannot devote himself to an order of activity which satisfies only one of his personal wants, thus ceasing the activities required for satisfying his other personal wants, unless those for whose benefit he carries on his special activity in excess, give him in return the benefits of their special activities.[2]

---

[1] See especially *S of S*, p. 332; *P of S*, I, 470-1, 507-8.
[2] *S of S*, p. 332.

Spencer's picture of social co-operation is founded on the idea of the economic division of labour; social roles, for him, mean specialization of *personnel*.

But if Spencer's conception of social functions in past stages of evolution is essentially modelled on the concepts of economics, the connection becomes even more obvious when he comes to discuss the present and the future in terms of the 'Militant' and 'Industrial' types of society. The evolutionists denounced the picture of society as held together by the rational calculation of advantages, and were fond of producing exotic examples in refutation, but they did not dispense with it altogether. It reappears as the eminently desirable end-product of the evolutionary process. Smellie's remarks on this aspect of Maine have already been noted.[1] They could equally well be applied to Spencer's conception of the 'Industrial Society', with one qualification. Whereas Maine, in his political thought, shares the assumptions of James Mill,[2] for Spencer the role of rational choice in the coming millennium is largely supplanted by the built-in habits and instincts which are the product of centuries of adaptation. In all else the parallel is perfect. Spencer's 'Industrial Society' is the liberal, individualistic, rational bourgeois society *par excellence*. Like Marx, Spencer was a sociologist of conflict who believed that conflict would ultimately cease, and the state, regarded essentially as a weapon in the conflict, would wither away, and with it the rituals, ceremonies, theologies and irrational sanctions with which authority, in the intermediate stages of development, had clothed itself.[3]

One institution, of course, Spencer the bourgeois could not allow to wither away. Property satisfied a permanent

---

[1] See above, p. 156.   [2] See above, p. 169.
[3] *Essays*, I, 137–8, 157; *S of S*, p. 348.

need in the nature of man. But the world of Spencer's 'Industrial Society' is a world bare of sociological furniture; a society with nothing but its naked economic bones showing. Man having become perfectly adapted to the social state, almost all the institutions in which his social life has clothed itself in its dangerous pilgrimage have become redundant and, now being seen for the irrationalities and superfluities they essentially are, can be cast off with a vote of thanks for past services.[1]

These old forms which it [society] successively throws off, have all been once vitally united with it—having severally served as the protective envelopes within which a higher humanity was being evolved. They are cast aside only when they become hindrances—only when some inner and better envelope has been formed.[2]

But is there a last envelope and, if so, what is the prize inside? Inside the last envelope there is written nothing but natural sympathy and the economic division of labour, for these seem, according to Spencer, to constitute the only social relations recognized in the perfect 'Industrial Society'. Even property, though still recognized, seems to imply no mystique of status.

It is essentially a new 'State of Nature', founded on the division of labour and akin to the utopia of the older utilitarians; only, for Spencer, instead of men being brought to it by rational perception of the laws of nature, or of the ultimate identity of interests, or coerced into it by a utilitarian legislator, it is the product of a long evolutionary process, in which conflict and the protective influences of irrational practices and taboos have been major factors.

At times, particularly in his earlier, more optimistic years, Spencer speaks in the genuine apocalyptic accents of

---

[1] *Ibid.* [2] *Essays*, I, 157.

nineteenth-century historicism. The day of deliverance is at hand. The Puritan ground-roots of Spencer's social thought become visible; it might be some ancestral Huguenot[1] denouncing the ceremonies, mysteries and hierarchy of the Scarlet Woman. Spencer's own vocabulary recognizes the similarity. 'There needs then, a protestantism in social usages. Forms that have ceased to facilitate and have become obstructive...have to be swept away; *and eventually are so swept away* in all cases.'[2] Nonconformists must rise against the tyranny of manners and fashions: 'In rules of living, a West End clique is our Pope; and we are all papists, with but a mere sprinkling of heretics....to free us from these idolatries and superstitious conformities, there has to come a protestation in social usages.'[3]

Spencer himself took pride in being such a heretic. On one occasion he refused to attend an 'At Home' at the Foreign Office, on the grounds that he had an insuperable objection to wearing *levée* dress. When Lady Derby kindly (it is to be hoped) offered to let him come in ordinary evening dress, however, he shrank from such *outré* nonconformism, worthy son of a quasi-Quaker though he was.[4] This incident is not trivial; it was of the utmost importance in Victorian social science that the men sufficiently detached to be able to believe in the possibility of such a science were likely to be agnostics and radicals, and hence unsympathetic to any kind of ritual or mystique. A Tractarian would probably have stood a better chance of understanding the part played in the life of a primitive people by its religion, had he not been incapable of the scientific detachment necessary for even contemplating doing so. And in the case

---

[1] *Autobiography*, I, 6.
[2] *Essays*, I, 152. Italics mine.
[3] *Ibid.* pp. 155–6.
[4] Duncan, *Life and Letters of Herbert Spencer*, pp. 185–6.

of Spencer and Tylor at least, rationalistic preconceptions were reinforced by the prejudices of an extreme Protestant background, and it is not fanciful to think that the effect can be seen in their writings.

But what were the goods enshrined in Spencer's Industrial Utopia, when the encrustations of the evolutionary process should finally have been pared away? What would life be like *without* them? Spencer answers in much the same terms as Engels. According to Spencer: 'We may regard it [civilization] as a progress towards that constitution of man and society required for the complete manifestation of everyone's individuality.'[1] The only point which emerges at all clearly from this is freedom—freedom from the coercion of nature—because complete adaptation to it has been achieved; freedom from the coercion of society, because perfect adaptation to the social state has been followed by the abolition of those coercive instruments necessitated by imperfect adaptation. Elsewhere, Spencer puts the case for freedom more clearly:

Everything shall conform itself to equity and reason; nothing shall be saved by its prestige.[2] Conceding to each man liberty to pursue his own ends and satisfy his own tastes, he [the reformer] demands for himself like liberty; and consents to no restrictions on this save those which other men's claims involve.[3]

It is apparent that Spencer regards the claims of society, the institutions—other than economic institutions—by which human energy is shaped and guided, as something essentially alien to the human personality, something from which it will ultimately liberate itself, and not as something integral to the whole notion of personality, something

---

[1] *SS*, p. 434.
[2] Cf. Tylor, below, p. 257.   [3] *Essays*, I, 137.

without which men can be neither human nor individual in any way which we can understand.

Broadly speaking, it is true of all the evolutionary social theorists that they could recognize the social functions of irrational, absurd and superstitious practices only provided that they were someone else's, or at least, if present in their own society, that they were merely transitory. This distinction enabled them to provide more satisfying explanations of them, as they occurred in alien societies, and in the past of their own, than their predecessors the philosophic radicals had been able to supply, while remaining essentially philosophic radicals in their attitude to their own society. The spectacle they present, generally speaking, is the familiar one of a philosopher of history insisting that his own age is the ultimate, or at least penultimate, stage of the whole process. It is possible to explain this apparent coincidence in Hegelian terms: a process can only be understood when completed, or nearing completion. A more satisfying, if more cynical, explanation is that this assumption enables the philosopher of history to have it both ways; to explain the past in gradualist, evolutionary terms, and at the same time to denounce the evils of his own society as if he were an ordinary radical rationalist. It is perhaps the only emotionally tolerable way in which reformist enthusiasm can be combined with adherence to a philosophy of history.

Spencer, it is true, admitted the necessity of the evolutionary process, even in its earlier, more repugnant phases, and was to that extent a relativist, and a student of the social functions of apparently undesirable institutions. In the final pages of *The Study of Sociology* he even went so far as to make out a kind of pragmatic case for conservatism. But generally speaking his approach to *contemporary* social institutions is that of an impatient *laissez-faire* radical, reconciling his almost instinctive political attitudes with his theory of gradual social evolution by the assumption that civilization was on the point of opening the last envelope. We have already noticed similar attitudes in Mill and Maine, and shall see them again in Tylor. It is, in fact, an attitude typical of evolutionary positivism—a curious compromise, as if one were to admit the validity of the theories of psychoanalysis as applied to children, but to talk to adults only of the virtues of cold baths and will-power.

CHAPTER 7

TYLOR AND THE GROWTH OF ANTHROPOLOGY

I. LUBBOCK AND McLENNAN

Apart from Maine, three major figures in the development of social anthropology during our period call for attention: Sir John Lubbock, J. F. McLennan and E. B. Tylor. Of these, Tylor is undoubtedly the most important, but the other two are worth at least a passing glance.

Lubbock[1] alone, and he was the one least concerned with purely sociological questions, had the kind of introduction to evolutionary social theory which is generally regarded as typical, i.e. he came to it from evolutionary biology and prehistoric archaeology. The son of a distinguished mathematician and astronomer,[2] Lubbock was born, as it were, with an F.R.S. in his mouth. It was Darwin himself, a near neighbour at Down, who guided his first steps in science.[3] At twenty-one he already knew Lyell, Hooker, Prestwich and Sir John Evans, and had become a member of the Geological Society, with Lyell himself as his sponsor.[4] In the following year he met Huxley and Tyndall. When the family went to Cambridge it was with Whewell that they stayed.[5] He was admitted into the secrets of the *Origin of Species* during the long years of its gestation, and in 1860 Darwin wrote to Lubbock, then twenty-six, 'I settled some time ago that I should think more of Huxley's and your

[1] Later Lord Avebury (1834–1914).
[2] Sir John Lubbock (1803–65).
[3] H. G. Hutchinson, *The Life of Sir John Lubbock, Lord Avebury* (2 vols. 1914), I, 23.
[4] *Loc. cit.*   [5] *Ibid.* I, 33.

opinion—than of that of any other man in England.'[1] He was one of the protagonists at the famous Oxford meeting of the British Association and in the same year he went with Prestwich, Galton and Busk to visit Boucher de Perthes at Abbeville.[2]

Following this latter experience he began systematically to comb Europe for evidence of prehistoric man, visiting Switzerland, Scandinavia and the Dordogne. Like the Danish archaeologist, Worsaae, he began to think that modern 'stone-age' peoples should be studied by archaeologists, and 'realised the complexity of the task he had undertaken; he had to explain not only the origin of man's dwellings, weapons, clothes and methods of gaining a livelihood, but also…marriage, religion, laws, and blood relationships'.[3]

Lubbock had been, as Sir Arthur Keith rather quaintly says, 'nurtured in the cradle of evolution'.[4] Evolutionary biology and prehistoric archaeology were the inspiration of such relatively slight excursions into social theory as he made, some of them rather bizarre.[5] His career admirably bears out the view that 'much of the concern with cultural evolution in all fields of thought in the late nineteenth century owes a great deal to the demonstration of technological development which archaeology now represented as early human history'.[6]

[1] *Ibid.* 50.   [2] *Ibid.* 51.

[3] Sir Arthur Keith in *The Life-Work of Lord Avebury*, ed. Mrs Adrian Grant Duff (1934), p. 77.

[4] *Ibid.* p. 68.

[5] See the prophecies in the final chapter of J. Lubbock, *Prehistoric Times* (1865).

[6] Glyn Daniel, *A Hundred Years of Archaeology*, p. 120. Andrew Lang made the same point in *Anthropological Essays presented to Edward Burnett Tylor* (O.U.P. 1907), pp. 1–2. Lubbock himself listed the uses of anthropology thus: 'The study of the lower races of men, apart from the direct importance which it possesses in an empire like ours, is of great interest…In the first

A rather different impression is given, however, by the career of another major social evolutionist of the eighteen-sixties, J. F. McLennan. His work is altogether more sociologically oriented than Lubbock's (he was a friend of, and was said to have influenced, that very sociologically minded orientalist, Robertson Smith[1]) and, so far as we know, evolutionary biology and prehistoric archaeology played little or no part in the formation of his ideas.

Born in 1827, the son of an insurance agent, he was a clever Scots boy who migrated from Aberdeen to Trinity, Cambridge, where he graduated as a wrangler in 1853. In 1857 he was called to the Bar. His career thus runs parallel to Maine's for a few years. Maine was resident in Cambridge, though not at Trinity, till 1854, when he moved to the Inns of Court, whither, in all probability, McLennan went also. There is, however, no record of any direct contact between the two at this time, though it is probable that McLennan knew of his senior.

His first published work was the article on 'Law' which he contributed to the *Encyclopaedia Britannica* (8th ed.) in 1857. It was apparently the research involved in writing this article which first interested him in primitive legal institutions, and particularly in the practice of collusive abduction.[2] The article, therefore, is in the nature of a prolegomenon to his subsequent writings. The sources it reveals are interesting. He refers to Comte, Savigny, Spencer

place, the condition and habits of existing savages resemble in many ways, though not in all, those of our own ancestors . . . in the second, they illustrate much of what is passing among ourselves, many customs which have evidently no relation to present circumstances, and even some ideas which are rooted in our minds, as fossils are imbedded in the soil; and thirdly, we can even penetrate some of that mist which separates the present from the future' (*The Origin of Civilization* (1870), p. 1).
[1] Lord Bryce, *Studies in Contemporary Biography* (1903), p. 320.
[2] *D.N.B.*

—though only to the essay on 'Over-Legislation'—and Mill's *Logic*. Some of the views he expresses are what one would expect from such sources. Thus, society is said to originate in the family, and social phenomena are pronounced to be subject to natural laws; he follows Mill in saying that these laws are 'derived from those of individual life'.

Most interesting of all, perhaps, is his suggestion that among the sources of information about early legal history are 'the descriptions of early societies in various degrees of savagery which have at different times been given by intelligent observers', though it is not clear what he means by 'early'—whether he is referring to descriptions of primitive peoples such as those to be found in Herodotus and Tacitus, or whether he is using it, as it was frequently to be used later, as equivalent to primitive though contemporary peoples.

On the other hand, there are some curious omissions— curious, at least, in the light of his later work. The section on Jurisprudence, far from being the tract on the historical method that Maine would almost certainly have made it, is severely analytic. The suggestions about the way laws may have developed are purely conjectural, and not eked out by reference to existing primitive peoples. Altogether, the article is an oddly Janus-faced document. McLennan may, of course, have thought it right to play for safety in an Encyclopaedia article, and suppressed his more original ideas. On the other hand, something of profound importance may have occurred in his intellectual history between 1857 and 1865, the latter being the date of *Primitive Marriage*.

If this is the case, there is no particular reason to think it was the publication of the *Origin of Species* in 1859, nor is there any evidence in McLennan's writing to support the view that it was the rapid strides made by prehistoric archaeology in these years. It is much more likely to have been the publication of Maine's *Ancient Law* in 1861, though, as we have seen, it would have been quite possible and natural for McLennan to have attended the lectures in which, from the early eighteen-fifties, Maine was expounding the gist of *Ancient Law*.[1]

However this may be, it is clear that McLennan went far beyond Maine in his acceptance of the assumptions of the Evolutionary Comparative Method. He criticized Maine's neglect of contemporary savagery, but he does not seem to have appreciated the reservations on which Maine's selectivity was based. Maine insisted that his comparisons were valid only within what philology had revealed as a single ethnic group—the Aryan. He hoped that with the aid of the comparative method, disciplined in this way, history might rival the achievements of philology.[2] McLennan believed it possible to 'draw a clear and decided outline of the course of human progress in times long antecedent to those to which even philology can make reference'.[3] Maine presented the validity of the historical comparative method as a corollary of the demonstration, by philology, of a racial affinity. McLennan's confidence in the method was much more broadly based. He has found, he says, 'such similarity, so many correspondences, so much sameness...that I have come to regard the ethnological differences of the several families of mankind as of little or no account compared with what they have in common'.[4]

---

[1] In his Encyclopaedia article McLennan refers to the Greek conception of 'Themis', which Maine discusses at some length in *Ancient Law*, but perhaps this is insignificant, as it is an example which would naturally occur to a classically educated lawyer.   [2] See above, p. 148.

[3] *Primitive Marriage* (1865), repr. in *Studies in Ancient History*, 1st series (1886), p. 4.   [4] *Primitive Marriage*, Preface.

This is the old Enlightenment belief in a universal human nature put on a basis of inductive comparison. Sometimes, in fact, McLennan's language is extremely close to that of his eighteenth-century predecessors.[1] It is true that he uses the concept of 'survivals',[2] whose introduction into anthropology is generally attributed to Tylor,[3] but his work is singularly lacking in those metaphors derived from geology, palaeontology and biology with which the pages of his contemporaries were freely sprinkled; metaphors and analogies —'strata', 'fossils', 'rudimentary organs' and the like— which seem to indicate a certain diffidence, a sense that anthropology was a junior science, needing models and guarantees of validity in the examples of more established disciplines.

Instead of these attempts to establish diplomatic relations with the *Zeitgeist*, we get from McLennan one of the clearest, most elaborate and least apologetic of all the expositions of the principles of the Evolutionary Comparative Method presented in the eighteen-sixties,[4] with acknowledgements to Dugald Stewart, Lafitau and Millar.[5]

It is tempting to regard McLennan, therefore, as a direct descendant of the Scottish school of conjectural historians of the later eighteenth century, rather than as a by-product of the intellectual ferment of the eighteen-fifties and eighteen-sixties. It would be ironical if the really important thing about him turned out to be not his period but his nationality. It is an attractive theory though it leaves much unexplained, but it has one major drawback. Unless the Encyclopaedia article is very misleading, his ideas underwent, if not a transformation, at least a rapid development

[1] See esp. *Primitive Marriage*, ch. 1.
[2] *Studies in Ancient History*, pp. 3–8.   [3] See below, p. 240.
[4] *Primitive Marriage*, ch. 1.
[5] *Ibid.* p. 161. *Studies in Ancient History*, 1st series, p. 420.

between 1857 and 1865. Nevertheless, whatever the catalyst may have been—and it was most probably *Ancient Law*—it still seems fairly evident that the roots of McLennan's thinking lay in social theory rather than in the contemporary natural sciences.

In spite of this, however, there are few indications in his work—far fewer than in that of the biologist-archaeologist Lubbock—of what one might call the ulterior motives of Victorian anthropology. His assumptions may be questionable and his theories, by the standards of modern anthropological fieldwork, over-ambitious, but his approach was severely academic. He cast his net wider than Maine, for the reasons given above, but he devoted himself with far greater concentration than Maine to the solution of a single problem—the phenomenon of marriage by capture. There are some signs of a broader approach in the studies published posthumously under the title *Studies in Ancient History—Second Series* (1896), under the aegis of his brother, but McLennan's ill health and premature death in 1881 really ensured that his treatment of this particular problem should remain his chief contribution to nascent anthropology.

2. TYLOR AND THE STUDY OF RELIGION

Very different from McLennan's was the career of the last of the writers of the eighteen-sixties whom we have to consider. Tylor owed the dominating position he came to enjoy in English anthropology in part to his longevity—he was born in 1832 and died in 1917. Tylor apart, only Spencer (1820–1903) and Lubbock (1834–1914) of the first generation of evolutionary social theorists lived on into the twentieth century; and Spencer would never have regarded himself, as Tylor came to do, as a professional anthropologist, though their preoccupations were sufficiently close for a rather rancorous dispute to arise between them over their respective priority in the use of the term Animism.[1] The use or non-use of the name anthropology, however, was not, perhaps, in itself, of much importance. Maine and McLennan, though always included among the precursors in histories of anthropology, did not use the name, and Lubbock, as President of the Ethnological Society, accepted it, when his society merged with the Anthropological Society, only with great reluctance.[2] Far more important than the fact that Tylor called himself an anthropologist was the fact that, from very early on, he behaved like a professional. Not only was he the only really distinguished figure in the history or prehistory of anthropology to be a member of the Anthropological Society in the eighteen-sixties, he was a member of the Ethnological Society as well. His appointment in 1884 to the newly created Readership in Anthropology at Oxford was a proper reward for such professional zeal, as well as for his writings. Cambridge, incidentally, did not create a comparable post till 1909, when A. C. Haddon was made Reader in Ethnology, by which time Tylor's Readership had become a chair (1896).

Tylor's rise to pre-eminence coincided with a shift in the emphasis and direction of anthropological studies. Not, it is true, such a radical revolution in social theory as had occurred in the eighteen-fifties and eighteen-sixties, but a shift nevertheless. The generation of writers who came to maturity in the eighteen-sixties had been composed, for the most part, of lawyers interested in primitive institutions as 'legal antiquities', or of scientists or archaeologists whose original interest had been in anatomy, biology or geology.

[1] See *Mind*, II (1877), 141–5, 415–23, 429, and *Academy*, II (1877), 367, 392, 416, 462.   [2] Hutchinson, *The Life of Sir John Lubbock*, I, 118.

The anthropologists who came to maturity in the last quarter of the century, however, included a number whose interest had been awoken in quite a different way. Andrew Lang, R. R. Marett and James Frazer had begun as classical scholars, and had become interested in folk-lore and primitive religion as an extension of the study of classical myth. The story that Marett tells was perhaps fairly typical. In the course of a tutorial, the discussion of certain Roman gentile names suggested a connection with animals and plants, and his tutor, Strachan-Davidson, recommended him to read Andrew Lang's *Custom and Myth*, and it was from this that his interest stemmed.[1] He was first really set working on anthropology by his work for the Green Moral Philosophy Prize, the subject for which, in 1893, was—a sign of the times—'The Ethics of Savage Races',[2] and it then occurred to him that 'there was clearly room in the Greats course for a lecture on ethics in its evolutionary aspect.'[3]

To what extent was Tylor, either through his position at Oxford—a number of the new generation were Oxford men; none of the earlier one had been—or through his writings, responsible for this shift in emphasis? Up to a point, of course, it needs no explanation. Sooner or later it was bound to occur to men whose education involved constant attention to classical mythology that the new anthropological writings were relevant to their own concerns. But there is evidence that Tylor's work played a crucial part in the transmission of ideas. To Marett he was 'the Father of Anthropology'.[4] Marett, it is true, had received his introduction to anthropology from Lang's *Custom and Myth*, but having done so he described himself as 'henceforth an enthusiastic if extremely ignorant disciple of the school of Tylor',[5] and even

---

[1] Marett, *A Jerseyman at Oxford*, p. 84.　　[2] *Ibid.* p. 115.
[3] *Ibid.* p. 116.　　　[4] *Ibid.* p. 167.　　　[5] *Ibid.* p. 84.

went so far as to say that 'anthropology was just "Mr Tylor's science" when Andrew Lang first wrote about it'.[1] Lang, it is true, might not altogether have liked the implications of these remarks. He was at pains to point out, when he came to write of his relations with Tylor, that when he first met him, at Oxford in 1872, he had not heard of any of Tylor's books, but was already interested in anthropology through McLennan's work on totemism.[2] Lang had in fact been interested in folk-lore from childhood, but according to his biographer 'it was from Tylor that Lang received the anthropological method'.[3]

But there is more evidence than such recollection or hearsay to establish Tylor as a key figure in the shift in emphasis in evolutionary social theory from the study of primitive legal institutions, or Spencerian inquiries into social structures and functions, to the study of primitive religion which was to reach its apogee in Frazer's *Golden Bough*. It was not merely that Tylor himself wrote primarily on this subject, but that it was Tylor who, by his attack on the hitherto dominant theory, propounded by Max Müller, that mythology was a 'disease of language' and hence fell within the domain of philology, threw open the subject of religion to anthropological treatment.

Religion can be treated sociologically as readily as any other aspect of social life; the names of Durkheim—'the egregious Durkheim', as Andrew Lang called him[4]—and Weber are sufficient reminders of that. But an ardent

---

[1] *Ibid.* p. 308.

[2] Andrew Lang, 'Edward Burnett Tylor' in *Anthropological Essays presented to Edward Burnett Tylor*, p. 1.

[3] R. Lancelyn Green, *Andrew Lang* (Leicester, 1946), p. 70. Marett calls him 'the devoted Tylorian, Andrew Lang' (R. R. Marett, *Tylor* (1936), p. 26).

[4] *Concerning Andrew Lang*. Andrew Lang Lectures, 1927–37 (O.U.P. 1949), p. 22.

functionalist, if there is anyone today who would be prepared to accept the designation, would have good reason to regard the shift in emphasis in Victorian anthropology described above as a disaster, and Tylor as the chief villain. Spencer's analyses of social structures and functions may have been overlaid by his evolutionary preoccupations, but they were something. The institutional studies of Maine and McLennan, though regarded as contributions to prehistory rather than as studies of living societies, were institutional studies nevertheless, involving constant attention to kinship and property relations, and the connections between them. There was no reason why interest in primitive religion should not have developed likewise into the study of religion as a social institution, but, broadly speaking, it did not. That it did not must be ascribed very largely to the work and influence of Tylor, and to the kind of interest that the classical scholars of the eighteen-eighties and eighteen-nineties brought to the anthropological study of religion,[1] though it might be pointed out that even Tylor's approach, basing explanations of primitive religion on hypothetical accounts of primitive psychology, was an improvement, from the sociological point of view, on Max Müller's.

Tylor was not, of course, the only one to write of primitive religion in this way. Spencer himself wrote about it in essentially the same way, but speculations of this kind were only a part of Spencer's work; they were absolutely central in Tylor's. The point is not so much, therefore, the sophistication or crudity of Tylor's explanations, but the direction in which his work pointed, the kind of phenomena on which it tended to focus attention. Although there was

[1] 'I long continued to regard anthropology from what I take to have been Lang's earlier point of view, that is, mainly as a background to the classics' (Marett in *Concerning Andrew Lang*, p. 3).

no reason why religion should not have been considered sociologically just as readily as law or property, it was perhaps easier and more tempting, particularly to men nurtured in a Protestant, even puritan atmosphere, to regard religion as the product of individual thoughts and fears. Not that anthropologists of religion were alone in using the hypothesis of the savage's faulty classifications and unsound explanations to account for social phenomena—we have only to recall Maine's explanation of the classificatory system of kinship—but the savage's legal and property institutions, however irrationally organized and mythically justified, could not simply be explained away as mere mistakes, as could his gods and magic.

Compare, for example, Tylor's psychological treatment of animism with McLennan's explanation of marriage by capture. After rebuking Max Müller for basing his account on a psychological conjecture,[1] McLennan goes on,

It must have been *the system* of certain tribes to capture their women—necessarily the women of other tribes—for wives. But we may be sure that such a system could not have sprung out of a mere instinctive desire of savages to possess objects cherished by a foreign tribe; it must have had a deeper source—to be sought for in their circumstances, their ideas of kinship, their tribal arrangements.[2]

However conjectural the subsequent argument, from population pressure, through female infanticide, to exogamy and the formation by long usage of a prejudice against intermarriage with kindred, the emphasis is on the tribe and its arrangements, rather than on the individual savage philosopher.

---

[1] 'Rejecting then, the primitive prudery hypothesis, which requires for its basis a declension from ancient standards of purity—of the existence of which we have no evidence' (McLennan, *Studies in Ancient History*, 1st series, p. 11).   [2] *Ibid.* p. 23. Italics original.

The other main aspect of Tylor's work, looked at from this point of view, is his use of the concept of 'survivals'. Malinowski claimed that the 'survivals' theory, the theory that there are elements of social life which now perform no social function but are simply relics of past states of society, inhibited the study of social facts as living items of a culture;[1] that it encouraged, in fact, an antiquarian rather than a sociological attitude to contemporary society. One does not have to subscribe to the view that every social institution *must* have a social function to agree with him. To be able to describe a puzzling social phenomenon with comfortable finality as a 'survival' converted into an intellectual resting-place what might otherwise have been a starting-point.[2] The theory of 'survivals' encouraged men to see parallels between primitive and civilized practices, but it drew the sting and the stimulus from the comparison by regarding the former as relics, aliens from another era. It seemed to broaden horizons, but in fact it was a device for keeping them in the same place. The epithet which naturally accompanies 'survivals' is 'mere'.

Tylor is sometimes claimed as the man who introduced the concept of 'survivals' into social anthropology.[3] This is not strictly true. McLennan had used the idea, though not the word, with great authority, in 1865[4] when Tylor had produced nothing in technical anthropology but papers for the Anthropological Society, of which McLennan was not a member. Herbert Spencer had used the idea in the

[1] B. Malinowski, *A Scientific Theory of Culture* (Chapel Hill, N.C. 1944), p. 31.

[2] S. A. Cook was led to a kind of tentative functionalism by assuming that there must be some reason why survivals still survived (S. A. Cook, *The Study of Religions* (1914), pp. 173–81).

[3] Hodgen, *The Doctrine of Survivals*, p. 34.

[4] McLennan, *Studies*, 1st series.

eighteen-fifties before Tylor had written anything at all.[1] It is an obvious corollary of the belief that present savagery represents the past of civilization—that both are points on essentially the same road. McLennan and Spencer had used the alleged existence of survivals as support for the hypothesis of social evolution, though Spencer had also drawn the same moral as Tylor was later to do. It was left to Tylor to make survival-hunting one of the major anthropological activities, and in this sense the tradition which ascribes to him the introduction of the concept is justified.

On both these counts, therefore, the psychological treatment of primitive religion and the introduction of the concept of 'survivals', Tylor's influence was a major factor in determining the direction taken by anthropological studies. Of course, the account given here of what we have rather loosely called 'the second generation' of anthropologists is not the whole story; they were not all Oxford classicists primarily interested in religion and folk-lore. The intellectual roots of the team which Haddon took to the Torres Straits (1899) lay primarily in the natural sciences. Institutional studies continued—Westermarck's *History of Human Marriage* (1891) is a case in point. Robertson Smith wrote on religion in a very un-Tylorian manner.[2] Nevertheless, Tylor was an outstandingly influential figure, and his intellectual history is therefore of peculiar interest.[3]

---

[1] H. Spencer, 'Manners and Fashion', *Westminster Review*, new series, v (1854).

[2] W. Robertson Smith, *Lectures on the Religion of the Semites*, 1st series (1899). As an example of the predominance of Tylor over the minds of the younger generation we may take the case of Frazer. Frazer's interest in anthropology was first aroused jointly by Tylor's *Primitive Culture* (2 vols. 1871), and by friendship with Robertson Smith (R. Angus Downie, *James George Frazer* (1940), pp. 9, 11). But Frazer wrote anthropology like Tylor, not like Robertson Smith.

[3] The chief source for information about Tylor's life is Marett, *Tylor*. See also *Anthropological Essays presented to E. B. Tylor*.

3. 'ANAHUAC' AND THE UNITY OF MANKIND

Edward Burnett Tylor was born in 1832, and was thus a decade younger than Maine and Spencer. His parents were well-to-do London Quakers, a fact which may have had something to do with his failing to go to a university. The other noteworthy member of the family was his elder brother, Alfred, who became a distinguished geologist.

It was sheer luck, in the well-disguised form of ill health, which released Tylor from the family business which he had entered at sixteen. The young man was thought to be delicate; the family was well off, and in 1855 he set out to travel in search of health. For some reason he went west rather than east, and in 1856 he met, quite by chance, in an omnibus in Havana, a fellow Quaker and enthusiastic archaeologist, Henry Christy.[1] Christy was going to Mexico in search of archaeological finds, and Tylor went with him. It was an important decision, even if Marett exaggerates when he says that 'on that chance hung his own fate together with the fate of British anthropology'.[2] *Anahuac*, the book which Tylor wrote as a result of this journey, was subtitled 'Mexico and the Mexicans, Ancient and Modern', but it was the ancient rather than the modern that stirred his curiosity, and the civilization of the Aztecs raises, sharply and unmistakably, the fundamental question of social evolution—has civilization spread outwards from a single centre, as Prichard and Latham had held, or does it develop autonomously along essentially the same lines in many different societies?

This was the problem at which Tylor nibbled inter-

[1] Henry Christy (1810–65). He had apparently become interested in primitive man and his implements as the result of the Great Exhibition of 1851! He excavated in the Dordogne with Lartet.

[2] Marett, *Tylor*, p. 29.

mittently throughout his book,[1] and though he ends with a caution, it is clear that his sympathies are with the hypothesis of autonomous development. Formal qualifications for tackling the problem, of course, he did not possess at all, but such formal qualifications as the age could have offered him would not, except possibly in philology, have been likely to be very relevant. The text of *Anahuac* makes it clear that he had the acquaintance with geology which the period, and his elder brother's interest, would lead one to expect. He and Christy seem to have behaved as collectors rather than as serious archaeologists, but Tylor was sufficiently aware of developments in archaeology by the time he came to write up his experiences to draw parallels with the findings of prehistoric archaeology in Europe,[2] and to argue for the autonomous development of Aztec civilization on essentially archaeological grounds.[3]

Less predictable, but almost equally noticeable, in *Anahuac* is Tylor's antiquarianism. His eye for 'survivals' is already developed. He mentions Shrove Tuesday and Guy Fawkes Day as derived from Catholic Holy Week practices,[4] and his attention is caught by the persistence of pre-scientific modes of thinking, such as astrology, surviving in civilized societies.[5] Examples of such survivals had, of course, a certain general relevance to the only academic problem treated at any length in *Anahuac*, the problem of the relation of European to Aztec culture, but *Anahuac* is a chatty travel-book with 'instructive' asides, not a formal treatise, and in it Tylor's interest in the 'antiquities' of culture is exhibited in a thoroughly informal and unsystematic manner. Antiquarianism and an interest

---

[1] *Anahuac* (1861), pp. 41, 100–3, 208, 242–4.
[2] *Ibid.* pp. 41, 100–1. [3] *Ibid.* p. 103.
[4] *Ibid.* pp. 49–50. [5] *Ibid.* p. 67.

in folk-lore first appear in Tylor's writing, not so much as tools deliberately wrought or adapted in the service of a new science, but as part of the ordinary texture of his thinking. Tylor was an antiquarian before he was a systematic anthropologist; it was the way his mind naturally worked. Hogden has traced[1] the history of the study of folk-lore and particularly the use of the concept of 'survivals' before Tylor, but it seems impossible to relate Tylor to this tradition in any very specific way.

The obverse side of Tylor's antiquarianism in *Anahuac* was his detachment from, and relative lack of interest in, contemporary Mexico as a living society. Very revealing in its unconscious arrogance is the remark: 'In these countries one is brought, in a manner, face to face with England as it used to be; and very trifling matters become interesting when viewed in this light.'[2] The curiosity of the future 'Father of Anthropology', to use Marett's phrase, virtually stopped short at the threshold of contemporary Mexico, except where it could be related to the past of his own country—a fact which gives one some idea of his probable progeny. It is true that when he was in Mexico, Tylor was a young man of twenty-five. His trip was for health rather than for study, and his book was obviously aimed at a public which wanted to be entertained at least as much as it was instructed. Moreover, the sociological approach to the study of contemporary society was in its infancy. It still remains strange that one of the founders of social anthropology should apparently have felt so relatively little temptation to even the most jejune sociological generalizations, so little inclination to write even the slenderest essay in the manner of de Tocqueville. It is almost inconceivable that Spencer,

---

[1] Hodgen, *The Concept of Survivals*, pp. 48–9.
[2] Tylor, *Anahuac*, p. 125.

Maine or J. S. Mill, had he set himself at a similar age to write such a book, should have been so sociologically incurious. Their interest in the possibilities and limitations of legal and political action would have forced them into some kind of social analysis, but Tylor's interests lay elsewhere. There is little indication in *Anahuac* that he knows anything of economics or political theory.

Even in such reflections on his experiences as he does allow himself, Tylor reveals all the limitations and prejudices to be expected of a mid-nineteenth-century Englishman of Quaker parentage and scientific interests—prejudices which, however natural, were perhaps not the best qualifications for the study of alien societies and primitive religion, though they provide a clue to his interest in them. He was, for instance, deeply anti-Catholic,[1] and had a strong aversion to religious ritual and display.[2] Indeed, the nonconformist background of Spencer and Tylor was perhaps as important as their rationalism in determining their attitude to primitive religion. It was an irony of the times that the men who had sufficient scientific detachment to treat religion as an element in social life essentially no different, from a sociological point of view, from any other, were, *ipso facto*, least likely to be able to appreciate what religion, particularly public, organized, ritualistic religion, meant to the worshippers themselves. This is perhaps likely to be the case at any time, but particularly so in a period when religious controversy was so vehement as in mid-Victorian England. The sympathetic detachment of a Matthew Arnold was perhaps relatively rare in any section of the Victorian intelligentsia; it was certainly scarce among the evolutionary social theorists.

It may be thought that to dwell to this extent on Tylor's

[1] *Ibid.* pp. 79, 126–8, 206.   [2] *Ibid.* pp. 46–7, 52–4.

first book is to place too much emphasis on what was, after all, primarily a work of entertainment rather than scholarship. In a way, however, it is this very fact which gives *Anahuac* its peculiar importance among Tylor's works. It offers a chance of catching him, at a crucial time in his mental history, with his intellect, as it were, unbuttoned. It makes clear that the notion of 'survivals' was not originally with Tylor, as it seems to have been with Spencer and McLennan, a way of guaranteeing the validity of the evolutionary comparative method, but part of the ordinary furniture of his mind. On the other hand, the lack of signs of sociological or even of political or economic interests, not perhaps overwhelmingly significant in itself, is thrown into sharp relief by the attention Tylor gives to archaeology and to the origins of Aztec civilization. Essentially, Tylor's interests are those of Prichard and Latham and the members of the Ethnological Society—he is concerned with the derivation and development of cultures. The chief difference is that whereas they had placed their emphasis on the former, Tylor placed his on the latter. As an anonymous reviewer of his *Researches into the Early History of Mankind* put it: 'The effect upon the author's mind of the body of evidence he has collected, appears to lead him to remark on the oneness of mental types in the races who in very different parts of the world have apparently invented independently very similar contrivances, rather than to deduce from similarity of work a distinct historical connection.'[1]

It was in the *Researches* that Tylor first appeared before the public as an anthropologist and practitioner of the evolutionary comparative method, but, despite the cautious conclusion of *Anahuac*,[2] he had really chosen his side by

---

[1] *AR*, III (1865), 264.
[2] 'We must wait for further evidence' (*Anahuac*, p. 244).

1861, at least so far as the specific question of the origin of Aztec civilization was concerned. Nothing gives a better idea of the complexity of the combinations of ideas involved in the development of evolutionary social theory, the inter-action of philosophical and scientific currents, and the inadequacy of any simple explanation than the intellectual supports of Tylor's evolutionism. We have already noticed the essentially historical cast of his mind, and its confronta-tion, at an early age, by the problem of the Aztecs. These things undoubtedly helped to prescribe the direction of his interests, but they did not, in themselves, determine his attitude to them. The chief argument in *Anahuac* is archaeo-logical, the problem being both put and solved in archaeo-logical terms: 'The family likeness that exists among the stone tools and weapons found in so many parts of the world is very remarkable. The flint arrows of North America... might be easily mistaken for the weapons of our British ancestors, dug up on the banks of the Thames.'[1] This simi-larity, Tylor says, has been used to support the idea of tribes migrating from a single centre. But 'the argument has not much weight, and a larger view of the subject quite supersedes it'.[2] Tylor's own 'larger view' runs as follows: The Mexicans did not use iron implements. But there is plenty of iron-ore in Mexico. Therefore they must have been ignorant of its use. Therefore the only civilization they could have received from the Old World must have been from very barbarous peoples. Therefore 'we must admit that the inhabitants of Mexico raised themselves inde-pendently, to the extraordinary degree of culture which distinguished them when Europeans first became aware of their existence'.[3]

[1] *Ibid.* pp. 100–1.   [2] *Ibid.* p. 102.
[3] *Ibid.* p. 103.

This argument tacitly assumed the falsity of the degenerationist view, a point which Tylor was later to make
more explicitly: 'The history of man, as...told by a study
of the implements he has used, is the history of an upward
development.'[1] His attitude to the archaeological record thus
led him to reject, at first implicitly and later explicitly,
the degenerationists' account of savagery,[2] and he made
specific use of it in his first book to confute the diffusionists.
His explanation, however, if it can be called that, of the
autonomous social development in which his archaeological
arguments led him to believe was a piece of dogma derived
from the doctrines of the Enlightenment rather than from
the discoveries of the eighteen-fifties and eighteen-sixties,
which set him decisively apart from the racialists of the
Anthropological Society: 'Human nature is similar everywhere, and the same wants and instincts often find their
development in the same way among nations totally
separated from one another.'[3]

It was an assumption which was to recur frequently in
his writings,[4] and was in fact a necessary presupposition,
not merely of his use of the evolutionary comparative
method but of his whole method of explanation: 'It is,
I think, a principle to be held fast in studying the early
history of our race, that we ought always to look for practical and intelligible motives for the habits and opinions we
find existing in the world.'[5] He tried rather tentatively to
give this belief in the psychological unity of mankind some

[1] Tylor, 'On Traces of the Early Mental Condition of Man', *Proceedings
of the Royal Institution*, v (1867), 84. Cf. Tylor, *Researches*, p. 364, and
Primitive Culture, I, 32–4. Tylor used the alleged existence of 'survivals' to
support the theory of social development.

[2] Cf. Lubbock, *The Origin of Civilization*, Appendix.

[3] Tylor, *Anahuac*, p. 208.

[4] 'General likeness in human nature' (*Primitive Culture*, I, 5).

[5] 'The Religion of Savages', *Fortnightly Review*, VI (1866), 86.

empirical backing,[1] but in his earliest work it appears quite nakedly as an *a priori* assumption, and it is reasonable to assume that the evidence offered subsequently was in the nature of a *post facto* justification. That Tylor's belief in the psychological unity of mankind was derived from the tradition of thought of the Enlightenment rather than from any particular evidence for it in the new biological or archaeological studies of his own time is borne out by his use of that old favourite of the philosophic radicals and of the empiricist philosophical tradition, the association of ideas. The theory of the association of ideas—'the very philosophy of the savage',[2] as he called it—was Tylor's chief analytical tool in those interpretations of primitive beliefs in which he tried to take the strangeness out of them and make them intelligible, as the beliefs natural to men whose mental processes were essentially the same as our own, though hampered by lack of proper information. Thus animism is 'a highly rational theory for men in a low state of knowledge'.[3] Association is the key to understanding of such beliefs because 'in this law and early mental state there reigns supreme the faculty of association of thoughts'.[4]

For Tylor, the validity of his use of the evolutionary comparative method was guaranteed in three ways. First, by the archaeological record, which seemed to indicate a gradual progression in civilization, in a sequence essentially similar in all societies. Secondly, by the presence in civilized life of practices and beliefs akin to those of contemporary savages, and intelligible only on the assumption that they

---

[1] 'Like the universal language of gestures, the art of picture writing tends to prove that the mind of uncultured man works in much the same way at all times and everywhere' (*Researches*, p. 88).

[2] 'On Traces of the Early Mental Condition of Man', *Proceedings of the Royal Institution*, v (1867), 91.

[3] *Ibid.* p. 524.

[4] *Ibid.* p. 92.

are relics (survivals) of a primitive past. And thirdly, by the analysis of such notions in terms which made them seem comprehensible and, in the circumstances in which they were presumed to have originated, natural, and hence made their holders acceptable as ancestors or proxies for ancestors.

This last step was important to Tylor, as indeed was the theory of survivals, to which we shall return later, not merely as evidence for the validity of the comparative method but as a vital part of the practice of it. If it was true that 'the European may find among the Greenlanders or Maoris many a trait for reconstructing the picture of his own primitive ancestors',[1] then to make those traits intelligible with the aid of the theory of the association of ideas, or in any way, was to go a long way not merely to reconstructing but to understanding the prehistory of civilization. 'Savages display thoughts and practices whose origin is comparatively intelligible; far more intelligible than in the modified form in which we have them as survivals at higher grades of culture.'[2]

It may seem ironical to see one of the 'universal laws of human nature' taking its place in the new science of social anthropology and Tylor himself, in later life, showed signs of scepticism, at least with reference to other people's work. Criticizing Spencer's account of 'Ceremonial Institutions', he wrote: 'My own impression is that our knowledge of the principles of human action is far from being ripe enough for thus constructing man's rules of life from the inside, as though one were demonstrating the action of a machine

---

[1] *Primitive Culture*, I, 19.

[2] 'The Survival of Savage Thought in Modern Civilization', *Proceedings of the Royal Institution*, V, 534. No more than in the use of the comparative method is there anything new in this use of accepted psychological doctrines to interpret the mentality of primitives. See Manuel, *The Eighteenth Century Confronts the Gods*.

from accurately known laws.'[1] The reservations, however, seem to have affected his own practice little.[2] In any case, even among the critics of the older tradition of social and political analysis based on the 'laws of human nature', the objection had been to a too crude and unhistorical use of them rather than to the 'laws' themselves.

4. THE ULTERIOR MOTIVES OF TYLOR'S ANTHROPOLOGY

The rise of evolutionary social theory has been represented in this book as, at least in part, a response to a crisis in social theory. This view gets little support from Tylor's writings. The sense of crisis, present at least implicitly in the work of Spencer and Maine, is absent here, though he was actively involved in one of the storm-centres, the Anthropological Society, and though admirers were later to see his work in terms of such a crisis. Thus Marett, estimating his work, wrote: 'The need of his age was to proclaim that mankind is a many in one, with the emphasis on the one',[3] and to Andrew Lang his achievement was to have 'proved that man, in Byron's phrase, is everywhere the same unhappy fellow, whatever the colour of his hair or skin, and the shape of his skull'.[4]

But if Tylor, less steeped in, and perhaps more naïve about, social and political philosophy than Maine or Spencer, and armed with archaeological arguments to set against those of the racialist anatomists of the Anthropological

[1] *Macmillan's Magazine*, XLVI (1882), 74. Note also the passage on p. 73. 'It is so easy to put ourselves in the place of others...'
[2] Cf. his reservations about diffusionism and the comparative method. 'The History of Games', *Fortnightly Review*, new series, XXV (1879). Also *Researches*, p. 369.
[3] Marett, *Tylor*, p. 48.
[4] *Anthropological Essays Presented to E. B. Tylor*, p. 6.

Society, felt little of the same sense of crisis,[1] and if his work, compared with Spencer's determinism or Maine's interest in Aryan institutions, has an eighteenth-century air, he shared with Spencer, and with his colleagues of the Anthropological Society, a sense of the possibilities of a science of man.

So far we have touched on the origins of Tylor's ideas, but not the inspiration. The sources of evolutionary social theory were various, but its inspiration was invariably the same—a profound belief in the necessity and possibility of a science of social development. Those who were most aware of the flaws in the traditional basis of ethical and social theory were conscious of the necessity. If for Tylor it was not a necessity, it was certainly a glowing possibility.

It is perhaps pedantic to ask for the reasons for his enthusiastic acceptance of this possibility, and his confidence that anthropology would show that 'the history of mankind is part and parcel of the history of nature, that our thoughts, wills and actions accord with laws as definite as those which govern the motion of waves, the combination of acids and bases, and the growth of plants and animals'.[2]

To some extent, we have already attempted an answer in discussing the arguments and assumptions which lay behind his use of the evolutionary comparative method, but attitudes and enthusiasms are less palpable, more amorphous, than concepts and methods. Something must be allowed to the irreducible factor—irreducible, at least, at this level of explanation—of individual temperament and cast of mind.

---

[1] But he was sufficiently a man of his time to remark: 'To ingenious attempts at explaining by the light of reason things which want the light of history to show their meaning, much of the learned nonsense of the world has indeed been due', and to cite Maine's improvement on Blackstone (*Primitive Culture*, I, 18).

[2] *Ibid.* p. 24.

Tylor's enthusiasm for scientific laws, and his belief that such laws could be found also in the development of human culture, were not the outcome of devotion to the methods of any particular science, but to optimism about the application of scientific methods generally. The mixture of similes in the passages quoted above is symptomatic. Probably Tylor had received his first serious introduction to scientific method, and its exciting possibilities, particularly for the discovery of laws of development and the reconstruction of a remote past, from uniformitarian geology,[1] and the phraseology of his profession of faith sometimes echoes that of Lyell.[2] But there is no need to postulate a master-science in Tylor's mind. Thus in *Primitive Culture* he compares the phenomena of the anthropologist to the naturalist's 'species'.[3] But compare this passage with the following: 'The study of languages has, perhaps, done more than any other in removing from our view of human thought and action the ideas of chance and arbitrary invention, and in substituting for them a theory of development.'[4]

But this is not the limit of Tylor's eclecticism. According to Marett, he was strongly influenced by Quételet,[5] and certainly he expressed admiration for him and agreement with his doctrines.[6] In view of this, it is not surprising to find him showing enthusiasm for Buckle or, at least, for the aims Buckle set himself.[7] But such 'evidence' really cancels

---

[1] See above, p. 243.

[2] E.g. 'If anyone holds that human thought and action were worked out in primeval times according to laws essentially other than those of the modern world, it is for him to prove... this anomalous state of things, otherwise the doctrine of permanent principle will hold good, as in astronomy or geology' (*Primitive Culture*, I, 29; cf. I, 144).

[3] *Ibid.* I, 7; cf. I, 33.   [4] *Ibid.* I, 17.

[5] Marett, *Tylor*, p. 28.

[6] Tylor in *Nature*, v (1872), 358. Cf. *Primitive Culture*, I, 10.

[7] *Researches*, p. 4.

itself out. The range of influences is so wide that it proves nothing, except that Tylor threw himself wholeheartedly and confidently into what he called 'that great movement of our time—the introduction of scientific evidence into problems over which theologians and moralists have long claimed exclusive jurisdiction'.[1]

But if there is no need to posit any specific source for Tylor's confident positivism, he was very explicit about what he regarded as the value and justification of the new science. As in the cases of Spencer and Maine, though with interesting variations, it was a justification which entailed a developmental rather than a purely analytic approach to social science.

Tylor concluded his most ambitious work, *Primitive Culture*, with the words: 'The science of culture is essentially a reformer's science.'[2] This declaration was not an after-thought, but an epigrammatic conclusion to a theme constantly touched on throughout the book and announced in its earlier pages: 'Not merely as a matter of curious research, but as a practical guide to the understanding of the present, and the shaping of the future, the investigation into the origin and early development of civilization must be pushed on zealously.'[3] At first sight, the contribution of Tylor's work to this 'practical guide' may not be immediately obvious. Compared with Spencer or Maine, Tylor was a-political. He made no attempt to infer from the laws of progress the necessity of any particular type of state or policy. The reformation to which he looked forward was not political but moral and intellectual, and its essence was the concept of 'survivals'. His recommendations were based, not like Spencer's, on the supposed laws of social develop-

[1] *Nature*, v. 360.   [2] *Primitive Culture*, II, 410.
[3] *Ibid.* I, 22.

ment, but on its stages. The validity of Spencer's argument depended upon an equation between social development and progress, and he had attempted, if in a rather perfunctory fashion, to demonstrate the connection. Tylor, however, offered no explicit justification of this equation, though he seems to have assumed it.[1]

For Tylor, as for Buckle and Condorcet, Comte and J. S. Mill, the central fact of progress seems to have been the discovery of truth and the advance of science: 'It is a law of human progress that thought tends to work itself clear.... Thus man has but to go on observing and thinking secure that in time his errors will fall away, while the truth he attains to will abide and grow.'[2]

But there is, according to Tylor, a flaw in this self-perfecting, self-correcting process; it is the tendency of past states of mind, and the practices to which they gave rise, to linger long after they have become incompatible with the most advanced scientific knowledge—to become, in fact, survivals. For this tendency, the remedy is provided by anthropology, which must reveal survivals for what they are—relics of more primitive modes of thinking: 'It is the practical office of ethnography to make known...the tenure of opinions in the public mind, to what is received on its own direct evidence, what is ruder ancient doctrine re-shaped to answer modern ends, and what is but time-honoured superstition in the garb of modern knowledge.'[3]

---

[1] Though it is interesting that Tylor, like Spencer, Lubbock and Huxley, was unable to resist the temptation to moralize the laws of nature. He refers to 'the great principle of moral science, that morality and happiness go together—in fact that morality is the method of happiness' (E. B. Tylor, *Anthropology*, 2 vols., Thinker's Library, no. 14, 1930), II, 136 (1881).

[2] *Ibid.* II, 86.

[3] *Primitive Culture*, II, 403. The words anthropology, ethnology and ethnography are used very loosely by Tylor here.

Tylor declared war on survivals with almost the fervour of George Fox denouncing steeple-houses and indeed there is something very characteristically puritanical, as well as rationalistic, about this attack on superstition and empty forms and rituals.[1] Theology was Tylor's particular concern, and he turned to it with the air of one about to cleanse the temple of the Lord, ominously remarking: 'It is with a sense of attempting an investigation which bears very closely upon the current theology of our own day, that I have set myself to examine systematically, among the lower races, the development of animism.'[2] Tylor had become a convinced Darwinian in the early eighteen-sixties, and it seems likely that this was his contribution to the battle. Huxley, indeed, had written of 'The Evolution of Theology'[3] in the service of the same cause, but his was a mere *jeu d'esprit* in this field compared with Tylor's contribution. Superstition, of course, and spiritualism were castigated: 'a modern medium is a Red Indian or a Tatar shaman in a dress coat',[4] but Tylor did not hesitate to trace also to savage origins such central practices of orthodox Christianity as baptism and consecration.[5] Lord Annan has called Frazer's *Golden Bough* an ironical epitaph on the Christian Religion,[6] but Frazer was only following in Tylor's footsteps. Tylor's own work might of course be seen essentially as a continuation of the new biblical criticism which had caused such a stir in the mid-century, but Tylor was no biblical scholar or orientalist, and his work really belongs

---

[1] Cf. Spencer, p. 224 above.   [2] Tylor, *op. cit.* I, 21

[3] T. H. Huxley, 'The Evolution of Theology: An Anthropological Study', *Nineteenth Century*, XIX (1886).

[4] 'The Survival of Savage Thought in Modern Civilization', *Proceedings of the Royal Institution*, V (1869), 528.

[5] *Ibid.* pp. 530–1.

[6] Annan, *The Curious Strength of Positivism in English Thought*, p. 11.

to another tradition—not to German historical scholarship, but to the Enlightenment. His phobias are the traditional victims of the Enlightenment—superstition, metaphysics, meaningless traditions, empty forms and ceremonies—all the practices of civilized life for which common sense can find no justification.

But Tylor's method of attack is different. Instead of a frontal assault, a logical or empirical demonstration of error, he suggests the historical method. Irrational practices are to be shown for what they are, relics of an earlier and inferior state—a state in which such practices were perfectly unobjectionable and natural. The defenders of survivals are to be put to shame by the demonstration of their kinship with the savage. This indeed is 'history as the emancipation from the past'. 'History...is an agent powerful and becoming more powerful, in shaping men's minds, and through their minds their actions in the world.'[1] A favourite method of the eighteenth-century *philosophe* has been turned upside down. Instead of comparing the condemned practices of civilization unfavourably with those of savages, the former are shown to be merely relics of the latter.

Tylor was not the first to make use of this method. We have already noticed Spencer's use of it in an essay in the eighteen-fifties[2] which Tylor may have read. But the assumption on which the method is based, that the different aspects of the intellectual life of a society may advance at different speeds, and therefore come to represent different, though co-existing, stages in intellectual development, is

---

[1] *Primitive Culture*, II, 404. Cf. 'The early history of man has its bearing ...on some of the deepest and most vital points of our social and intellectual state' (*ibid*. p. 402).
[2] See above, p. 241, n. 1.

irresistibly reminiscent of Comte. For Spencer, believing in the automatic adjustment of life to its conditions, intellectual development was of only secondary interest, but for Tylor, as for Comte, it was the essence of progress itself, and the precondition of all progress in other respects.[1] It is quite possible to account for Tylor's intellectual development, as we have done hitherto, without reference to Comte, and certainly his own references to him are scanty and insignificant.[2] It is unlikely that Tylor's intellectual career would have been materially altered had he never heard of Comte; at most Comte's influence was only one ingredient among many. Nevertheless, in respect of this particular doctrine, the parallel is impossible to ignore.

Unless a religion can hold its own in the front of science and morals, it may only gradually, in the course of ages, lose its place in the nation, but all the power of statecraft and all the wealth of the temples will not save it from eventually yielding to a belief that takes in higher knowledge and teaches better life.[3]

This may have seemed mere common sense in 1881, but it also sounds remarkably like Comtism expressed in the cadences of Victorian prophecy.

For Tylor, anthropology had two main functions—to inspire and to criticize. It was to 'impress men's minds with a doctrine of development'. On the other hand, 'it is a harsher, and at times even painful, office of ethnography to expose the remains of crude old culture which have passed into harmful superstition, and to mark these out for destruction'.[4] Both these tasks entail an essentially historical approach to anthropology. It would probably be an over-statement to claim that it was considerations such as these

---

[1] But see *Nature*, XXVIII (1883), 8, where Tylor seems to accept Spencer's view.

[2] He is quoted, *Primitive Culture*, I, 18. See also *Mind*, II, 145.

[3] *Anthropology*, II, 109.   [4] *Primitive Culture*, II, 410.

which determined his whole attitude to the subject. His was, initially at least, a historical rather than a sociological cast of mind in any case.[1] But they are typical of his generation, and of the kind of interests and motives which were leading hopes for a social science to realize themselves in the form of conjectural history. If the critical aspect of Tylor's use of anthropology is the more obvious; if the function of prophecy was overshadowed—as sometimes happens with prophets— by that of denunciation; it does not mean that for him the other aspect was less important. Anthropology was to provide 'the means of understanding our own lives, and our place in the world'.[2] Like Spencer and Hobhouse[3], though perhaps less insistently, Tylor wanted to make out the plot of human history.

[1] One obvious qualification is called for, in respect of his article 'On a Method of Investigating the Development of Institutions', *Journal of the Anthropological Institute*, XVIII (1889).

[2] *Anthropology*, II, 160.

[3] See below, p. 276.

CHAPTER 8

CONCLUSION

Evolutionary social theory, and the positivist assumptions about the nature of science and of society which gave it vitality, died, in England, slowly and unspectacularly. It is impossible to discuss its demise in terms of the emergence of outstanding new, creative theoreticians, as Professor Parsons and Professor Stuart Hughes have treated, in two striking studies,[1] the general European recession from positivism in the eighteen-nineties. There is, at the turn of the century, no English Weber and no English version of the *Année Sociologique*. Parsons' chapter on Alfred Marshall in *The Structure of Social Action* is not essential to the development of his theme in the way that the chapters on Durkheim and Weber are.

In philosophy the only Anglo-Saxon version of the recession from positivism with any pretensions to originality —pragmatism—was not English but American. In England, in the eighteen-nineties, the prevailing anti-positivist philosophical doctrines represented not a new breakthrough but a rehash of Hegelianism. Even this was soon to be superseded by the reinvigorated positivism of Russell's logical atomism.

Why should this have been so? Why did England make no distinctive contribution to the rethinking of the fundamental concepts of social thought at the turn of the century? Obviously it is out of the question to attempt to provide an adequate explanation here, but it is tempting at this point to provide a pseudo-explanation—the natural disposition of

[1] Parsons, *The Structure of Social Action* and R. Stuart Hughes, *Consciousness and Society* (1959).

the English intellectual climate to positivistic modes of thinking. This may be worth saying if it draws our attention, for example, to the fact that England, unlike Germany, never produced a counterpart in technical philosophy to the Romantic Movement. In the Romanticism of the early nineteenth century one finds adumbrated many of the themes which emerge again, in new and subtler forms, at the end of the century. But only in Germany in the early nineteenth century was there a major attempt to think through, in technical, philosophical terms, the Romantic notions of human freedom, of the organic character of society, of the importance of aesthetic experience, and of the autonomous yet meaningful character of history, and to give them a theoretical status as formidable and systematic as the empiricist and materialist philosophies which drew their inspiration from the natural sciences. Before Germany produced Weber it produced Kant and Hegel.

But what of France, with her strong positivist intellectual tradition? Here two factors are worth comment, though either might turn out to be misleading if too much weight were placed upon it. First, France never capitulated to the Darwinian, materialist version of evolution to the same extent as England and Germany. There was a strain of vitalist evolutionary thinking, stemming from Lamarck, which re-emerged in Bergson. Secondly, apart from Durkheim and Bergson, the major figures in French intellectual life before the First World War who may be taken to represent a break, in some sense or other, with positivism as a framework of ideas were closely concerned with the heated political extremism of the Dreyfus period.

It will not do to suggest a simple correlation between political extremism and the breakdown of positivist determinism. Durkheim was no extremist, and in Germany the revisionist Bernstein was a neo-Kantian who renounced revolution and Engels's determinist Marxism at one and the same time. Lenin, on the other hand, was a positivist to the core. Nevertheless, in France, in the case of, for example, Barrès on the right and Sorel on the left, their violent repudiation of political orthodoxy, republican and Marxist respectively, was directly related to their anti-deterministic irrationalism.

The conditions of French social and political life gave such attitudes an importance which English political life did not allow.[1] Irrationalist fascism or near fascism and revolutionary syndicalism found no such congenial soil in England as in France; both were condemned to neo-medievalism and quaintness, whether of the right—Chesterton and Belloc— or of the left, in the watered-down syndicalism of Guild Socialism (Gild Socialism, as it was originally called). The most notable English political theorists of the left, the Fabians, were as firmly wedded to positivist as to gradualist attitudes. Shaw, it is true, professed a vitalist, Bergsonian version of evolution, and Graham Wallas's studies of the non-rational aspects of political behaviour broke with the Spencerian tradition, but his *Human Nature and Politics* provided stimulating insights rather than a new theoretical framework. *Fabian Essays* (edited by George Bernard Shaw, 1889) is a very positivist document, and Sidney Webb's contribution is the most positivist and evolutionist of all. Indeed, the Essays as a whole have a far closer intellectual kinship with the *laissez-faire* Spencer than with the revolutionary socialist Sorel.

Of course, evolutionary positivism in England died. Or

---

[1] Literature was another matter. Compare the relative importance in literary history of Sorel's translator, T. E. Hulme, with his insignificance in the history of political thought.

rather it petered out, giving way, for a while, in professional anthropology, not to a new theoretical synthesis—that was only provided, in the work of Malinowski and Radcliffe-Brown, after the First World War[1]—but to a revival of the study of cultural diffusion. As Professor T. H. Marshall says, speaking of 'the rejection of the bold evolutionary theories of the Tylor-Morgan type', there was a revolution 'amounting almost to a disintegration of anthropology itself, and of sociology too'.[2] It would take us too far afield to consider the development of anthropology in the twentieth century. Nevertheless, some attention must be paid to the disintegration of evolutionary positivism.

Theories of social evolution had provided for the Victorians an intellectual resting-place, a point of repose at which the tension between the need for certainty and the need to accommodate more diverse social facts, and more subtle ways of interpreting them, than the traditional certainties allowed for reached a kind of temporary equilibrium.

They provided a way of being both relativist and not relativist; of admitting that many diverse modes of organizing and interpreting social life might have something to be said for them, and might play vital roles in the lives of human beings, while continuing to maintain the absolute validity of one such mode—the positivist. The Victorian social evolutionists achieved this *tour de force* by admitting that other modes of thought and social behaviour might have been valid *once*, but asserting or assuming that these were only part of a larger process—social evolution—which had to be understood in a positivist manner, and which led

[1] See Firth (ed.), *Man and Culture*, and E. H. Ackerknecht, 'On the Comparative Method in Anthropology' in R. F. Spencer (ed.), *Method and Perspective in Anthropology* (Minneapolis, 1954).

[2] T. H. Marshall, 'Anthropology Today', *British Journal of Sociology* (1956), p. 61.

ultimately in a direction satisfying to those who cherished an ideal of absolutely rational—which in this context means primarily economic—social behaviour.

Social theory, in fact, was still being required to produce a great deal more than explanations of how society works, or even of how it changes. Typically, the nineteenth-century intellectual required from social science, assuming he happened to believe in its possibility, which of course a great many did not, not merely techniques of social engineering but a basis for ethics and political theory and an account of the human situation in relation to the rest of creation. Social science grew, not merely out of emulation of other, more successful sciences, but out of the collapse or revaluation of the older theories, philosophical and religious, which in the past had satisfied these needs. Much of what now seems the astonishing ambitiousness of nineteenth-century social theory arose from its attempt to fill their place.

In the earlier part of this book attention was concentrated on the decline of the social theory of philosophic radicalism, on the assumption that it was more directly related to the growing demand for a social science, rather than on the more general malaise and excitement caused by the disturbances to orthodox faith and the revision of established views about the cosmos. The latter, however, must constantly be borne in mind as a background to what has been said.

The disintegration of philosophic radicalism as a relatively self-contained and self-confident intellectual system created a problem for those who, like J. S. Mill and Spencer, inherited the aspirations of Bentham and James Mill without their confidence in the adequacy of Benthamite methods and concepts. For the conservative, or for an empiricist like Macaulay who found English Whiggism a satisfactory intellectual resting-place, there was, of course, no problem. Many of the insights which became central to nineteenth-century social theory were initially propounded as part of the reaction against the terrifying certainties of the Jacobins. Indeed, an insistence on the importance of historical and social conditioning, the consequent diversity of men and societies, and the extreme folly and danger of drastic interference with existing social and political arrangements in the name of *a priori* moral and psychological dogmas is still the hall-mark of a certain kind of sceptical conservatism. The conservative can rest here in comfort. But for men who share some of the aspirations of Jacobinism without its sociological naïveté, this is intolerable.

The revival, in the nineteenth century, of intellectually formidable radical political theories came about not through a revival of *a priorism* but by a substantial acceptance of the sceptical arguments; for once it was the radicals who borrowed the conservatives' clothes.

Marx standing Hegel on his head is the most obvious example. Marx's criticisms of the utopian socialists parallel in many respects Burke's attack on the National Assembly. Ignorance of history, overestimation of the ability of men to mould social circumstances, overestimation of the rationality of men, these are the charges in both cases. The new radicalism accepted the intractability of social material, the futility of *a priori* theorizing and the importance of historical understanding. It simply rewrote the philosophy of history to a radical tune, and by doing so made political radicalism intellectually respectable in an intellectual climate dominated by a conviction of the importance of historical conditioning.

J. S. Mill's intellectual career exhibits this process in microcosm. Stirred by doubts partly personal, partly philosophical in origin, it became vital to him to convince himself that his values were not mere prejudices, and ultimately only some theory of *progress* could provide reassurance. Such a theory alone could show that the formation of ends was not random, that it fell into a pattern as little arbitrary as that of causes and effects. Theories of progress lay ready to hand, in the work of Comte and the Saint-Simonians, and J. S. Mill modified his social views accordingly. The task of political theory as he now saw it 'was to supply, not a set of model institutions, but principles from which the institutions suitable to any given circumstances might be deduced'.[1] The criterion in any given case should be 'what great improvement in life and culture stands next in order for the people concerned, as the condition of their future progress, and what institutions are most likely to promote that'.[2] Such a criterion obviously implies a belief in a 'natural' order of development; it requires a philosophy of history and a system of classifying societies as 'stages' in the natural order. J. S. Mill elaborates his new opinions in a passage which, though hackneyed, deserves to be quoted in full:

That the human mind has a certain order of possible progress, in which some things must precede others, an order which governments and public instructors can modify to some, but not to an unlimited extent; that all questions of political institutions are relative, not absolute, and that different stages of human progress not only *will* have, but *ought* to have, different institutions: that government is always in the hands, or passing into the hands, of whatever is the strongest power in society, and that what this power is does not depend on institutions, but institutions on it: that any general theory or philosophy of politics supposes a previous theory of human progress, and that this is the same thing with a philosophy of history.[3]

[1] J. S. Mill, *Autobiography*, p. 136.　　[2] *Ibid*. pp. 144–5.
[3] *Ibid*. p. 137. Italics original.

An English radical has accepted the conservative's insistence on the intractability of social material, his belief in an inherent social dynamic which cannot be diverted at will by shallow, *a priori* rationalists. But the philosophic conservative's criterion of judgement—the intimations of a tradition —is too vague and passive to satisfy a man with an appetite for progress. A knowledge of the laws of social dynamics is required, a philosophy of history capable of classification and prediction.

As so often, J. S. Mill is a convenient microcosm of the transition from typically eighteenth- to typically nineteenth-century ways of thinking. Ethics, according to Mill, must be grounded on 'the permanent interests of man as a progressive being'.[1] But such a criterion implied a theory of human progress. The rise of evolutionary social theory must be seen in terms of these needs and aspirations.

There were, of course, more ways than one of deriving an ethical and political theory from evolutionary sociology. Perhaps the crudest way is to deduce it from the supposed mechanism of the evolutionary process—natural selection, for example. This is essentially the method of the Social Darwinists, from Bagehot to Benjamin Kidd. Spencer too, though a pre-Darwinian evolutionist, argued in a way which was essentially similar. Progress, the argument runs, is produced by the operation of certain laws; to ensure the continuation of progress we must allow those laws free operation. Of course even this theory could yield conflicting recommendations according to how certain ambiguities were solved. For example, the struggle for existence between whom? individuals? or groups? or nations? In logical type, however, the theories are similar.

A slightly different type of argument could be produced

[1] J. S. Mill, *On Liberty*, p. 9.

if you assumed that evolutionary social theory held the possibility of prediction in greater detail. Then you had your goal in front of you, as it were. You know, as Mill put it, what great improvement lay next in order. Or, even if you did not claim to be able to infer the future of the process from its past, and hence the future of the Victorian Englishman, 'heir to all the ages, in the foremost files of time', then surely you could at least predict the future of the more backward peoples, since it had already been realized by the more progressive ones.

Yet another variant of the theory starts from the assumption that not all the elements of a society advance simultaneously. Even the most progressive societies carry traces of past barbarism in their social systems. The task then is seen as the eradication of such vestiges, and the creation of a homogeneous modern society.

All these theories, of course, depend upon the identification of social evolution with progress, which raises an obvious difficulty. It is possible to talk of the progress of science, because there exist fairly clearly defined criteria according to which scientific theories and methods are judged successful or unsuccessful. This is not very obviously the case with the total life of man in society.

There are at least two ways in which the equation of social evolution with progress might be made. First, by taking an ethical attitude towards the evolutionary process because of its contribution to the achievement of some good, and second, by an ethical attitude to the process for its own sake—i.e. an attitude such that the question, 'Why do you approve?' would be, to the man who held it, unanswerable. It is good *because* it is good (in itself).

It is obvious that the distinction is not easy to draw. A writer who actually held the first attitude might appear to be holding the second simply because he did not make his principles explicit. Another might begin by holding the first but become less and less interested in the grounds for his approval and eventually lose sight of them altogether. Or another might hold the first intellectually, but reserve all his enthusiasm for the second. Probably there was no social evolutionist who would have confessed to having no answer to the question 'Why do you approve of the process you describe?'. In a number of cases the justification was utilitarian. Spencer could write: 'The conduct to which we apply the name good, is the relatively more evolved conduct; and bad is the name we apply to conduct which is relatively less evolved';[1] but then quickly asserted that 'the good is universally the pleasurable'.[2] The first statement is only true because more 'evolved' conduct is that which has more pleasurable rewards attached to it for oneself and fewer painful consequences for others. It must be remembered that Spencer regards evolution as adaptation, and 'all evil results from non-adaptation of constitution to conditions'.[3] For the time being, one of the ways in which this adaptation is achieved is by the struggle for existence and the elimination of the unfit, but 'the development of the higher creation is a progress towards a form of being capable of a happiness undiminished by these drawbacks'.[4]

Lubbock, too, refers to the utopia towards which evolution is infallibly moving, in terms of 'the future happiness of our race'.[5] Others have a different criterion but, nevertheless, a criterion. Thus, Lecky writes: 'The superiority of a highly civilized man lies chiefly in the fact that he belongs to a higher order of being, for he has approached

---

[1] H. Spencer, *The Data of Ethics* (1879), p. 25.
[2] *Ibid.* p. 30. Cf. Spencer, *Autobiography*, II, 88.
[3] *Social Statics*, p. 59.   [4] *Ibid.* p. 322.   [5] See below, p. 275.

more nearly to the end of his existence, and has called into action a larger number of his capacities. And this is itself an end.'[1] Lecky has here essentially the same thought as J. S. Mill when he prefixed to his essay *On Liberty* Wilhelm von Humboldt's phrase: 'Human development in its richest diversity.' Similar, too, is Hobhouse's description of the rational good as the development of the greatest possible number of non-conflicting human purposes.[2]

It is difficult, however, in many cases, to separate approval of the results of the process from enthusiasm for the process itself. In his last illness the only thought that could cheer Spencer was Development,[3] though according to his theory, it must inevitably be followed by dissolution, and the whole process of adaptation, with all its suffering, must begin again. The urge to endow the universe with moral qualities was still strong. The intellectual inheritance of centuries of Natural Law weighed still on minds which had dismissed the theoretical foundations of the doctrine. Even Huxley, who held that 'social progress means a checking of the cosmic process at every step and the substitution for it of another, which may be called an ethical process',[4] could in another context endow that same process with ethical attributes. 'The absolute justice of the system of things', he wrote to Charles Kingsley, 'is as clear to me as any scientific fact. The gravitation of sin to sorrow is as certain as that of the earth to the sun.'[5] His meaning is not in doubt—he has

[1] W. E. Lecky, *History of European Morals* (New York, 1955), p. 87 (1869).
[2] L. T. Hobhouse, *Social Development* (1924), pp. 85-7. A non-conflicting purpose is one which conflicts neither with the purposes of others nor with the latent potentialities, as it were, of the individual subject.
[3] B. Webb, *My Apprenticeship*, pp. 30-1.
[4] T. H. Huxley, *Evolution and Ethics*, p. 81.
[5] L. Huxley, *Life and Letters of T. H. Huxley*, I, 317. See on this point Oma Stanley, 'T. H. Huxley's Treatment of Nature', *Journal of the History of Ideas*, XVIII (1957).

explained himself a little earlier: 'Life cannot exist without a certain conformity to the surrounding universe—that conformity involves a certain amount of happiness in excess of pain. In short, as we live we are paid for living.' In other words, there are certain inescapable conditions of life; if we do not respect them, they will take a toll of pain; if we do we shall be paid by a balance of pleasure over pain. Even allowing the last point, which is highly dubious, it is difficult to see why any man from Huxley's intellectual standpoint should regard the result as 'justice'. Certain consequences follow certain actions—that is all. Even if Huxley is using 'sin' metaphorically, he surely cannot mean anything by 'justice' other than to speak in a normative manner of the processes of Nature. Lubbock, too, speaks of Nature's retribution in almost identical terms: 'That suffering is the inevitable consequence of sin, as surely as night follows day, is, however, the stern yet necessary teaching of science',[1] but in his case it is less surprising, since far from regarding 'natural laws' as opposed to the purposes of man, he believes that they will inevitably conduct him to utopia. But often it seems as though the evolutionary process is being approved simply for itself, because it provides a plot for the cosmic drama, without reference to an ulterior end. The demand that the universe must not be indifferent to the concerns of man survived the destruction by Darwin of the argument from design. There is an ambiguity in the proposal to trace the 'natural' (normal/essential) course of human development. It may be based on a teleology. On the other hand, it may merely represent the attempt to discover what *would* be the course of development in the absence of 'disturbing causes'. There is a consistent tendency for the latter to pass over into the former and be regarded normatively. Much of

[1] *Prehistoric Times*, p. 489.

the concern with tracing the course of social development seems to have involved, and drawn its inspiration from, an implicit denial that—to take a classic formulation of the opposite view—'The sense of the world must lie outside the world... If there is any value which is of value, it must lie outside all happening and being so. For all happening and being so is accidental.'[1] The appeal of the idea that Nature holds the secret of right conduct if men can only learn it was not dead. Professor Lovejoy, in a famous phrase, described the rise of evolutionary doctrines in biology as 'the temporalization of the Chain of Being'.[2] It would be almost equally apt to describe nineteenth-century theories of social evolution as 'the temporalization of Natural Law'. Certainly contemporary critics seemed to assume that evolutionary social theorists were attempting (illegitimately) to derive their values directly from the process they described.[3] The most famous criticism of all, Huxley's 1893 Romanes Lecture on *Evolution and Ethics*, seems to make this assumption.

Perhaps it is no coincidence that the evolutionary social theorist who saw the issue most clearly was also virtually the last. Hobhouse, more philosophically self-conscious than most of his colleagues, was aware of the danger of arguing in a circle. 'We must find some element, not itself ethical, occupying a leading place in social development and enabling us by its changes to measure the distance which any given society has travelled from the primitive condition of man.'[4] He was careful himself to point out that he had established his criterion of ethical progress and his 'objective' criteria of social development independently of one another.

---

[1] L. Wittgenstein, *Tractatus Logico-Philosophicus* (1922), 6.41.
[2] Lovejoy, *The Great Chain of Being*.
[3] See above, pp. 96–7.
[4] L. T. Hobhouse, *Morals in Evolution* (7th ed. 1951), p. 34 (1906).

He was also, however, anxious to prove the optimistic conclusion that there was, *on the whole*, a correlation between the two series—the ethically better and the structurally and chronologically more advanced.[1] In fact it would be no exaggeration to say that a major part of his work was devoted to an attempt to prove such a correlation.

But why? What good will it do him? He will not be able to deduce his values from it, since he has already had to establish them independently in order to avoid the circular argument he has foreseen. Does he want factual predictions? If so, why bother to correlate his sociological theory with his ethical one? This is not, after all, what a modern sociologist, however anxious to put his discipline at the service of a political programme, or a modern political theorist, however sociologically sophisticated, would be likely to try to do. All that either of them requires is that the proposed programme should be sociologically *possible*. Compare this attitude with the following passage from Hobhouse:

To form by a philosophic analysis a just conception of human progress, to trace this progress in its manifold complexity in the course of history, to test its reality by careful classification and searching comparison, to ascertain its conditions and if possible to forecast its future—this is the comprehensive problem towards which all sociological science converges, and on the solution of which all reasoned sociological effort must finally depend.[2]

To test the reality of a conception of progress arrived at philosophically can only mean, in this context, to show that what has been ought (broadly speaking) to have been, and what ought to be, will be. By forecasting the future, it is

---

[1] Hobhouse, *Social Development*, pp. 12, 88, 89, 92, 93.
[2] Hobhouse, Editorial Introduction to the *Sociological Review*, quoted H. E. Barnes, *An Introduction to the History of Sociology* (Chicago, 1948), p. 621.

clear that Hobhouse means not merely predicting the consequences of some particular social policy, but forecasting
the whole future trend of social development. But if it is
possible to make, or even aspire to, such a forecast, we know
that what ought to be will be, or else that it will not. If the
future is predictable, we are deprived, except in minor and
peripheral matters, of hope. We are forced either into
confidence or into gloom. Things are going to get either
better or worse, generally speaking, and if we can predict
the future we know *which* it is to be.

It could not be a matter of indifference to the Victorian
social evolutionists what type of development it was whose
course they plotted, for they believed it was not only the
past but to some extent the future of their species that they
revealed; it followed from the doctrine that past changes
had been brought about by laws still in operation. As Tylor
put it, 'the thing that has been will be; and we are to study
savages and old nations to learn the laws that under the
new circumstances are working for good or ill in our own
development'.[1] In fact they had few doubts whether it had
been good or ill. There are normative connotations in the
very words they used: 'primitive', 'advanced', to say nothing
of 'progress,' just as there were in the older term 'savage'.
In the eighteen-sixties and eighteen-seventies, the degenerationist school of Archbishop Whately and the Duke of
Argyll was still considered important enough for Tylor and
Lubbock[2] to bother to refute it, but among the anthropologists themselves there was optimism varying only in its
degrees of confidence and sophistication. Spencer's system
included dissolution as well as evolution, but almost all his

[1] Tylor, *Primitive Culture*, I, 144.
[2] *Ibid*. I, 32–4. *Researches*, p. 364, and Lubbock, *The Origin of Civilization*,
Appendix.

writings and his emotional commitments are concentrated on the latter.

The inference that as advancement has hitherto been the rule, it will be the rule henceforth, may be called a plausible speculation. But when it is shown that this advancement is due to the working of the universal law; and that in virtue of that law it must continue until the state we call perfection is reached, then the advent of such a state is removed out of the region of probability into that of certainty.[1]

More rhapsodically, Lubbock wrote:

The future happiness of our race, which poets hardly ventured to hope for, science boldly predicts. Utopia, which we have long looked upon as synonymous with an evident impossibility, which we have ungratefully regarded as 'too good to be true', turns out on the contrary to be the necessary consequence of natural laws.[2]

Hobhouse was not a determinist in the sense that Spencer was. Rather he seems to have held with J. S. Mill that 'the human mind has a certain order of possible progress' and that it was up to human beings to find and follow it. But he shared the common tendency of the nineteenth-century social scientist to talk in terms of a rigid dichotomy of social law or social chaos.

Is there any unity or significance in the drama as a whole?... Can we under all these difficulties of involvement, form any notion of the plot? Are we sure that there is a plot at all, and that our play is not a tale told by an idiot, signifying nothing? These, as I conceive the subject, are the questions which sociology has to resolve.[3]

In other words, there can be no half measures—no understanding of this or that chunk of social reality. Ultimately, according to Hobhouse, sociology stands or falls according

---

[1] *SS*, p. 64. [2] Lubbock, *Prehistoric Times*, pp. 491–2.
[3] Hobhouse, *Social Development*, p. 31.

to whether it can make intelligible the course of social development, according to whether it can reveal *the* (note the use of the singular) plot.

But more is involved here, surely, than simply intellectual understanding. If social development were not ultimately good, it would indeed, for Hobhouse, be a tale told by an idiot. It would be meaningless in the sense that evil and suffering themselves often seem meaningless. The Victorians often, perhaps usually, required that social theory should *mean* something in this sense of being meaningful. This it could not do unless it both revealed social laws of a very high level of generality and showed that man's future as a social animal was a glorious one. Both these requirements demanded a concentration on the problem of social change and the relative neglect of social coherence and stability. They do much to explain why nineteenth-century social theory should have taken the idea of social evolution as its key concept. They also help to explain the persistence. of evolutionary positivism long after alternative theories had arisen on the continent. Theories do not automatically disappear because more sophisticated theories are put forward, at least in fields as closely connected as evolutionary social theory with some of the emotionally most heavily charged hopes and beliefs of mankind.

The changes in the intellectual climate which led to the displacement of evolutionary positivism as the current sociological orthodoxy are beyond the scope of this book. They were part of the general assault on positivistic thinking which ranged from literature to the philosophy of science. In particular, it was the severance of sociology and political theory, the acceptance of the degree of relativism which is involved in the study of societies as working systems, which helped to kill evolutionary social theory. The critics of evolutionary ethics, and indeed of naturalistic ethics generally, have been victorious, and even as Hobhouse was joining social improvement and social development by a kind of *tour de force*, ethics and sociology were falling apart. Victorian theories of progress were not simply the expression of an overflowing optimism, but a basically optimistic climate of opinion was probably necessary to their growth. Already when Hobhouse's *Social Development* was published (1926), the First World War had cast doubt on the belief that there was any necessary connection between technological achievement and moral improvement, between sweetness and light and efficiency in face of the environment. The new prophet was not Spencer but Spengler.

The belief that what ought to be necessarily would be was perhaps most acceptable, like the kindred assumption in a certain kind of fiction that happiness is invariably the reward of virtue, while it remained implicit. In Hobhouse's careful distinction of 'ought' and 'is', despite his attempt to reunite them *de facto*, we can see the incipient collapse of an assumption which gave much of its meaning and purpose to that view of social science which saw its essential task as plotting the course of man's destiny as a social animal.

BIBLIOGRAPHY[1]

1. SOURCES BEFORE 1900[2]

ARNOLD, M. *Culture and Anarchy* (2nd ed. 1875).

AUSTIN, J. *Lectures on Jurisprudence* (3rd ed. 1869).

BAGEHOT, W. *Literary Studies* (3 vols. 1884).

—— *Physics and Politics* (2nd ed. 1872) (1869).

BAIN, A. *James Mill* (1882).

BECKER, B. H. *Scientific London* (1874).

BENDYSSHE, A. T. *A History of Anthropology* (1865).

BENN, A. W. *A History of English Rationalism in the Nineteenth Century* (2 vols. 1906).

BENTHAM, J. *Collected Works* (ed. J. Bowring, 11 vols. 1843).

BIRKS, T. R. *Modern Utilitarianism* (1874).

BLUNT, J. J. *Vestiges of Ancient Manners* (1823).

BRIDE, T. F. *Letters from Victorian Pioneers* (Melbourne, 1898).

BRISTED, C. A. *Five Years in an English University* (N. Y., 1852).

BUCKLE, T. H. *The History of Civilization in England* (2 vols. 1857–61).

—— *Miscellaneous and Posthumous Works* (ed. H. Taylor; 1872).

CAIRD, E. *The Evolution of Religion* (2 vols. Glasgow, 1893).

Cambridge Essays (1856).

CLIFFORD, W. K. *Lectures and Essays* (1879).

CLODD, E. *Myths and Dreams* (1885).

COLUMBUS, CHRISTOPHER. See under *Select Letters*.

COMTE, A. *Cours de Philosophie Positive* (6 vols. Paris, 1830–42).

—— *Positive Philosophy*. Freely translated and condensed by H. Martineau (2 vols. 1853).

CONDORCET, MARQUIS DE. *Sketch for a Historical Picture of the Progress of the Human Mind* (tr. J. Barraclough; 1955) (1794–5).

---

[1] Unless otherwise stated, the place of publication is London.

[2] Works by an author whose first cited work appeared before 1900 are all included in this section, even though his later works may have been published after 1900.

CROSS, J. W. *Life and Letters of George Eliot* (3 vols. Edinburgh, 1885).

DARWIN, C. *The Origin of Species* (1859).
—— *The Descent of Man* (2nd ed. 1874).
—— *The Expression of the Emotions in Man and Animals* (1872).
—— *Autobiography. 1809–82* (revised ed. 1958).

DIDEROT, D. *Selected Philosophical Writings* (ed. J. Lough; C.U.P. 1953).

DUBOIS, (ABBÉ) J. A. *Manners and Customs of India* (1817).

DUFF, SIR M. E. GRANT. *Sir Henry Maine. A Brief Memoir of his Life.* With speeches, etc., ed. Whitley Stokes (1892).
—— *Notes from a Diary, 1858–1901* (14 vols. 1897–1905).

DURKHEIM, E. *Les formes élémentaires de la vie religieuse* (Paris, 1912).
—— *On the Division of Labour in Society* (tr. E. G. Simpson; New York, 1933).
—— *The Rules of Sociological Method* (8th ed. tr. S. A. Solovay and J. H. Mueller; Chicago, 1938).
—— *Sociology and Philosophy* (tr. D. F. Pocock; 1953).

EDMONDS, T. R. *Practical, Moral and Political Economy* (1828).

ENGELS, F. *The Origin of the Family, Private Property and the State* (selected works of K. Marx and F. Engels, 2 vols. Moscow, 1958, vol. II).

FERGUSON, A. *An Essay on the History of Civil Society* (Basel, 1789) (1767).

FLINT, R. *The Philosophy of History in Europe* (Edinburgh, 1874).

FUSTEL DE COULANGES. *La Cité Antique* (2nd ed. Paris, 1866).

GROTE, G. *History of Greece* (12 vols. 1846–56).

GROTE, H. *The Personal Life of George Grote* (1873).

GROTE, J. *Exploratio Philosophica* (2 vols. 1865).
—— *Examination of the Utilitarian Philosophy* (C.U.P. 1870).

HAMILTON, R. *The Progress of Society* (1830).

HARRISON, F. *The Meaning of History* (1894).
—— *Autobiographic Memoirs* (2 vols. 1911).

HOBBES, T. *Leviathan* (ed. M. Oakshott. Blackwell, Oxford, 1946).

HUMBOLDT, A. VON. *Cosmos* (tr. E. C. Otté; 5 vols. 1849–58).

HUME, D. *A Treatise of Human Nature* (ed. Selby-Bigge; O.U.P. 1888).

HUME, D. *Essays, Literary, Moral and Political* (1870 ed.).

HUTH, A. H. *Life and Writings of Thomas Henry Buckle* (1880).

HUXLEY, T. H. *Man's Place in Nature* (1863).

—— *Lay Sermons* (1871).

—— *Evolution of Ethics*, repr. in T. H. Huxley and Julian Huxley, *Evolution and Ethics, 1893–1943* (1947).

KIDD, B. *Social Evolution* (1894).

—— *Principles of Western Civilization* (1902).

KIPLING, R. *Plain Tales from the Hills* (3rd ed. 1890).

KNOX, R. *The Races of Man* (1850).

LANG, A. *Custom and Myth* (1884).

—— *Myth, Ritual and Religion* (1887).

—— *Concerning Andrew Lang*. The Andrew Lang Lectures, 1927–37 (O.U.P. 1949).

LANGE, F. *A History of Materialism* (tr. E. C. Thomas; 1925).

LATHAM, R. G. *The Natural History of the Varieties of Man* (1850).

LECKY, W. E. *A History of European Morals* (New York, 1955) (1869).

LEWES, G. H. *A Biographical History of Philosophy* (2 vols. 1845–6).

LONSDALE, H. *The Life and Writings of Robert Knox* (1870).

LUBBOCK, SIR J. (LORD AVEBURY). *Prehistoric Times* (1865).

—— *The Origin of Civilization* (1870).

LYTTON, E. R. *Julian Fane. A Memoir* (1871).

MACAULAY, T. B. *Miscellaneous Writings* (2 vols. 1880).

MACKINTOSH, JAMES. *A Dissertation on Ethical Philosophy* (Edinburgh, 1836).

MACKINTOSH, R. *From Comte to Benjamin Kidd* (1899).

McLENNAN, J. F. *Primitive Marriage* (Edinburgh, 1865).

—— *Studies in Ancient History*, comprising a reprint of *Primitive Marriage* (1876).

—— *The Patriarchal Theory*, ed. and completed by D. McLennan (1885).

—— *Studies in Ancient History*, 2nd series (1896).

MAINE, SIR HENRY. *Plato*. Written for the Chancellor's Medal for English Verse (C.U.P. 1843).

—— *H. F. Hallam, A Memoir*, by H. S. Maine and F. Lushington (1851).

—— *Ancient Law* (O.U.P. 1954) (1861).

—— *Village Communities in the East and West* (1871).

—— *Lectures on the Early History of Institutions* (1875).

—— *The Effects of Observation of India on Modern European Thought.* The Rede Lecture 1875 (1875).

—— *Dissertations on Early Law and Custom* (1883).

—— *Popular Government* (1885).

—— *International Law* (1888).

MALLOCK, W. H. *Aristocracy and Evolution* (1848).

MARSHALL, A. *Principles of Economics* (2 vols.).

MARTINEAU, H. *Autobiography* (3 vols. 1877) (1898).

MÜLLER, F. MAX. *Lectures on the Science of Language* (1861–4).

—— *On the Stratification of Language.* The Rede Lecture 1868 (1868).

—— *Chips from a German Workshop* (2nd ed. 2 vols. 1868).

—— *Introduction to the Science of Religion* (1873).

MILL, JAMES. *The History of British India* (1817).

—— *Essay on Government* (C.U.P. 1937) (1820).

—— *A Fragment on Mackintosh* (1835).

MILL, J. S. *A System of Logic* (9th ed. 2 vols. 1875) (1843).

—— *On Liberty* (Blackwell, Oxford, 1946.) (1859).

—— *Auguste Comte and Positivism* (1865).

—— *Autobiography* (O.U.P. 1954) (1873).

—— *Mill on Bentham and Coleridge.* Intr. F. R. Leavis (1950).

—— *Earlier Letters, 1812–48* (ed. F. E. Mineka; 1963).

MORGAN, L. H. *Ancient Society* (1877).

MURRAY, H. *Enquiries Historical and Moral respecting the Character of Nations and the Progress of Society* (Edinburgh, 1808).

OSBORN, H. F. *From the Greeks to Darwin* (New York, 1894).

POLLOCK, SIR F. *Oxford Lectures* (1890).

PRICHARD, J. C. *Analysis of Egyptian Mythology* (1819).

—— *The Natural History of Man* (1843).

QUÉTELET, L. A. *Physique Sociale* (2 vols. Brussels, 1869) (1835).

RITCHIE, D. G. *Darwinism and Politics* (1889).

—— *Hegel and Darwin* (1893).

ROBERTSON, J. M. *Buckle and his Critics* (1895).

ROBERTSON, W. *A History of America,* (1777).

ROBERTSON SMITH, W. *Lectures on the Religion of the Semites.* First series (1907) (1899).

ROUSSEAU, J.-J. *Discours sur l'origine et les fondements de l'inégalité parmi les hommes* (C.U.P. 1941), p. 29 (1755).

Select Letters of Christopher Columbus (tr. R. H. Major; 2nd ed. 1870).

SHAW, G. B. (ed.). *Fabian Essays* (1889).

SMITH, ADAM. *Lectures on Justice, Police, Revenue and Arms* (ed. E. CANNAN; O.U.P. 1896).

—— *Essays on Philosophical Subjects to which is prefixed a Life and Writings of the Author by Dugald Stewart* (1795).

SORLEY, W. R. *On the Basis of Ethics,* with special reference to the *Theory of Evolution* (1884).

—— *The Ethics of Naturalism* (1885).

SPENCER, H. *Social Statics* (1851).

—— *The Principles of Psychology* (3rd ed. 2 vols. 1881) (1855).

—— *Essays,* scientific, political and speculative (3 vols. 1858–74).

—— *The Classification of the Sciences* (1861).

—— *First Principles* (4th ed. 1880) (1862).

—— *The Principles of Biology* (1864).

—— *The Study of Sociology* (2nd ed. 1874) (1873).

—— *The Principles of Sociology* (3 vols. 1876–).

—— *The Data of Ethics* (1879).

—— *The Man versus the State* (1884).

—— *The Principles of Ethics* (2 vols. 1892–3).

—— *Various Fragments* (1894).

—— *An Autobiography* (2 vols. 1904).

—— *Descriptive Sociology* (1931–4).

STEPHEN, J. F. *Essays by a Barrister* (1862).

STEPHEN, L. *Sketches from Cambridge,* by a Don (O.U.P. 1932) (1865).

—— *The Science of Ethics* (1882).

—— *Life and Letters of Sir J. F. Stephen* (1895).

—— *The English Utilitarians* (3 vols. 1950) (1900).

—— *Some Early Impressions* (1924) (1903).

—— *History of English Thought in the Eighteenth Century* (2 vols. 3rd ed. 1902).

TREVELYAN, G. O. *Life and Letters of Lord Macaulay* (1908) (1876).

TYLOR, E. B. *Anahuac* (1861).

—— *Researches into the Early History of Mankind and the Development of Civilization* (1865).

—— *Primitive Culture* (2 vols. 1871).

—— *Anthropology* (1881). (Thinker's Library no. 14, 2 vols. 1930.)

—— *Anthropological Essays Presented to Edward Burnett Tylor* (O.U.P. 1907).

VOLTAIRE. *Essai sur les Mœurs* (*Œuvres*, Paris, 1878).

WAITZ, T. *Introduction to Anthropology* (tr. J. F. Collingwood; 1863).

WAKE, C. S. *Chapters on Man* (1868).

WARD, H. (ed.). *The Reign of Queen Victoria* (2 vols. 1887).

2. SOURCES AFTER 1900

ALLEN, C. K. *Law in the Making* (2nd ed. O.U.P. 1930).

ANNAN, N. G. *Leslie Stephen* (1951).

—— *The Curious Strength of Positivism in English Political Thought.* (L. T. Hobhouse Memorial Trust Lecture no. 28) (O.U.P. 1959).

AYER, A. J. *Philosophical Essays* (1954).

BARKER, E. *Political Thought in England, 1848–1914* (O.U.P. 1915).

BARNES, H. E. *An Introduction to the History of Sociology* (Chicago, 1948).

BARNETT, S. A. (ed.). *A Century of Darwin* (1958).

BAUMGARDT, D. *Bentham and the Ethics of Today* (Princeton U.P. 1952).

BEARCE, G. D. *British Attitudes towards India, 1784–1858* (O.U.P. 1961).

BEVINGTON, M. M. *The Saturday Review* (Columbia, 1941).

BROWN, J. *The Austinian Theory of Law* (1906).

BRYCE, J. *Studies in Contemporary Biography* (1903).

BRYSON, G. *Man and Society. The Scottish Enquiry of the Eighteenth Century* (Princeton U.P. 1945).

CARTER, G. S. *A Hundred Years of Evolution* (1958).

CLIVE, J. *Scotch Reviewers. The Edinburgh Review, 1802–1815* (1957).

COOK, S. A. *The Study of Religions* (1914).

CRICK, B. *The American Science of Politics* (1959).

DANIEL, GLYN E. *A Hundred Years of Archaeology* (1950).

DAVIE, G. E. *The Democratic Intellect* (Edinburgh U.P. 1961).

DOWNIE, R. A. *James George Frazer* (1940).

DUNCAN, D. *Life and Letters of Herbert Spencer* (1908).

DURAND, H. M. *Life of Sir Alfred Lyall* (Edinburgh, 1913).

EASTWOOD, R. A. and KEETON, G. W. *The Austinian Theories of Law* (1920).

EVANS-PRITCHARD, E. E. *Social Anthropology* (1954).

FAIRCHILD, H. N. *The Noble Savage* (New York, 1928).

FEAVER, G. A. *From Status to Contract*, A biographical study of Sir Henry Maine 1822–1888 (1962) (L.S.E. unpub. thesis.)

FIRTH, R. (ed.). *Man and Culture* (1957).

FORBES, D. *The Liberal Anglican idea of History* (C.U.P. 1952).

FRANKEL, C. *The Faith of Reason* (New York, 1948).

FRAZER, J. G. *Lectures on the Early History of the Kingship* (1905).

—— *Psyche's Task* (2nd ed. 1913).

GARDINER, A. G. *Life of Sir William Vernon Harcourt* (1923).

GARDINER, P. (ed.). *Theories of History* (1959).

GILLISPIE, C. C. *Genesis and Geology* (Harvard, 1951).

GINSBERG, M. *The Diversity of Morals* (1956).

GLASS, D. (ed.). *Introduction to Malthus* (1953).

GOLDENWEISER, A. A. *Anthropology* (New York, 1937).

GOMME, G. L. *Folklore as an Historical Science* (1908).

GOOCH, G. P. *History and Historians in the Nineteenth Century.*

GRANT DUFF, MRS ADRIAN (ed.). *The Life-Work of Lord Avebury* (1931).

GRAVE, S. A. *The Scottish Philosophy of Common Sense* (O.U.P. 1960).

GREEN, R. LANCELYN. *Andrew Lang* (Leicester, 1946).

HADDON, A. C. *A History of Anthropology* (1934).

HALÉVY, E. *The Growth of Philosophic Radicalism* (tr. M. Morris; 1952).

HANKE, LEWIS. *Aristotle and the Indians* (1959).

HARRISON, A. *Frederic Harrison. Thoughts and Memories* (1926).

HEARNSHAW, F. J. C. (ed.). *Social and Political Ideas of the Victorian Age* (1933).

HOBHOUSE L. T. *Mind in Evolution* (1901).

—— *Morals in Evolution* (7th ed. 1951) (1906).

—— *Development and Purpose* (1913).

—— *Social Development* (1924).

HOBSON, J. A. and GINSBURG, M. *L. T. Hobhouse, his Life and Work* (1931).

HODGEN, M. T. *The Doctrine of Survivals* (1936).

HOLDSWORTH, W. S. *Some Makers of English Law* (C.U.P. 1938).

HUBERT, R. *Les Sciences sociales dans l'Encyclopédie* (Paris, 1923).

HUGHES, R. STUART. *Consciousness and Society* (1959).

HUTCHINSON, H. G. *Life of Sir John Lubbock, Lord Avebury* (2 vols. 1914).

HUXLEY, L. *Life and Letters of T. H. Huxley* (3 vols. 1900).

—— *Ideas and Beliefs of the Victorians* (1949).

JESPERSEN, O. *Language, its Nature, Development and Origin* (1922).

KITCHEL, A. T. *George Lewes and George Eliot* (New York, 1933).

KROEBER, A. L. (ed.). *Anthropology Today* (Chicago, 1953).

KUBITZ, O. A. *The Development of J. S. Mill's System of Logic* (Univ. of Urbana, Ill., 1932).

LEHMANN, W. C. *Adam Ferguson and the Beginnings of Modern Sociology* (New York, 1930).

—— *John Millar of Glasgow, 1735–1801* (C.U.P. 1960).

LÉVY-BRUHL, A. *The Philosophy of Auguste Comte* (1903).

Life and Letters of F. Max Müller, by his wife (2 vols. 1902).

LOVEJOY, A. O. *The Great Chain of Being* (Harvard, 1936).

LOWIE, R. H. *The History of Ethnological Theory* (1938).

McGEE, J. E. *A Crusade for Humanity* (1931).

MACK, MARY P. *Jeremy Bentham. An Odyssey of Ideas, 1748–1792* (1962).

MAITLAND, F. W. *Life and Letters of Leslie Stephen* (1906).

MALINOWSKI, B. *A Scientific Theory of Culture* (Chapel Hill, N.C. 1944).

MANUEL, F. E. *The Eighteenth Century Confronts the Gods* (Harvard, 1959).

MARETT, R. R. *Tylor* (1936).

—— *A Jerseyman at Oxford* (O.U.P. 1941).

—— (ed.). *Anthropology and the Classics* (O.U.P. 1908).

MARVIN, S. F. *Comte* (1936).

MAX MÜLLER, F., see under *Life and Letters*.

MEINECKE, F. *Die Entstehung des Historismus* (Munich, 1959).

MITCHELL, D. *Sociology* (1959).

MUELLER, I. W. *J. S. Mill and French Thought* (Univ. of Ill. 1956).

MURRAY, R. H. *Social and Political Thinkers of the Nineteenth Century* (2 vols. C.U.P. 1929).

MYERS, J. L. *The Influence of Anthropology on the Course of Political Science* (Berkeley, Calif. 1916).

NADEL, S. F. *Foundations of Social Anthropology* (1951).

NEW, C. W. *The Life of Henry Brougham to 1830* (O.U.P. 1961).

NICHOLSON, J. A. *Some Aspects of the Philosophy of L. T. Hobhouse* (Univ. of Urbana, Ill. 1928).

OGDEN, C. K. *Bentham's Theory of Fictions* (1932).

PACKE, M. ST J. *The Life of John Stuart Mill* (1954).

PARSONS, T. *The Structure of Social Action* (New York, 1937).

—— *Essays in Sociological Theory, Pure and Applied* (Univ. of Ill. 1949).

PEDERSEN, H. *The Development of Linguistic Science in the Nineteenth Century* (tr. J. W. Spargo; Cambridge, Mass. 1931).

PENNIMAN, T. K. *A Hundred Years of Anthropology* (1951).

PITT-RIVERS, A. H. (LANE FOX). *The Evolution of Culture* (O.U.P. 1906).

POCOCK, D. F. *Social Anthropology* (1961).

The Pollock-Holmes Letters (2 vols. C.U.P. 1942).

POPPER, K. R. *The Open Society and Its Enemies* (2 vols. revised ed. 1952).

QUIGGIN, A. HINGSTON. *Haddon the Head-Hunter* (C.U.P. 1942).

RADCLIFFE-BROWN, A. R. *Structure and Function in Primitive Society* (1956).

—— *Method in Social Anthropology* (Chicago, 1958).

ROACH, J. P. C. *Sir James Fitzjames Stephen* (unpub. Cambridge Ph.D. thesis, 1954).

ROBBINS, LIONEL. *The Theory of Economic Policy in English Classical Political Economy* (1952).

ROUCEK, J. S. (ed.). *Contemporary Sociology* (1959).

RUMNEY, J. *Herbert Spencer's Sociology* (1934).

RUSSELL, E. S. *Form and Function* (1916).

SAVILLE, J. (ed). *Democracy and the Labour Movement* (1954).

SCHUMPETER, J. *Economic Doctrine and Method* (tr. R. Aris; 1954).

SEWARD, A. C. (ed.). *Darwin and Modern Science* (C.U.P. 1909).

Henry Sidgwick, A Memoir, by A.S. and E.M.S. (1906).

SIMEY, T. S. and M. B. *Charles Booth—Social Scientist* (O.U.P. 1960).

SPENCER, R. F. (ed.). *Method and Perspective in Anthropology* (Minneapolis, 1954).

STARK, W. *The Sociology of Knowledge* (1958).

STOKES, E. *The English Utilitarians and India* (O.U.P. 1959).

TEGGART, J. F. *Theories of History* (New Haven, 1925).

VINOGRADOFF, SIR P. *The Teaching of Sir Henry Maine* (O.U.P. 1904).

WALLAS, G. *Human Nature and Politics* (1908).

WEBB, B. *My Apprenticeship* (1950) (1936).

WEBB, G. *Herder and After* ('s Gravenhage, 1959).

WEBB, R. K. *Harriet Martineau. A Radical Victorian* (1959).

WILLEY, B. *The Seventeenth Century Background* (1934).

—— *The Eighteenth Century Background* (1940).

—— *Nineteenth Century Studies* (1949).

—— *More Nineteenth Century Studies* (1956).

INDEX